THE SCANDINAVIAN REFORMATION

*from evangelical movement to
institutionalisation of reform*

EDITED BY

OLE PETER GRELL

*Carlsberg Research Fellow, Wellcome Unit for the History of Medicine,
University of Cambridge*

CAMBRIDGE
UNIVERSITY PRESS

Published by the Press Syndicate of the University of Cambridge
The Pitt Building, Trumpington Street, Cambridge CB2 1RP
40 West 20th Street, New York, NY 10011–4211, USA
10 Stamford Road, Oakleigh, Melbourne 3166, Australia

© Cambridge University Press 1995

First published 1995

Printed in Great Britain at the University Press, Cambridge

A catalogue record for this book is available from the British Library

Library of Congress cataloguing in publication data
The Scandinavian Reformation: from evangelical movement to
institutionalisation of reform/edited by Ole Peter Grell.
    p.   cm.
Includes index.
ISBN 0 521 44162 5
1. Reformation – Scandinavia.   2. Scandinavia – Church history – 16th
century.   I. Grell, Ole Peter.
BR400.S29   1995
274.8′06–dc20   94–14116 CIP

ISBN 0 521 44162 5 hardback

CPSL

Contents

Notes on contributors

OLE PETER GRELL is a Carlsberg Research Fellow at the Wellcome Unit for the History of Medicine at the University of Cambridge. He is the author of *Dutch Calvinists in Early Stuart London* (1989). His publications include a number of articles on the Danish and Scandinavian Reformation, and he has recently co-edited the volume, *Medicine and the Reformation* (1993).

JENS CHR. V. JOHANSEN is a Research Fellow in the Department of Legal History at the University of Copenhagen in Denmark. He has written a number of articles on witchcraft and superstition in Denmark and has recently published *Da Djævlen var ude ... Trolddom i det 17. århundredes Danmark* (1991).

E. I. KOURI is Professor of History at the University of Helsinki in Finland. He is the author of *England and the Attempts to Form a Protestant Alliance in the late 1560s* (1981), *Elizabethan England and Europe* (1982), and he has co-edited *Politics and Society in Reformation Europe* (1987). He is also an editor of the forthcoming *Cambridge History of Scandinavia*.

MARTIN SCHWARZ LAUSTEN is Associate Professor of Church History at the University of Copenhagen in Denmark. Among his books on Danish and northern German Reformation history are *Christian den 3. og Kirken 1537–1559* (1987) and *Bishop Peder Palladius og Kirken 1537–1560* (1987).

THORKILD LYBY is Associate Professor in Church History at the University of Aarhus in Denmark. He has written a number of articles on the Reformation in Denmark and has recently published a major monograph, *Vi Evangeliske. Studier over samspillet mellem udenrigspolitik og kirkepolitik på Frederik I's tid* (1993).

INGUN MONTGOMERY is Professor of Church History at the University of Oslo in Norway. She has written extensively on religion and politics in late sixteenth- and early seventeenth-century Sweden. She is the author of the most recent book on the relationship between church and state in early modern Sweden, *Värjestånd och Lärostånd. Religion och politik i meningsutbytet melan kungamakt och prästerskap i Sverige 1593–1608* (1972).

Preface

It is well over a century ago that the Danish historian, C. F. Allen, published his seminal five-volume study of Scandinavia in the Reformation period, entitled: *De tre nordiske Rigers Historie*. Since then, however, hardly any works, apart from a few surveys, have focussed on the Reformation of Scandinavia as a whole. Instead, subsequent scholars of Scandinavian Reformation history have restricted their research to one or, at most, two of the Nordic countries, normally their own country, thus reflecting a national division which in many ways was a product of the Reformation. This volume will remedy this situation by providing, for the first time in English, a detailed history of the Scandinavian Reformation from its evangelical beginning in the 1520s until its institutionalisation in the first half of the seventeenth century, when Protestant territorial churches had been firmly established in the Nordic kingdoms. At the same time it will, of course, also make available in English the most recent research into the Reformation of the Nordic countries.

In such a tightly conceived volume as the present a considerable amount of flexibility and co-operation from my five contributors has been absolutely essential for the successful conclusion of this enterprise. For this, I thank them, and also for the patience and generosity with which they have accepted most of my editorial interventions.

Apart from those contributing I have also benefited from discussions with Dr P. Ingesman of Aarhus University and my colleague at the Wellcome Unit for the History of Medicine, Dr A. Cunningham, who has patiently listened to much talk about the Scandinavian Reformation.

For her expert linguistic assistance in translating and editing the papers I thank Dr Helen A. Brown; in this connection I gratefully acknowledge a grant towards the translation of the present work from the Danish Research Council for the Humanities.

I have also benefited from the practical advice and support of Richard Fisher of Cambridge University Press throughout the editing of this book. None of this, however, would have been possible without the financial support I have enjoyed from the Carlsberg Foundation in Copenhagen to whom I dedicate this volume with gratitude.

Ole Peter Grell
Cambridge

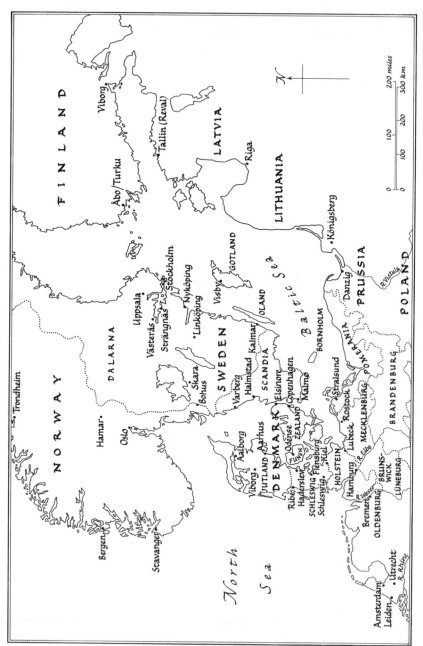

Scandinavia during the Reformation

CHAPTER 1

Introduction

Ole Peter Grell

Evangelical ideas first reached Scandinavia around 1520. At this time, this vast and sparsely populated region was of only marginal political and religious significance in Europe. The Reformation of the Nordic countries which followed was largely a by-product of Luther's Reformation. The Nordic countries still remained of little importance for the Reformation in general, when, in 1555, the Peace of Augsburg guaranteed the survival of European Protestantism for the immediate future. However, by the early seventeenth century and the Thirty Years War, it was the political and military intervention of Lutheran Scandinavia, together with militant Calvinism in south and southwest Germany, which eventually secured the survival of Protestantism at the peace negotiations in Münster and Osnabrück.[1] The importance of Scandinavia to European Protestantism less than a century after Luther's death was, in other words, paramount. Even if the interventions of Christian IV of Denmark and Gustavus Adolphus of Sweden in the Thirty Years War were dictated as much by political as by religious ambitions, their decisions to take up arms for the Protestant cause would hardly have been imaginable without their Lutheran upbringing and power bases, as kings of strongly Lutheran states. With regard to Gustavus Adolphus, it is probably more telling that the king chose to wear a black breast plate in battle which proclaimed him to be the champion of God, i.e. Protestantism, than his constant reassurances to the German princes and the emperor that his reasons for intervening in the war were purely political.[2] Gustavus Adolphus undoubtedly believed that he acted as God's instrument, chosen to defend all Protestants, Calvinists, as well as Lutherans.[3]

[1] See, for instance, H. A. Oberman, *Luther. Man between God and Devil*, London 1989, 10–12.
[2] For this breast plate with Jehovah written in capital letters across it, see H. Langer, *The Thirty Years War*, Dorset 1978, plate 110; for an emphasis on the political motives of Gustavus Adolphus, often to the exclusion of any religious motivation, see G. Parker, *The Thirty Years War*, London 1984, 121–2.
[3] M. Roberts, *Gustavus Adolphus. A History of Sweden*, II, London 1958, 788.

In Scandinavia, as well as in Germany, the new evangelical ideas benefited from the social and political upheavals which had begun in the late Middle Ages. The defeudalisation process saw a growing confrontation between lay and ecclesiastical aristocracy, peasants, burghers and the crown in the Nordic countries during this period. As in Germany, the political centre came under ever greater pressure from the periphery. Whereas in Germany, by 1520, Luther had already, willingly or unwillingly, become a pawn in the political struggle between the territorial princes and the emperor, the Reformation in Scandinavia became intrinsically linked to the weakening of the political centre, and helped to accelerate the dissolution of the Scandinavian Union, which had been created in 1397, into territorial/national states.[4]

The attempts of the Danish king, Christian II, to secure and expand his control over the Union of the Scandinavian Kingdoms through increasingly absolutist policies only served to antagonise the lay and ecclesiastical nobility in his realms. His harsh repression of those who wanted greater Swedish independence led to the massacre of more than eighty members of the Swedish lay and ecclesiastical aristocracy in Stockholm in November 1520. This sparked a revolt under the leadership of Gustav Vasa, whose father had been among those executed in Stockholm, which eventually saw Sweden re-established as an independent kingdom in 1521. By April 1523, royal policies which sought to restrict the political influence of the Danish aristocracy forced Christian II to seek refuge in the Netherlands after he had been deposed by the Danish Council (*Rigsrådet*). The Council immediately proceeded to elect their ally, and Christian II's uncle, Duke Frederik of Schleswig and Holstein, as king. Thus by the summer of 1523 two usurpers, Gustav Vasa and Frederik I had succeeded to the thrones of Sweden/Finland and Denmark/Norway and the Union of the Scandinavian Kingdoms had collapsed. Both monarchs were positively inclined towards the new evangelical ideas and wanted to establish some form of national church under royal control.[5] They appear, however, to have differed significantly in religious commitment. Where Gustav Vasa's interest in Protestantism was predominantly determined by political and economic

[4] For Germany, see W. Borth, *Die Luthersache (causa Lutherani), 1517–1524*, Lübeck and Hamburg 1970, 75–7 and 106–14; see also P. Blickle, 'Social Protest and Reformation Theology', in P. Blickle (ed.), *Religion, Politics and Social Protest*, London 1984, 1–23. For Scandinavia, see O. P. Grell, 'Scandinavia', in A. Pettegree (ed.), *The Early Reformation in Europe*, Cambridge 1992, 94–119.
[5] See chapters 2 and 3.

considerations, Frederik I's, and later his son, Christian III's, views were dictated as much by religious, as by political priorities.

Until the danger, which the deposed king, Christian II, and his Habsburg family continued to present for the new Scandinavian rulers, eventually disappeared during the 1530s, some hesitant, political co-operation existed between Gustav Vasa and Frederik I. Gustav Vasa, however, always doubted the political sincerity of Frederik I and later, even more so, that of his son, Christian III who, he was convinced, nurtured secret ambitions of re-establishing the Union under Danish hegemony. Yet, it has to be borne in mind that Gustav Vasa's position remained exposed, at least until the 1540s, facing, as he did, constant internal revolts, and lack of external recognition of the legitimacy of his rule. Frederik I and later his son, Christian III, never encountered similar domestic problems and, while their legitimacy could also be questioned, they, at least, belonged to the royal family and were next in the line of succession to Christian II. These circumstances undoubtedly helped to make their rule internationally more acceptable in an early modern Europe, which was increasingly dominated by dynastic ideas.[6]

Both Gustav Vasa and Frederik I were seriously in debt by the time they succeeded to the throne; Gustav more so than Frederik because of the protracted military campaign necessary to oust the supporters of Christian II; but even Frederik I's largely unopposed military advance through Denmark to Copenhagen proved costly. In Sweden, as well as in Denmark, this caused serious fiscal problems for years to come. These difficulties were further aggravated by the need for constant extra defence expenditure during the 1520s because of the threat of an invasion by Christian II.[7] Furthermore, the many rebellions in Sweden by a dissatisfied, predominantly conservative and Catholic population, not to mention the civil war in Denmark (*Grevens Fejde*) of 1534–6, which followed the death of Frederik I and eventually saw Christian III enter Copenhagen victoriously, added to the economic woes of the countries. Economic necessity alone would have dictated some form of inter-vention against a wealthy Catholic church in both countries, simply in order to foot the bills.[8] Thus, both governments had sound financial reasons for supporting the evangelical movement. Consequently, the

---

[6] Grell, 'Scandinavia', 117; for the growing European dynasticism, see R. Bonney, *The European Dynastic States 1494–1660*, Oxford 1991.

[7] For Sweden, see M. Roberts, *The Early Vasas. A History of Sweden 1523–1611*, Cambridge 1968, 92–3; for Denmark, see T. Lyby, *Vi Evangeliske. Studier over Samspillet mellem Udenrigspolitik og Kirkepolitik på Frederik I's Tid*, Aarhus 1993, 33–4.

[8] See chapters 2, 3 and 4.

leaders of the Catholic church in Scandinavia already found themselves on the defensive for economic and political reasons, before the evangelical movement undermined their position further.[9]

Popular support for the Reformation was undoubtedly strongest in Denmark, where, by the second decade of the sixteenth century, Catholicism seems to have been unable to generate much grass-roots support, as opposed to Sweden. Furthermore, only in Denmark does anti-clericalism appear to have been a significant phenomenon. This is to some extent explained by the fact that Denmark was the most urbanised of the Nordic countries. More than 10 per cent of the population lived in towns here, several of which such as Copenhagen, Malmø, Elsinore, Odense, Aalborg, Aarhus and Ribe ranged in size from 2,000 to 8,000 inhabitants. In Sweden less than 5 per cent of the population lived in towns and only Stockholm, which had between 4,000 and 6,000 inhabitants, could lay any real claim to urban status, while most other Swedish towns were little more than large villages.[10] Norway and Finland were even more rural in character. As in Germany, it was in the urban environment that evangelical ideas first took root and spread. Thus Denmark, with its relations with the German urban centres much closer than the other Scandinavian countries, provided social conditions which proved particularly conducive to Protestantism. Further proof that popular support for Protestantism was much stronger in Denmark than in Sweden can be found in the evangelical literature published in the two countries. The Danish literature is doctrinally more diverse than the Swedish, even if the confessional significance of these differences have often been overemphasised by modern church historians. The variations in emphasis and doctrine of these works, however, can be seen to confirm the relative strength of popular support for the Reformation in Denmark, whereas the uniformity of the Swedish literature is indicative of an evangelical movement which, apart from developments in Stockholm, depended primarily on princely initiatives.[11]

Consequently Denmark witnessed a full Reformation well before the other Nordic countries and became the first country in Scandinavia to receive a Protestant Church Order in 1537/9, written under the

[9] See chapter 4.
[10] For the urbanisation of Sweden, see Roberts, *The Early Vasas*, 28–30; for Denmark, see E. Ladewig Petersen, *Dansk Social Historie*, III, Copenhagen 1980, 47 and 199–202; A. E. Christensen *et al.* (eds.), *Gyldendals Danmarkshistorie*, II, Copenhagen 1980, 376–7. See also O. P. Grell, 'The Emergence of Two Cities: The Reformation in Malmø and Copenhagen', in L. Grane and K. Hørby (eds.), *Die dänische Reformation vor ihrem Internationalen Hintergrund*, Göttingen 1990, 129–45.
[11] For Sweden, see chapter 3.

supervision of Luther's colleague and friend, Johannes Bugenhagen. The new Lutheran church in Denmark closely followed the Wittenberg model. It was a church fully controlled by the crown, where the ministers and superintendents/bishops were loyal servants of the government, swearing allegiance to the king. In the Request of 1536, the evangelical preachers wanted the new church to be given control over spiritual affairs, ecclesiastical appointments, and to be allowed an arch-bishop/head superintendent. This was ignored by Christian III. The king, who saw himself as *custos utriusque tabulae* (keeper of the two tablets of the Law of Moses), often deliberately ignored the advice of his clergy and personally intervened in ecclesiastical affairs.[12]

The route of the Reformation in Sweden was far more tortuous and much slower than in Denmark. The country did not receive a Church Order until 1571 and then only in a confessionally vague form. It was not until the Uppsala Assembly of 1593 that it finally opted for Lutheran-ism.[13] Consequently, Sweden became the most heterodox of the Scandi-navian countries, dithering between Lutheranism, Calvinism and Catholicism throughout most of the second half of the sixteenth century. This was in many ways a bequest from the reign of Gustav Vasa (1521–60). During the last twenty years of his reign, Gustav Vasa had been firmly in control of all ecclesiastical matters in his realm, but he had avoided making any final decisions with regard to ecclesiastical organis-ation and confessional matters. That he chose Calvinist tutors, such as Dionysius Beurreus and Jan van Herboville, for his sons Erik, later King Erik XIV, and Karl, later King Karl IX, is yet another sign that Gustav Vasa was less concerned about confessional orthodoxy than his royal counterparts in Denmark.[14] The result was that the Swedish church did not, either legally, or in practice, become part of the state. Instead it continued to be led by the archbishop of Uppsala. Given the right political and ecclesiastical circumstances, this guaranteed that the Swed-ish church would pursue its own church policy, as it did in the reigns of Gustav Vasa's three sons, Erik XIV (1560–8), Johan III (1568–92), and Karl IX (1599–1611).

Similarly, the lack of proper institutionalisation of the Reformation in the country made the Swedish church susceptible to greater changes in royal church policy. Following the death of Gustav Vasa, Reformed or

[12] M. Schwarz Lausten, *Christian den 3. og Kirken 1537–1559*, Copenhagen 1987, 109–10, and 215–16.
[13] See chapter 6.
[14] For Beurreus, see *Svensk Biografisk Lexikon* (Swedish Dictionary of National Biography), henceforth *SBL*.

Calvinist ideas appear to have gained ground during the first years of the reign of Erik XIV, not least via his influential Huguenot tutor and advisor, Dionysius Beurreus. Eventually, Beurreus and his followers, many of whom were immigrants from East Friesland who had been encouraged to settle in Sweden during the last years of Gustav Vasa's reign, were confronted by Archbishop Laurentius Petri and the predominantly Lutheran hierarchy of the Swedish church, forcing Erik XIV to halt the propagation of Reformed doctrine in the country. Calvinist teachings were declared false, but the Reformed immigrants were guaranteed freedom of conscience.[15]

Later in the 1570s, after the accession of Johan III, the crown sought to bring the Swedish church closer to Catholicism, via amendments to the Church Order of 1571, the *Nova Ordinantia*, and a new liturgy, the so-called Red Book.[16] Even if Johan III probably never intended a full return to the Catholic fold, he encouraged secret Jesuit attempts to introduce the Counter Reformation in Sweden. Thus the Norwegian Jesuit, Laurentius Nicolai ('Klosterlasse'), who arrived in Stockholm in 1576, proved an immediate success with Johan, who allowed him to open a theological college in the former Franciscan monastery in the city. As could be expected from a good Jesuit, Laurentius Nicolai had quickly identified one of the major weaknesses of the Swedish Reformation: the shortage of evangelical secondary and tertiary education in the country. The University of Uppsala had been closed since 1516 and, in spite of attempts by both Erik XIV and Johan III to invigorate it, there was nowhere that the Swedish clergy could be properly educated. During the two years he was active in Sweden, Laurentius Nicolai's Jesuit academy in Stockholm proved highly successful, until riots, which followed Nicolai's admission of being a Jesuit, forced Johan III to close the college. It was not until the Uppsala Assembly in 1593, which finally confirmed the Swedish church as Lutheran, that a decision was taken to re-open the University of Uppsala. The official opening of the university took place in 1595 on the initiative of Duke Karl, the later King Karl IX.[17]

If anything, the Jesuit attempt to infiltrate Sweden served only to undermine the reign of Johan's son, the Catholic King Sigismund of Poland, who was deposed in 1598/9 after only six years on the throne.

[15] G. Annell, *Erik XIV:s Etiska förestillinger och deras inflytande på hans politik*, Uppsala 1945, 182–202.
[16] See chapter 6.
[17] For Laurentius Nicolai's activities in Sweden, see V. Helk, *Laurentius Nicolai Norvegius*, Copenhagen 1966, 80–153; for the deplorable state of evangelical education in Sweden, see S. Lindroth, *Svensk Lärdomshistoria. Medeltiden. Reformationstiden*, Stockholm 1975, 208–22 and 340–6. See also C. Annerstedt, *Uppsala Universitets Historia*, I, Uppsala 1877.

The Protestant opposition to the crypto-Catholic policies of Johan and Sigismund had been openly encouraged by Duke Karl. Several leading members of the Swedish Church had sought refuge in Karl's duchy from where they emerged during the 1590s. Karl, however, found that when he became ruler of Sweden many of the Lutheran theologians to whom he had offered protection against Johan and Sigismund turned out to be his most ardent antagonists. Not only did they outspokenly defend the independence of the church, but they also accused him of crypto-Calvinism. They obstructed all his attempts to impose royal supremacy on the church and resented his, in their eyes, heterodox doctrinal views.[18]

Karl, however, appears to have supported a scheme for the unification of the Protestant churches, faced as they were with resurgent Catholicism. In 1608 he ordered a religious dispute to take place between the Scottish Reformed minister, John Forbes, who had arrived in Stockholm, and his Lutheran archbishop, Olaus Martini. Karl appears to have been interested in a unification scheme until at least 1610, when John Forbes, who later became minister to the English Reformed church in Middleburg in the United Provinces, made a second visit to Sweden.[19] The Swedish government retained its interest in unifying the different Protestant denominations in the reign of Gustavus Adolphus. Not only the king, but also his closest advisors, Axel Oxenstierna and Johan Skytte, actively promoted John Dury's well-known plan for the unification of the Protestant churches and later invited Amos Comenius to Sweden. This was all done in spite of strong opposition from the Lutheran leadership of the Swedish church.[20]

Denmark witnessed no such changes in church policy. The Church Order of 1537 provided the foundation for a flexible anti-doctrinal Lutheranism which, seen from the government's perspective, remained unchanged throughout this period, even if the dominant theology of the church gradually moved in a more liberal, Philippist, crypto-Calvinist direction, as can be seen from the example of Niels Hemmingsen.[21] Christian III and his son, Frederik II, actively discouraged religious debate, and not until the second decade of the seventeenth century, in the reign of Christian IV, as a reaction to Counter Reformation

---

[18] See H. Block, *Karl IX som teolog och religiös personlighet*, Uppsala 1918.
[19] For John Forbes's visits to Sweden, see *SBL*; for Forbes's career, see also *Dictionary of National Biography*.
[20] See S. Lindroth, *Svensk Lärdomshistoria. Stormaktstiden*, Stockholm 1975, 168–70.
[21] See chapter 5.

Catholicism on one hand, and Calvinism on the other, did the Danish church witness a struggle over doctrine. Then, however, the outcome was a foregone conclusion. Bishop Hans Poulsen Resen's drive for Lutheran uniformity constituted an integral part of the government's absolutist policies. In many ways it was a policy which had much more in common with that of Archbishop William Laud in England in the 1630s, than the move towards a narrow Lutheran orthodoxy which took place in a number of German territorial states in the same period.

Furthermore, Denmark benefited from an extended period of internal peace and stability, which made it possible for the government gradually to put a new Lutheran ecclesiastical administration in place, and to build up a network of evangelical Latin schools.[22] The University of Copenhagen which had been closed since 1531 was re-opened in 1537, re-modelled on the Lutheran University of Wittenberg. This evangelical preoccupation with the creation of an educational and ecclesiastical framework for the new Lutheran church was only temporarily halted by the Seven Years War with Sweden from 1563 to 1570. Following the peace of Stettin in 1570, however, the efforts to improve both secondary and tertiary education, as well as the economic conditions for the new church, such as minister's salaries, gathered pace in Denmark.[23]

Some of the differences between the Lutheran Reformations in Denmark/Norway and Sweden/Finland are illustrated by the countries' contrasting reactions to the growing number of Protestant refugees who sought a safe haven in the second half of the sixteenth century. Already in 1553 fear of Anabaptists and 'Sacramentarians' (Reformed) made the Danish government issue an injunction against foreigners settling in the country without prior proof of their orthodoxy. The arrival in Copenhagen of Johannes a Lasco with approximately 200 Reformed refugees from London, who had fled England after the accession of the Catholic Queen Mary, in July 1553, provoked an immediate government response. Not only were the refugees expelled from Denmark/Norway and the duchies of Schleswig and Holstein after having refused to accept the Order and doctrines of the Lutheran church,[24] but the affair probably encouraged the government to re-issue the Injunction of 1553 with

---

[22] See L. Grane, 'Teaching the People – the Education of the Clergy and the Institution of the People in the Danish Reformation Church', in Grane and Hørby (eds.), *Die dänische Reformation*, 164–84.

[23] See chapter 5; see also O. P. Grell, 'Scandinavia', in R. W. Scribner, R. Porter and M. Teich (eds.), *The Reformation in National Context*, Cambridge 1994, 111–32.

[24] For the arrival in Denmark of Johannes a Lasco and the Reformed refugees from London, see M. Schwarz Lausten, *Biskop Peder Palladius og Kirken 1537–1560*, Copenhagen 1987, 206–24.

the added threat of capital punishment for offenders. Later, in 1569, the growing number of heterodox Protestant refugees from the Netherlands who sought shelter from the persecution of the Duke of Alva in Denmark caused the government to issue the Strangers' Articles which obliged immigrants to accept the Augsburg Confession and the Danish Church Order.[25] Evidently the government had no intention of accepting Protestant refugees, who, even if their economic benefit to the country would be considerable, might destabilise the religious equilibrium.

The Swedish government's approach to such immigrants was totally different. Gustav Vasa invited Calvinist exiles from the Netherlands to settle in Sweden in 1559. This policy was continued by Erik XIV who asked Dionysius Beurreus, who then served as Swedish ambassador to Queen Elizabeth of England, to recruit Reformed refugee craftsmen in London, promising them that they would be allowed to profess their faith openly, while enjoying full civil rights on a par with the king's subjects, if they were to settle in Sweden. The charter Erik XIV issued on 5 March 1561 inviting those who had been exiled 'for the sake of devotion and truth' to emigrate to Sweden, if they would 'live in peace according to the gospel and the true religion of God' and, of course, 'conduct themselves as pious Christians, and swear and preserve allegiance to us and our kingdom', in effect offered religious toleration for Reformed Protestants in Sweden.[26] However, Archbishop Laurentius Petri's intervention against Calvinism in 1565 caused Erik XIV to halt this initiative.

This policy was eventually resurrected by his brother, Karl IX, in the 1590s. In spite of the antagonism towards Calvinism espoused by the leading Lutheran theologians in Sweden during his reign, the demands of the Lutheran church were largely subordinated to the mercantilist policies of the crown. Thus, one of the leading Dutch entrepreneurs, Willem de Bessche, who managed to improve Swedish weapon production and obtained a virtual monopoly on Swedish iron production, settled in the country in 1595 on the invitation of Karl. De Bessche, however, was only the most successful of the many, primarily Reformed, craftsmen and entrepreneurs whom Karl IX encouraged to settle in Sweden.[27] Gustavus Adolphus continued his father's mercantilist policy, inviting Reformed immigrants to Sweden, and in 1627 the Reformed

---

[25] See chapter 6.
[26] O. P. Grell, 'Huguenot and Walloon Contributions to Sweden's Emergence as a European Power, 1560–1648', in *Proceedings of the Hugeunot Society*, 25, 4 (1992), 378–9.
[27] K. Kilbom, *Vallonerne. Valloninvandringen. Stormaktsvældet och den svenska Järnhanteringen*, Stockholm 1958, 168–85.

merchant and entrepreneur, Louis de Geer, made Sweden his home. It was thanks to de Geer that the military–industrial complex was established in Sweden which made it possible to supply the Swedish armies during the Thirty Years War. In this connection it proved important that Gustavus Adolphus, on his accession in 1611, managed to secure some measure of toleration for the Reformed, even if they were not allowed their own church and were excluded from government jobs. This limited religious liberty was later confirmed in 1615.[28] In practice, however, the toleration granted the Reformed immigrants was considerably greater and the government connived at the existence of Reformed congregations and services in Stockholm and Gothenburg. In November 1627, a low point for the Protestant cause in the Thirty Years War, Gustavus Adolphus even issued a proclamation offering all persecuted German Protestants refuge in Sweden.[29]

During the early part of Christian IV's reign a similar toleration for Calvinist immigrants, dictated by mercantilist policies, appears to have been considered by the Danish government. Thus, in 1607 when the government dispatched the diplomat, Jonas Charisius, to the United Provinces, to recruit Reformed craftsmen and merchants, these prospective immigrants were promised religious freedom.[30] However, the prospect of toleration quickly evaporated when the Strangers' Articles of 1569 were re-issued as part of the series of laws which the government issued from 1617 onwards, in order to enhance uniformity in state and church. Thus, no similar promises appear to have been offered when, in the early 1620s, new attempts were made to encourage Dutch merchants and craftsmen to settle in Denmark and Norway.

In spite of these major differences in pace and impact between the Reformations in Denmark/Norway and Sweden/Finland, they shared a number of identical difficulties, especially concerning the problems their governments and churches faced when trying to convert the population to the new evangelical faith. It proved difficult to eradicate Catholic traditions and superstition. The Lutheran clergy in Scandinavia had to fight a constant battle against the adoration of images, and the worship of saints and relics throughout the sixteenth century. In some cases such beliefs and superstitions continued well into the seventeenth century.[31] It

[28] Grell, 'Huguenot and Walloon Contributions to Sweden', 375–84.

[29] M. Roberts, *Gustavus Adolphus*, I, London 1953, 370.

[30] Ladewig Petersen, *Dansk Social Historie*, III, 299 and S. Ellehøj, *Politikens Danmarks Historie*, VII, Copenhagen 1970, 224.

[31] See chapter 7; see also H. J. Frederiksen, 'Reformationens Betydning for den Kirkelige Kunst i Danmark', in Reformationsperspektiver, *Acta Jutlandica*, 62, 3, Aarhus 1987, 100–26.

quickly became evident that the population needed a replacement for the rituals and traditions they had lost at the Reformation. This explains why a cult developed around holy springs which was eventually grudgingly accepted by the Lutheran church.[32] It may also account for the emergence of dozens of Lutheran popular prophets in sixteenth- and seventeenth-century Scandinavia, who, in spite of their often problematic character, originating mainly from the lower strata of the population, were not only tolerated, but often actively used by the Lutheran clergy.[33]

The Lutheran clergy, however, encountered fierce opposition in all the Nordic countries to their attempts to suppress 'cunning folk', not least because these people represented the population's only access to healing. This, however, was not the case with witches; here the population became actively involved in the witchcraft trials of the period, even if the trials in Denmark and Sweden/Finland followed distinctly different routes.[34]

Yet, by the early seventeenth century the Lutheran Reformation had demonstrated its durability in Scandinavia, and succeeded to an extent which many of the first evangelical superintendents/bishops in these countries would only have dreamed of in their more optimistic moments.

[32] Chapter 7.
[33] See J. Beyer, 'Luherske Folkelige Profeter som Åndelige Autoriteter', in B. P. McGuire (ed.) *Autoritet i Middelalderen*, Copenhagen 1991, 157–81. See also J. Beyer, 'Lutherische Propheten in Deutschland und Skandinavien im 16. und 17. Jahrhundert. Entstehung und Ausbreitung eines Kulturmusters zwischen Mündlichkeit und Schriftlichkeit', forthcoming in *Europa in Scandinavia. Kulturelle Dialoge Während der frühen Neuzeit, 1520–1720*, (Studia Septentrionalia, II) Frankfurt.
[34] See chapter 7.

CHAPTER 2

The early Reformation in Denmark and Norway 1520–1559

Martin Schwarz Lausten

The Reformation in the kingdom of Denmark–Norway was closely linked to the developments in the duchies of Schleswig and Holstein. The reason for this is not only to be found in the geographical position of the duchies between Germany and Denmark and their close political affiliation with Denmark in particular, but also in the fact that the evangelical movement made its earliest impact here.

In 1460 the nobility of the duchies had secured the constitutional position of Schleswig and Holstein as inseparable and indivisible. This decision was of considerable importance to the Danish king who, as duke of Schleswig and Holstein, was a vassal of the emperor, since Holstein constituted part of the Holy Roman Empire. However, even if the duchies remained a united administrative territory in a personal union with Denmark until 1848, dynastic interests meant that parts of the duchies continued to be ruled by younger members of the royal family. Thus, while Christian II was king of Denmark and Norway and duke of only parts of Schleswig and Holstein, his uncle resided in the castle of Gottorp and controlled substantial parts of the duchies. When, in 1523, the Danish lay and ecclesiastical nobility had forced Christian II into exile in the Netherlands, his uncle, the later Frederik I, was the obvious choice as king, strongly supported as he was by the aristocracy in Schleswig and Holstein. Consequently, the kingdoms of Denmark and Norway and the duchies once more became united under one ruler.

The beginnings of the evangelical movement in the duchies coincided with the political turmoil of the early 1520s. By 1522 evangelical preaching had begun in Holstein. Among the first evangelical ministers was the Wittenberg-educated, Hermann Tast, who began his preaching in Husum. Within the next couple of years the movement spread rapidly in Holstein where it found fertile soil, often prepared by the criticism of Christian humanists within the church. At the Diet of Rendsburg, in May 1525, the prelates complained not only about difficulties in collecting tithes and other spiritual fees, but also about regular disturbances of church services. They found little support among the laity. The lay aristocracy even pointed out that the Catholic church failed in its duty to provide the parishes with trained clergy who could preach. The considerable tension between lay and ecclesiastical aristocracy which had already existed for some time by 1525 grew during the following years, not least because of the financial and fiscal difficulties which confronted Frederik I's government. The king, as well as the lay aristocracy, wanted the church, to provide an increasing share of the government's expenses. The costs of keeping large forces ready and equipped to prevent a possible invasion by the exiled king, Christian II, and his brother-in-law, the emperor Charles V, were considerable. Accordingly, Frederik I could ill afford to antagonise the ecclesiastical aristocracy, since he depended on their economic and political support. However, the emerging evangelical movement, towards which he proved increasingly sympathetic, provided the king with a welcome lever to force concessions out of the prelates in 1525. They promised to increase their financial contribution to the government and to remedy the shortcomings of the church, promising to provide priests who could preach 'the word of God'. In return the Diet guaranteed the prelates their tithes and other spiritual income, offering the church protection against derision of 'God and his saints' by the laity.

The meeting in Rendsburg in 1525 gave the first indications of Frederik I's positive attitude towards the evangelicals and his willingness to undermine the position of the Catholic church in order to improve his and the realm's financial position. Such royal views were to be more pronounced in the years to come.

The king's desperate need for extra capital was further in evidence during the next Diet of Kiel in February 1526. Here he demanded yet another special tax from the lay and ecclesiastical nobility, as well as the burghers. This time he used the threat of the evangelical movement to even greater effect. For the first time both Frederik I and the prelates referred specifically to a 'Lutheran movement' in the duchies. One of the king's advisors declared that so far Frederik I and his son, Duke Christian, had only been able to contain and suppress 'the Lutheran sect', which might do irreparable damage to the duchies, with the greatest difficulty. The church's response was delivered by the bishop of Schleswig, Gottschalk Ahlefeldt, who offered economic assistance on the condition that the protection of all traditional ecclesiastical liberties and privileges could be guaranteed, not to mention the suppression of 'the martinists', as Ahlefeldt labelled the evangelicals. After having received promises for further financial support from the lay and ecclesiastical aristocracy, as well as the burghers, Frederik I promised the diet that he would uphold and protect the traditional rights of all estates. Nothing, however, was mentioned about the repression of 'the Lutheran sect'.

Similarly, the earlier statement at the diet, pointing to Frederik I's and his son's attempts to contain the evangelical movement, should probably not be taken at face value. By 1526, Duke Christian was fully committed to Protestantism and was already enticing Lutheran theologians to settle in Haderslev.[1] We know of no royal or ducal attempts to limit the effects of the evangelicals. Frederik I, however, had admonished his son the previous year to make sure that the peasants in his parts of the duchies continued to pay that third of their tithes which went to the bishops. In this connection the king had specifically referred to the dangers posed by the contemporary peasant revolts in Germany.

Frederik I's use of the evangelical movement to scare the Catholic clergy and their friends among the aristocracy at the Diet of Kiel became a dress rehearsal for the application of similar policies in Denmark.[2]

Duke Christian, the later Christian III (1503–59), had benefited from having a Wittenberg graduate, the evangelically inclined Wolfgang Utenhof, as tutor. Utenhof had taken up his position in 1518 after having graduated in canon law from the university. Not only was he well versed in Christian humanism, but he had also witnessed Luther's attack on scholasticism and the *Curia*. He was evidently a strong influence on his young pupil. As a member of the delegation of his uncle, Duke Joachim of Brandenburg, Christian attended the Diet of Worms in April 1521 and was moved by Luther's bold defence. His Protestant orientation was further in evidence when he married the evangelical Dorothea of Saxony-Lauenburg in 1526. In connection with his marriage he was given the small fief of Haderslev/Tørning. It consisted of approximately sixty parishes and presented the young duke with an excellent opportunity to introduce the Reformation as a controllable experiment in the wake of the Diet of Rendsburg. Among his first acts was the dismissal of the dean of the collegiate chapter in Haderslev. As early as August 1525 he began to assume the right of patronage to appoint evangelical ministers to

---

[1] See p. 15.
[2] For Denmark, see p. 20; notes from the diets were taken by the canon, Johann Parper, see W. Leverkus (ed.), 'Berichte über die Schleswig-Holsteinischen Landtage von 1525, 1526, 1533, 1540', in *Archiv für Staats-und Kirchengeschichte der Herzogthümer Schleswig, Holstein Lauenburg...*, IV, 1840, 453ff. See also W. Göbel *et al.*, *Schleswig-Holsteins Kirchengeschichte*, III, Neumünster 1982.

vacant positions, while during the first months of 1526 he managed to attract two German evangelical theologians to Haderslev. They were Johann Wenth, a recent graduate from Wittenberg, and Eberhard Weidensee, who held a doctorate in canon law from the University of Leipzig and had spent time in Wittenberg, playing an important part in the Reformation of Magdeburg (1524–6).

Assisted by these two, Duke Christian was able to initiate a regularised and controlled Reformation of his fief. He proceeded to establish a school for evangelical ministers in Haderslev. It was not only aimed at new recruits for the evangelical ministry, but also at local Catholic priests who had to be re-trained. The school proved a success, providing teaching in Latin and Greek and, of course, the Bible. It attracted evangelical pupils from as far afield as Malmø, among them some of Malmø's leading reformers. The duke's newly recruited theological advisors, Weidensee and Wenth, produced a Church Ordinance in 1526 which was introduced in most of Haderslev/Tørning.

The duke, however, was forced to exclude those parishes which belonged to the see of Ribe, because of protests from its bishop, Iver Munk. Such temporary setbacks, however, do not appear to have worried Duke Christian. In 1527 he was personally involved in the expulsion of the mendicant orders from Haderslev. The duke was evidently prepared to take direct action against Catholic institutions where necessary. According to a canon from Ribe, Christian was responsible for plundering many churches of their treasures and for summarily dismissing fully ordained priests. A year later Haderslev/Tørning had witnessed a full Reformation. Duke Christian had undoubtedly been inspired by the recent decisions of the Diet of Speyer in Germany, which had opened the possibility for all territorial rulers in Germany to order their own church affairs, provided they could defend their actions in front of God and the emperor. Simultaneously, the decisions made in Denmark at the two parliaments which met in Odense in 1526 and 1527, which had shown the Catholic church in Denmark to be incapable of resisting continued royal and lay political pressure, would have removed any remaining doubts the duke may have had about introducing the Reformation in his fief.[3] At a synod of the clergy of Haderslev/Tørning which met in the spring of 1528, the duke presented them with the Haderslev Ordinance, which gave firm instructions on how the Lutheran faith should be preached, what ceremonies should be used, how the

---

[3] For the parliaments of 1526 and 1527, see pp. 19–21.

clergy were to live, and a section about ecclesiastical organisation. It is the first evangelical Church Ordinance to emerge in Scandinavia and its dependence on Wittenberg and Luther is obvious. A visitation system on a par with that in Saxony was introduced and the ministers were obliged to swear an oath of obedience to the duke, repudiating false religious teachings.

Thus Duke Christian had established a princely, Lutheran territorial church in his tiny duchy in Schleswig which was identical to similar much larger territorial churches in Germany. The Catholic establishment in Denmark–Norway must have been deeply worried by this Protestant experiment on their doorstep, conducted, if not with royal assent, then certainly without any attempt by Frederik I to hinder his son's evangelical undertakings.[4]

An important prerequisite of the evangelical movement in Denmark–Norway was Christian humanism. Students who returned from universities such as those of Paris, Louvain, Wittenberg, Leipzig and Rostock brought back humanist ideas. Nearly 1,700 matriculated at European universities in the period 1451–1535. Most famous among them is Christiern Pedersen, who graduated from Paris and published a number of mainstream humanist books, apart from several devotional works strongly influenced by Christian humanism. Another Danish humanist, Petrus Parvus Rosæfontanus, offered an abridged humanist education in his 1519 introduction to a work, *Hortulus Synonymorum* (1520), by Henrik Smith, another humanist. He emphasised the importance of studies in Latin, Greek, Hebrew, rhetoric and classical authors, and he praised some of the famous humanists such as Erasmus, 'the learned, great general for the literary army, the object for all Christendom's enthusiasm', Petrus Mosellanus, and Johannes Rhagius Æsticampianus. Rosæfontanus cited Wittenberg as a centre for humanist learning and referred to Melanchthon as 'the most learned' while Martin Luther is mentioned as 'the theological doctor who most excellently seeks the truth of God'.

It was around this time that Christian humanism started to have an impact within the University of Copenhagen. It had been encouraged by King Christian II, who wanted to improve the quality and standing of the university. He encouraged the Carmelite friars to establish a college in the vicinity of the university. The leader of this college, Paulus Helie (c.1485–c.1535) was given a lectureship in theology at the university.

---

[4] M. Schwarz Lausten, *Christian den 3. og kirken 1537–1559*, Copenhagen 1987, 9–12 and H. V. Gregersen, *Reformationen i Sønderjylland*, Aabenraa 1986, 49–173.

Christian II was instrumental in bringing the Wittenberg-educated Martin Reinhard to Denmark, as royal chaplain, and Mathias Gabler, as lecturer in Greek. Briefly, the king also managed to entice Andreas Karlstadt to Copenhagen. Karlstadt seems to have been intended for a position as royal advisor and court preacher with special responsibility for a new ecclesiastical appeal court which Christian II intended to create. It was to have been part of a new set of laws which the king planned to introduce and which also determined that old scholastic textbooks were to be burned and replaced by modern humanist text-books. Students were to be taught classics, to read Terence, Virgil, Cicero, history and the Old and New Testaments. However, before these laws could be fully introduced Christian II had been forced into exile.[5]

The most influential of all the humanists was Paulus Helie. He shared the Christian humanist platform of his idol, Erasmus, and criticised traditional Catholic theology and Catholic piety. He was hostile to scholastic theology, because it failed to unite true piety with the curriculum. Scholasticism was seen as barbaric because it relied on medieval commentators rather than the texts. Instead, Helie wanted to focus on the text of the New Testament, emphasising the significance of understanding 'Christ, Peter and Paul' and advocating the teaching of the classical languages. Occasionally, he would also give weight to the apostolic tradition, the Fathers and decisions of the church councils, but these aspects always remained secondary and could only be used to support evidence drawn from scripture. On the question of faith and the important doctrine of free will, he followed Erasmus closely, but that did not prejudice his view of Luther, whose theology he agreed with on a number of points. Like Luther, Paulus Helie, was of the opinion that Man was saved by faith alone; but simultaneously he underlined the necessity of true piety. Like Erasmus he attracted great importance to the ethical behaviour of Man. Faith should express itself in godly living. Good works could not be discarded in connection with salvation, despite the overpowering importance of faith and grace. Helie was also strongly critical of traditional Catholic piety, but had no intention of leaving the church. The church had to be reformed from within through pious theological learning and pious living.

Through his teaching and criticism of the church, Paulus Helie proved immensely influential, not only at the University of Copenhagen, but

---

[5] For these laws and the scholarly debate, see A. E. Christensen *et al.* (eds.), *Danmarks Historie*, II, part I, Copenhagen 1980, 240–4 (K. Hørby).

more significantly and unintentionally, on the evangelical movement, where several of his pupils came to play an important part.[6]

THE CHURCH POLICY OF FREDERIK I AND HIS GOVERNMENT

By the end of 1522 the Danish lay and ecclesiastical aristocracy was in rebellion against Christian II. The cumulative effect of the king's autocratic rule and his often brutal actions against opponents generated the revolt. Christian II's recent actions in Sweden where, in 1520, he had executed around eighty members of the nobility including two bishops, had caused European consternation, while his high-handed treatment of the archbishopric of Lund had angered the *Curia*. In Denmark the Catholic prelates had been deeply worried by the king's new laws which would have interfered directly with the church's legal status and introduced Christian humanist reforms. It is significant that these laws were ceremoniously burned and accusations of heresy were emphasised by the rebels. Abroad, the king had not only antagonised the Hanseatic cities of the Baltic, especially Danzig, but also his sister-in-law, Margaret of Austria, the regent of the Netherlands, by augmenting the toll paid by ships passing through the Sound.

Thus it was a deeply isolated Christian II who fled Copenhagen in March 1523 only to see his uncle, Frederik I (1523–33), succeed him on the throne. Frederik I was obliged to sign a coronation charter which confirmed the traditional rights of the lay and ecclesiastical aristocracy. The charter also offered special guarantees for the prelates and the Catholic church against the new heretical teachings which had been promoted by Christian II. The new king promised:

not to allow any heretics, disciples of Luther or others to preach or to teach secretly or openly against the heavenly God, the church, the holiest father, the pope, or the Catholic church, but where they are found in this kingdom, We promise to punish them on life and property.[7]

In spite of this coronation charter forced upon Frederik I by a conservative Catholic Council, it was during his reign that the evangelical movement started to advance in Denmark. While Duke Christian in Schleswig was introducing a princely, Lutheran Reformation, a popular

---

[6] For the influence of these pupils, see p. 23; for Rosæfontanus's preface, see H. Smith, *Hortolus Synonymorum* (1520) in I. Bom (ed.), *Det 16. årh.'s danske Vokabularier*, II, Copenhagen 1974. See also M. Schwarz Lausten. 'Die Universität Kopenhagen und die Reformation', in L. Grane (ed.), *University and Reformation*, Leiden 1981, 99–113 and K. Hørby, 'Humanist Profiles in the Danish Reform Movement', in L. Grane and K. Hørby (eds.), *Die dänische Reformation vor ihrem internationalen Hintergrund*, Göttingen 1990, 28–38.

[7] For the coronation charter, see *Aarsberetninger fra Geheimearchivet*, II, Copenhagen 1856–60, 65–79.

evangelical movement was gaining support in his father's kingdom to the north. Undoubtedly, the popular evangelical movement benefited from the general feudal crisis which characterised Danish society in this period. A growing economic and political tension, which was mainly rooted in conflicts over trade, is in evidence between the aristocracy and the lower nobility on one hand, and the nobility and the burghers of the main towns and cities on the other. Similarly, antagonism between the Catholic church and the magistracies of the major towns and cities was on the increase as a result of the church's expanding ownership of urban properties. Likewise, the lay nobility was deeply worried about the growing ownership of arable land by the bishops in particular.

Furthermore, there was the constant threat of an invasion from the exiled Christian II who could still muster substantial internal support among the lower nobility, burghers and peasants. The exiled king constituted a major security problem which was particularly worrying for the lay and ecclesiastical aristocracy who had been instrumental in his deposition. This constant threat resulted in considerable financial demands, especially extra taxes, by the government. Similarly, news about the progress of the Reformation in the duchies must have caused the bishops and the Catholic majority of the Council further anguish.

Frederik I's confessional attitude has been a point of debate among scholars. For political reasons the king often took, officially at least, a neutral position in the religious domain; but several incidents illustrate his sympathy for the evangelical cause. For instance, he never tried to interfere with the princely Reformation his son was busily implementing in Schleswig, and in 1526 he married his daughter to Duke Albrecht of Prussia, the former Grand Master of the Teutonic Knights, who had recently converted to Lutheranism and was one of the most vilified Catholic apostates of the time. Paulus Helie informs us that the King also started to eat meat on Fridays that year and that his chancellor, Mogens Gøye, had begun taking communion in both forms. Furthermore, in October 1526 Frederik I offered the evangelical preacher, Hans Tausen, a former member of the Order of St John of Jerusalem, his personal protection by issuing a letter of protection.[8]

Far-reaching decisions were made during the parliament which met in Odense in November 1526. Here the prelates were given promises of support from the nobility, 'especially against the unchristian teaching of Luther which is now being used against the Holy Church'. It was,

---

[8] For the evangelical attitude of Frederik I, see the recent work by T. C. Lyby, *Vi Evangeliske. Studier over Samspillet mellem Udenrigspolitik og Kirkepolitik på Frederik I's Tid*, Aarhus 1993.

however, support which came at a price, since the church had to accept restrictions on its ownership of land, originating from the nobility. Of even greater significance was parliament's decision that annates in future should be paid to the government rather than Rome. In this decision lay the foundation for the creation of a national church independent of the pope and the *Curia*.[9]

The attempt of the Council to force Frederik I to respect the jurisdiction of the bishops and not to act contrary to his coronation charter and canon law, by interfering through his letters of protection for the evangelical preachers, failed. The Council's attempt to offer some form of compromise, whereby it would serve as a court of appeal for the ecclesiastical courts, fared no better. The king refused to compromise, proclaiming that he had always been a staunch supporter of the church and that he had never given his letter of protection to anyone who had acted wrongly. He had never encouraged anyone to preach anything but 'God's word and the gospel'. This was a policy he had no intention of changing.

As if to prove his sincerity he issued a further letter of protection during parliament. The recipient was another apostate monk, Jørgen Jensen Sadolin (*c*.1499–1559) who, like Hans Tausen, was active in the town of Viborg. He was given permission 'to teach young people'. This was undoubtedly an oblique reference to the evangelical school for ministers which was quickly established in Viborg by Sadolin. The two reformers demonstrated their confidence and disregard for the Catholic establishment, first when Tausen ordained Sadolin as a minister, and second when Tausen married Sadolin's sister. Both men continued to play an important part in the evangelical movement and later in the reign of Christian III as superintendents/bishops in the post-Reformation Lutheran church.[10]

Meanwhile the traditional hostility among the peasantry towards the payment of that third of the tithes which went to the bishops flared up. Together with the increased tax burden it generated disturbances in Jutland, Funen and Scania which also fed on a growing dissatisfaction with the provisions of the Catholic church at parish level.[11] By now the evangelical movement was spreading rapidly in the major towns and cities. The Council complained to Frederik I that the people were

---

[9] For further details about the decisions made in Odense in 1526, see chapter 4.
[10] See pp. 22 and 41.
[11] For the growing hostility towards the Catholic church among the peasants, see chapter 4.

disobedient 'especially towards the Holy Church and the prelates in the Kingdom to an extent which had never occurred before'.

During the following parliament in August 1527 the Council blamed the king for not having done enough to rein in disobedient peasants and for allowing 'evil councillors' to advise the people to refrain from giving alms to the mendicant orders. The Council demanded that the episcopal jurisdiction should be preserved and that payment of the tithes should be enforced. Frederik I offered full support for the church on the issue of tithes whereas he was only prepared to protect the mendicant friars against violence. Of greater significance, however, was the king's refusal to halt his protection of the evangelical preachers and to allow the Catholic bishops to exercise their jurisdiction over them.

It is important to note that Frederik I took the opportunity in August 1527 to make a general statement about his confessional position: the king refused to side with either the Catholic or the evangelical side, pointing out that the Christian faith was free, and that neither side would like to be forced to abandon their faith. Furthermore, the king could not intervene, because he is 'king and governs life and property, but not the soul'. Everyone had to act in accordance with his conscience and what he could defend before God on the day of judgement. As had been the case at the recent Diets of Schleswig and Holstein, this decision was to be adhered to until a General Council of the church decided otherwise. The use of a reference to the decisions of a future General Council of the whole church was no more than an insurance policy which had already been used in Germany. What it offered was in effect a protective umbrella for the free development of the evangelical movement.

It has been a highly disputed issue within Danish Reformation scholarship whether or not a general 'edict of toleration' was issued for the benefit of the evangelical preachers during the parliament in 1527. No such document has survived and the documents we have would mitigate against such a conclusion. Furthermore, the decisions of parliament would have made such an edict obsolete, since they permitted the evangelical movement to establish itself freely, while re-affirming the existence of an 'official' Catholic church under episcopal jurisdiction.[12]

---

[12] See especially J. O. Andersen, *Overfor Kirkebruddet*, Copenhagen 1917; S. Scharling, Frederik I's Kirkepolitik', *Kirkenhistoriske Samlinger*, 1974, 40–88 and O. P. Grell, 'Herredagen 1527', *Kirkehistoriske Samlinger*, 1978, 69–88. See also M. Schwarz Lausten, *Reformationen i Danmark*, Copenhagen 1987, 33–42. For an English version of the ordinance of the parliament in Odense in 1527, see B. J. Kidd (ed.), *Documents Illustrative of the Continental Reformation*, Oxford 1967, no. 100.

THE REFORMATION OF THE TOWNS AND CITIES

The confrontation between Catholicism and Protestantism came to characterise the next decade. For the evangelical movement it was a period of great popular involvement and appeal. In his chronicle (*Skibyk-røniken*) Paulus Helie wrote under 1526 that 'the poison of Lutheranism was sneaking through the whole of Jutland'; while in one of his first polemical pamphlets against the evangelicals (*Answer to Hans Mikkelsen*, (1527)) he bitterly concluded that 'the word of God is now freely discussed in inns, bath-houses, barber shops, forges, mills, custom houses, burgher-houses, in guilds, at banquets, among drunkards and gamblers, dancers and acrobats, courtiers, cacklers and fools, and shopkeepers', and even by 'such noble and learned men where he who shouts, cackles and blasphemes the loudest is counted the wisest'. Clearly, Helie was against any lay involvement in matters of doctrine and faith, 'especially since wise men could hardly agree on a single article which guaranteed that the ignorant, stupid wags and the mad would never agree'. Being a good humanist, he granted that the holy gospel had been neglected for a while, but that did not imply that 'peasants, burghers, shopkeepers or water-men, horsemen or muskeeters could make it good'.[13]

Paulus Helie had, in other words, no sympathy for the popular evangelical movement, but his influence was limited. By 1530 all major towns in Denmark were affected by the Reformation, if not already fully reformed. Viborg became the centre for the evangelical movement in the western part of the kingdom. The Catholic church had a strong presence here, including the bishop and the cathedral chapter, three major monasteries, the Franciscan, the Dominican and the Order of St John of Jerusalem, plus twelve churches. Furthermore, Viborg was an important administrative seat, where the high court assembled and the nobility gathered regularly. In spite of this the town had been fully reformed under the guidance of Hans Tausen and Jørgen Jensen Sadolin, who, protected by the king and assisted by the magistracy, had generated considerable support for the evangelical cause. Frederik I single-hand-edly allowed the demolition of a number of churches which the magis-tracy considered surplus to requirement and allowed the reformers to take over the monastic churches. Meanwhile, the burghers also occupied the cathedral and introduced evangelical services there.

In the eastern part of the kingdom the city of Malmø became the centre of the Reformation. Malmø, by then the largest Scandinavian

[13] M. Kristensen and N. K. Andersen (eds.), *Skrifter af Paulus Helie*, II, Copenhagen 1932, 65–6.

city, was home for neither bishop nor chapter and was ideally suited to offer full protection for its evangelical preachers. As in Viborg the evangelical movement was strongly encouraged here by the king and the magistracy. During 1529 all monasteries and churches were taken over by the magistracy and the evangelical preachers and a school for ministers was established on a par with those in Haderslev and Viborg. Here the leading reformers were Claus Mortensen, Frants Vormordsen, Peder Laurentsen and Oluf Chrysostomus, who, with the exception of Mortensen, were all former pupils of Helie.

The sermon became the most important tool in the hands of the reformers. It is significant that they labelled themselves preachers, and sermons came to dominate the Protestant services. In the cathedral in Viborg, sermons were given each morning at five and eight o'clock, while shorter services, where hymns in Danish were sung, took place in the morning, at noon, and in the evening. On Sundays the main service should take place in the cathedral when services had ended in the parish churches, while at noon a special service for the young should warn against vices such as drunkenness. In Malmø sermons were given in three churches every morning and hymns were sung in Danish. On Sundays and other holy days no fewer than four sermons before noon and two or three in the afternoon were given. This tightly packed schedule had been decided by the magistracy 'in order that we may be able to exercise the true Christian worship and get to know our blessed God and saviour, Jesus Christ'.[14]

Violent clashes between Catholics and evangelicals took place, especially in Malmø and Copenhagen; but we have little evidence of iconoclasm, apart from minor incidents, such as in Our Lady's Church in Copenhagen around Christmas 1530. Considerable violence, however, seems to have been used against the mendicant orders in particular. The evidence, however, has to be treated with caution, since it comes solely from the Catholic side. A contemporary pamphlet, entitled *The Chronicle of the Expulsion of the Grey Friars from their Monasteries in Denmark* describes the attacks on fifteen Franciscan monasteries in the period 1528–32. It puts the blame squarely on the burghers who masterminded the attacks, inflamed by the preachers, while the king failed to intervene.

Apart from the above mentioned acts to encourage the evangelical movement, Frederik I made increasing use of his right of patronage to

---

[14] See Peder Laurentsen, *Malmøbogen* (1530), ed. H. F. Rørdam, Copenhagen 1868.

promote evangelical ministers. From 1528 we find letters of appointment
for ministers, emphasising that the candidate should 'teach and preach
the pure word of God to the people'. Later, in 1532, we have examples
which are even more evangelical in their phrasing, stating that the
minister should preach purely and comprehensibly and offer the baptism
and the eucharist 'according to the pure word of God, and as a true
evangelical and Christian preacher, pastor and servant ought and is
obliged to do'. Frederik I undoubtedly favoured the evangelical party by
then. It is, however, important to note that from the late 1520s the king
was supported and encouraged in his evangelical initiatives by a small,
but influential number of aristocrats within the Council.

In addition to the sermons and the evangelical schools for ministers
described, the other main evangelical propaganda in Denmark was
printing. The Danish reformers made good use of this, as did their
colleagues in the rest of Europe. Scores of translations of German
evangelical pamphlets were published by the print shops in Viborg and
Malmø, as were locally produced evangelical pamphlets and broad-
sheets of a polemical, satirical and devotional nature, not to mention
manuals for the evangelical services. A considerable proportion of these
publications survive. Among the most important is the so-called *Malmøbook* (full title: *The reason and true explanation of the Reformation, usage and
practice of the mass, sermon and other true divine service and Christian devotion which
has been introduced in the Christian city of Malmø*), published in 1530 by Peder
Laurentsen. He provides a description of the Reformation recently
introduced by 'mayors, magistracy, preachers and teachers'. Laurentsen
gives us not only the main theological tenets of the new evangelical faith,
he also tells the reader about the acts and changes undertaken in the city
in connection with the Reformation, such as within schooling and poor
relief. Central to his pamphlet was the introduction of the evangelical
sermon and Danish hymns sung by the congregation, in addition to the
abolition of all the sacraments except baptism and the eucharist; but the
social undertakings of the reformers are also given prominence. Thus
Laurentsen explains how confiscated church property has been used for
the establishment of schools for children and the new evangelical clergy,
salaries for the ministers, and for provisions for the poor and sick. In a
small section concerned with the ringing of bells Laurentsen provides a
glimpse of how the Reformation in Malmø had come to affect the daily
lives of its inhabitants in often unexpected ways. The dismantling of a
considerable number of churches and monasteries had led to the silenc-
ing of many bells, which had hitherto served to divide the day's activities

for the city's inhabitants. The magistracy had been forced to step in to provide a new system of bell-ringing, performed partly by the watchmen and partly by the remaining churches. Thus, the *Malmøbook* provides a practical handbook of how the Reformation was introduced in the city, its religious content, and its local consequences. Given the right circumstances it may well have become a manual of Reformation for the other Danish towns and cities. It must have been concern about this which prompted a group of Catholic prelates to commission Paulus Helie to write a response. Helie's treatise, *Answer to the book which mayors and councillors in Malmø published about the Reformation of their city*, was highly polemical and aggressive, and remained unprinted until a manuscript copy was finally discovered in the late nineteenth century.[15]

The parliament which met in Copenhagen in the summer of 1530 became another important benchmark in the struggle between Catholics and evangelicals. The danger of an invasion led by the exiled Christian II, who had recently returned to the Catholic church on the instigation of his brother-in-law, Charles V, was increasing. Once more Frederik I had to resort to extra taxes in order to raise much-needed capital. In this situation it was in the king's interest to try to resolve the religious crisis. Frederik seems to have intended a religious disputation on a par with what had already occurred in a number of places in Germany.[16] Representatives of both sides were summoned to Copenhagen in order to produce their 'Christian faith and confession, and to defend and discuss them, in order that a Christian Reformation in religion can be introduced and identically taught and preached in this Kingdom'. The disputation, however, never took place because, among other things, no agreement could be found on who should judge it and what language was to be used. The Catholics wanted the disputation to take place in Latin before a traditional ecclesiastical court, while the evangelical preachers wanted lay judges and a vernacular debate. The preachers

[15] *Cronica seu breuis porcessus in causa expulsionis fratrum Minoritarum de suis cenobiis prouincie Danice*, in *Scriptores minores historiæ Danicæ medii ævi*, II, Copenhagen 1920, 325–67; H. F. Rørdam (ed.), *Skrifter fra Reformation*, I–V, Copenhagen 1885–90; Peder Laurentsen, *Malmøbogen*, Malmø 1530, facsimile edition by K. Gierow, Malmø 1979. See also Lausten, *Reformationen*, 42–97; O. P. Grell, 'The City of Malmø and the Danish Reformation', *Archiv für Reformationsgeschichte*, 79 (1988), 311–39; O. P. Grell, 'The Emergence of Two Cities: The Reformation in Malmø and Copenhagen', in Grane and Hørby, *Die dänische Reformation*, 129–45; H. Lundbæk, *Såfremt som vi skulle være deres lydige borgere. Rådene i København og Malmø 1516–1536 og deres politiske virksomhed i det feudale samfund*, Odense 1985; and M. Winge, 'Das mittelniederdeutsche Gesangbuch König Friederichs von Dänemark', *Jahrbuch des Vereins für niederdeutsche Sprachforschung*, 107, 32–59.
[16] For a different causation and rationale behind these events, see O. P. Grell, *The City of Malmø*, 322–3.

took the opportunity when gathering in Copenhagen to produce their own confession divided into forty-three articles, the so-called *Confessio Hafniensis*. The occasion also resulted in a number of polemical tracts from both sides.

The theology of the evangelical preachers has been debated in recent scholarship. Traditionally, the Danish reformers had been considered 'Lutheran' until N. K. Andersen in 1954 demonstrated that this was far from a satisfying label. Since then the evangelical preachers have been seen as having been closer to the humanist-evangelical movement, which differed from Luther on several important points. According to this concept the preachers, most of whom had been educated within the Christian humanist tradition espoused by their teacher, Paulus Helie, advocated a Protestant theology which had merged organically with their humanist background. This evangelical theology had reached Denmark from southern via northern Germany where it proved particularly important in the costal towns and cities of Zealand and Scania.

The preachers differed from Luther in their emphasis on the Bible, which they considered to be 'the law of Christ'. For them the Bible offered directions for the spiritual, as well as the material domain. The authority of the Bible could not be questioned. They remained unaffected by Luther's more flexible attitude to the Bible and his concept of the Word as means of grace, not to mention his distinction between law and gospel. Likewise, they differed from Luther in their understanding of Christ, the salvation and the sacraments, to mention some of the most important points. This view, however, has been criticised by some scholars. On one hand it has been argued that one of the most prominent reformers, Peder Laurentsen, did not differ from Luther in his concept of the eucharist (T. Christensen); on the other, it has been pointed out that the reformers' view of secular authority corresponds to the Lutheran position (O. P. Grell). These differences were probably of little or no consequence to the reformers. They considered themselves to be 'Lutheran' and that was also how their Catholic antagonists perceived them.[17]

Of greater significance, however, is the social concern which dominates the writings of the evangelical preachers. They appear deeply concerned about the social injustice of contemporary society and there is a close interrelationship between their evangelical theology and their fight for social justice. While advocating religious reform, the evangelical

[17] N. K. Andersen, *Confessio Hafniensis. Den københavnske Bekendelse af 1530*, Copenhagen 1954; T. Christensen, 'De captivitate Babylonica og Peder Laurentsens sakramentsopfattelse', in *Festskrift til K. E. Skydsgaard*, Copenhagen 1962, 136–59 and O. P. Grell, 'The City of Malmø', 328–39.

preachers also gave voice to the dissatisfaction with which most of the urban population viewed the wealthy Catholic institutions and clergy. Their social awareness is demonstrated by their plans for a social re-organisation of society in the fields of education, poor relief and health care. Repeatedly the preachers return to the dichotomy between the wealthy Catholic clergy who have corrupted the Christian faith and the impoverished laity who uphold the evangelical truth. They underline how the Catholic prelates, on the pretext of their false teaching, have crudely exploited the laity, especially with regard to requiem masses, images of saints, tithes, indulgences, and the establishment of confraternities. Apart from the indignation caused by this exploitation of the common people, the preachers were particularly angered by the clergy's negative attitude to physical work. They claimed that the poor peasants in particular were troubled by the many Catholic holy days and fasts, not least during harvest time when, according to Peder Laurentsen, the clergy was troubling the consciences of poor people with sin and torment if they carried out necessary work.

For the evangelical preachers, the Catholic distinction between lay and clerical was false. With reference to the New Testament, they emphasised the priesthood of all believers. Similarly, they wanted services to be held in the vernacular rather than Latin, which they considered to be an expression of Catholic clerical arrogance and contempt for the laity. They stated:

that a poor person, boy or girl, who sits on a cartload of dung and sings the Ten Commandments or some other praise from the gospel, he or she is better esteemed by God than many priests, monks or canons who grumble and shout from morning till night without true Christian faith and godliness, because they do not contemplate in the least what they sing and read.

Closely connected with these questions was the issue of the proper use of land and property which had hitherto belonged to the Catholic church. The Malmø reformer, Frants Vormordsen, demanded that this property be used for the salaries of evangelical bishops and ministers, for schools and tertiary education and for the support of hospitals and care for the poor, as had already been done in Malmø.[18]

POLITICS AND RELIGION IN NORWAY

Developments in Norway in the Reformation period were largely similar to those in Denmark. They were determined by a mixture of economic,

[18] See *Malmøbogen*, fol. 42. See also Lausten, *Reformationen*, 70–87.

political and religious factors. Added to that there was a distinct and significant move towards a more independent and nationally dictated policy. The Union Treaty of 1450, which remained in force until 1536, stated that the two kingdoms should remain united, equally, in eternity under the same king. The decisive political power was bestowed on the Council (*Rigsrådet*) under the leadership of the Norwegian archbishop. In reality, Norwegian independence was nullified during the reign of Christian II (1513–23). Even if Frederik I had to sign a coronation charter for Norway which was similar to the one he had to accept for Denmark, his promise to fight 'Lutheranism' proved as empty as it did in Denmark.

The evangelical movement, however, did not manage to generate much popular support in Norway. Evangelical preaching probably began in 1526 and between 1527 and 1529 a number of evangelical preachers were active and found adherents among leading noble families. However, the support for the evangelical cause was meagre.

Archbishop Olav Engelbriktsson became the main defender of the Catholic church and national independence during the reign of Frederik I. Engelbriktsson demonstrated a hostile attitude towards Frederik I from the outset and seems early on to have come to consider the king a heretic. Politically, the archbishop sought support from Christian II, in spite of the exiled king's already proven hostility to the Norwegian Catholic church and its prelates. Engelbriktsson evidently considered Christian II's re-conversion to Catholicism sincere (1530). Furthermore, the reconciliation between the exiled king and his brother-in-law, Emperor Charles V, suddenly made it possible for Christian to make an attempt to recapture Denmark/Norway. When Christian II arrived in Norway in 1531 with an expeditionary force, Engelbriktsson's influence on the political and ecclesiastical situation in Norway was considerable. While in Norway, however, Christian disclosed that he had not shed all his evangelical sympathies. In spite of quickly conquering parts of southern Norway and being strongly supported by most of the Catholic prelates, plus nobles and burghers, Christian II's invasion failed, and he ended up imprisoned at Sønderborg Castle in Jutland.

The archbishop and his supporters were politically strong enough to survive this crisis. They submitted themselves to Frederik I, but following the king's death in 1533, Olav Engelbriktsson once more made an attempt to secure an independent Catholic Norway. This time the archbishop wanted Christian II's son-in-law, Friedrich of the Palatinate, to become king of Norway. Christian III's victory in the civil war in Denmark, however, totally undermined Olav Engelbriktsson's political position and the archbishop fled to the Netherlands. As a result of Engelbriktsson's political adventure, Norway lost its independence. On the accession of Christian III it became a province of Denmark.[19]

THE ROYAL REFORMATION IN DENMARK

The Catholic bishops and the predominantly Catholic majority of the lay nobility attempted to put back the clocks at the parliament which met following the death of Frederik I in 1533. They avoided electing a successor to the king and took temporary control of the government. The bishops wanted their traditional jurisdiction over the clergy re-established. Likewise, property which had been taken from the church was to be returned and the evangelical preacher, Hans Tausen, was convicted by the Council. However, the Catholic majority on the Council quickly lost control over the developments and civil war broke out. The underlying social and political tensions exploded and spawned an alliance of Lübeck and the rebellious cities of Malmø and Copenhagen. These cities hired Duke Christopher of Oldenburg to lead their army in the name of the imprisoned king, Christian II. Faced with this dangerous rebellion, the lay and ecclesiastical aristocracy were forced to elect Frederik I's oldest son, the Lutheran Duke Christian to protect their interests. In July 1534 they hailed him as King Christian III of Denmark after he had guaranteed them their privileges. Concerning the religious issues, the new king's promises were unusually vague when he pointed out that following victory he would introduce 'a good Christian order in every way'. Religion, which had played an important part in the outbreak of the civil war, was of no significance from the summer of 1534. From then on both sides supported the Protestant cause, and no one could be in doubt that the kingdom would eventually be fully reformed.

On 6 August 1536 a victorious Christian III could make his entry into Copenhagen which had been the last place to surrender after nearly a year's siege. Together with his closest advisors from Holstein and his military leaders, he took a decision which was to change the political and religious map of Denmark. We are well informed about this event from

---

[19] See chapter 4; see also A. C. Bang, *Den norske Kirkes Historie i Reformations-Aarhundredet*, Christiania 1895; A. Holmsen, *Norges Historie fra de eldste tider til 1660*, Oslo 1977, 374–92; O. J. Benedictow, 'Fra Rike til Provins 1448–1536', in K. Mykland (ed.), *Norges Historie*, V, Oslo 1977, 395–457; O. Garstein, 'Reformasjon og Motreformasjon i Norge', *Tidsskrift for Teologi og Kirke*, 37 (1966), 209–44; K. Brandi, *Kaiser Karl V*, I, Munich 1937, 278, 302–4, 342, 354, and M. Spindler (ed.), *Handbuch der Bayerischen Geschichte ... Oberpfalz*, Munich 1971, 1302–3.

an account written by one of the participants, the Prussian admiral, Johann Pein. It was decided to imprison all the Catholic bishops and hold them responsible for the devastation of the civil war. The rest of the Council were forced to accept this procedure and had to sign letters of obligation to Christian III. The letters contained three main points. 1) The king had decided that the government of Denmark should be changed. In future only lay members of the Council would be allowed and no bishop should ever sit on the Council again. 2) This decision was to stand until 'a general, Christian Council', recognised by all Christian nations, decided otherwise. This reference to a General Council is very much in tune with the times. Plans for such a Council were once more being drawn up. The conditions set up by the evangelicals for an acceptance of such a Council were, however, that it should be free of papal control and that evangelicals and Catholics should be evenly represented. Furthermore, the Council's decisions had to be based on the Bible solely. Whether or not some of Christian III's councillors believed in the value of such a gathering or the reference was simply inserted for diplomatic and political reasons is of little consequence, since the Council never met. 3) Finally, the lay councillors had to promise not to oppose the preaching of the gospel and evangelical teachings and to accept the confiscation of all episcopal property and estates.

Christian III used the parliament which met in Copenhagen in October 1536 to explain publicly the changes he intended to introduce within church and state and how the change from Catholicism to Lutheranism was to take place. The importance of the occasion can be seen from the expanded gathering which met in Copenhagen and which included representatives from all estates. This also helped to give the occasion added legality.

The meeting in Copenhagen appears to have started with detailed accusations against the individual bishops being read out publicly. The charges were predominantly of a political nature – the bishops were responsible for the Council's decision to postpone the election of a successor to Frederik I, they had shown an unbearable tyranny towards nobility, burghers and peasants and they had committed both economic and religious crimes, having prevented the preaching of the gospel. Apart from a number of individual shortcomings of a moral nature, the main thrust of Christian III's accusations against the bishops was centred around their insubordination towards the crown and their disloyalty to the people.

The decisions of the estates were expressed in the bill of 30 October

1536. This bill describes itself as a new constitution for the kingdom, and contained among other things a new distribution of power between church and state, and provisions for church government. The bishops were dismissed 'because of their evil deeds'. The country was never to have such bishops again. Instead, 'Christian bishops and super-intendents who could teach and preach the holy gospel, the word of God and the holy Christian faith to the people' were to be employed. Further-more, since the bishops were dismissed, the episcopal estates would fall to the crown and be used for the benefit of the king and the common good. However, property and estates donated for requiem masses could be reclaimed by the donors' families, as long as they could document their cases. Tithes still had to be paid. The two-thirds which went to the local church and minister should continue to do so, while the third which went to the bishops in future should be paid to the king. Other minor spiritual fees were to be abolished, while the nobility retained their traditional privilege of not having to pay tithes on their private estates. Concerning patronage, it was decided that the king and the nobility should keep their traditional rights while the king should take over the bishops' patronage. Cathedral chapters and monasteries should continue until the king introduced reform, but individual monks and nuns were free to leave their orders. Finally, in the social domain it was decided that hospitals in the towns were not to be used as fiefs, but would keep their income and have qualified principals appointed, while beg-ging should be restricted.

This bill signalled the abolition of the Catholic church in Denmark, but said little about the evangelical settlement which was to follow. As such, it only provided a framework. By the imprisonment and conviction of the bishops, Christian III solved several problems at once. He achieved a legal settlement of the civil war and found a solution to most of his economic problems, such as war debts and money to pay his foreign troops, not to mention a solution to the religious problems. It was certainly not a just settlement, since the bishops had shared the responsi-bility for the postponement of the election of a new king in 1533 and the subsequent civil war with a substantial number of lay members of the Council. That these Catholic aristocrats supported the king's actions in 1536 is hardly surprising. Christian III was in a strong position after the upheaval. Victory had, after all, been achieved by his armed inter-vention. However, the king needed the support of the nobility in order to secure his position, while the nobility benefited from enhanced privileges which improved their political and economic position significantly.

The following year the kingdom's break with Catholicism and the creation of a Lutheran state church was celebrated by four ceremonies: 1) the coronation and anointing of the royal couple in a 'Protestant' ceremony led by the Wittenberg theologian, Johannes Bugenhagen, at Our Lady's Church in Copenhagen; 2) Bugenhagen ordained the seven new superintendents or Lutheran bishops in the same church; 3) Christian III signed the new Lutheran Church Ordinance; 4) the University of Copenhagen was re-opened as a Lutheran university. All these events took place within the months of August and September 1537.[20]

THE ROYAL REFORMATION IN NORWAY

Apart from the political decision to incorporate Norway into the kingdom of Denmark, Christian III and his advisors also formulated a strategy for introducing the Reformation in Norway. A special chapter was inserted in the Danish Church Ordinance. It stated that the king should appoint superintendents as quickly as possible. They should ensure that evangelical ministers, who would act in accordance with the Church Ordinance, were found for all Norwegian parishes. Furthermore, it was decided that Christian III should personally visit Norway and together with the new superintendents introduce a Church Ordinance tailored specifically to Norwegian conditions. Christian III, however, never found the time nor inclination to go to Norway and the Norwegian church was left to follow the Danish Church Ordinance until 1607 when the country finally received its own Church Ordinance. Concerning the economic foundation of the Norwegian church the same principles were applied as in Denmark. Ministers and parish churches kept their endowments while the king expropriated all property which had belonged to the Catholic bishops and considerable parts of what had formerly belonged to the cathedral chapters. Simultaneously, changes were introduced to the Norwegian tithes, in spite of vehement objections from the peasantry. As in Denmark, it was divided into three parts, with the king taking over the third which had traditionally gone to the bishops.

[20] For Christian III's letter of assurance, issued when elected king, 18 August 1534, see *Aarsberetninger*, 79–82; for his coronation charter, see *ibid.*, 82–9. For the charges against the Catholic bishops, see H. F. Rørdam (ed.), *Monumenta Historicæ Danica*, I, Copenhagen 1873, 135–256. For the Bill of 30 October 1536, see J. L. A. Kolderup-Rosenvinge (ed.), *Gamle Danske Love*, IV, Copenhagen 1824, 157–71. A translation of some of these documents is available in Kidd, *Documents*, nos. 131–3. See also M. Schwarz Lausten (ed.), *Kirkeordinansen 1537/39*, Copenhagen 1989 and M. Schwarz Lausten, 'Weltliche Obrigkeit und Kirche bei König Christian III. von Dänemark. Hintergründe und Folgen', in Grane and Hørby, *Die dänische Reformation*, 91–107.

The central principle behind the introduction of the Reformation in Norway was the gradual and piecemeal approach by the government. Christian III emphasised in his instruction to the Danish nobleman, Esge Bille, in Bergen, that he should allow Catholic priests to continue with Catholic services and ceremonies and avoid appointing new preachers in order not to 'worry and disturb the poor, simple and uneducated people'. Even then, the few gradual changes there were caused serious difficulties. The lower and middle strata of the Norwegian population demonstrated a much firmer and more lasting commitment to Catholicism than did their counterparts in Denmark.

However, the government's original plan to make the Norwegian superintendents responsible for the introduction of the Reformation was never executed. Apart from appointing Geble Pederssøn superintendent of Bergen, the other posts remained vacant for years. For instance, Trondheim only had its first evangelical superintendent appointed in 1546. Evidently the new government in Copenhagen did not attach much importance to ecclesiastical matters in Norway.

Even if the Norwegian superintendents were appointed by Christian III personally, the supervision of them and the Norwegian church fell to the first evangelical superintendent of Zealand, Peder Palladius. He took care of the Norwegian superintendents when they arrived in Copenhagen to be consecrated and to swear their oath of allegiance to the king. Likewise, Palladius took a special interest in Norwegian students of theology at the re-opened University of Copenhagen and produced pamphlets specifically aimed at the nascent Lutheran church in Norway; but like his king and master, Peder Palladius never visited Norway. Undoubtedly the protracted weakness of the Lutheran church in Norway during the sixteenth century is intricately linked to the government's wish to keep it on some sort of remote control from Copenhagen.[21]

REFORMATION AND SOCIETY

The bill of 30 October 1536 created the foundation for a new constitution. It regulated the relationship between state and church to use two anachronistic concepts. The Catholic position, that the pope and his bishops should hold power within lay as well as ecclesiastical

---

[21] See Bang, *Den norske Kirke* and Lausten, *Kirkeordinansen*, 233–4. See also M. Schwarz Lausten, *Biskop Peder Palladius og Kirken 1537–1559*. Copenhagen 1987, 380–6; O. Koldsrud, 'Guds ords prediken i norsk reformasjon', *Norsk teologisk Tidsskrift*, 39 (1938), 3–23; C. F. Wisløff, *Norsk Kirkehistorie*, I, Oslo 1966, 405–30; S. Imsen, *Superintendenten. En studie i Kirkepolitik, Kirkeadministration og Statsudvikling mellom Reformasjon og eneveldet*, Oslo 1982 and Garstein, 'Reformasjon'.

government, was rejected. Lay and ecclesiastical authority were separated and the clergy were excluded from direct influence on the kingdom's political affairs. This domain now fell solely to the king and his lay councillors. This, of course, did not mean a separation of religion and politics – a concept which would have made little or no sense in early modern society. Instead it implied that society was governed by a Christian authority which was responsible to God. This was a position which did not differ materially from Luther's. However, Christian III and his advisors seem to have been worried about how to justify the imprisonment of the Catholic bishops. For a while the government contemplated the publication of a pamphlet which would explain and justify the king's actions to foreign governments. It was eventually abandoned and instead Christian III requested Luther's verdict on his actions. In a letter of 2 December 1536, Luther offered his support to Christian III, using arguments from his own theological concept on the relationship between spiritual and temporal government: 'It delights me that your royal Majesty has eradicated the bishops, who refused to halt their persecution of the word of God and caused confusion in secular government'. Luther, however, took the opportunity to request the king to use the sequestered property of the bishops to support the new evangelical church.

The official introduction of the Reformation in Denmark heralded the end of the medieval feudal state and the creation of a modern territorial monarchy. This puts the events of October 1536 on a par with other major epoch-making events in Danish history, such as the introduction of absolutism in 1660, the passing of the constitution (*Grundloven*) in 1849, and the introduction of cabinet responsibility in 1901.

The exclusion of the new Lutheran church from direct political influence, however, did not mean that Christian III was prepared to leave the church to its own devices. He continued the late medieval tradition of trying to maximise royal domination and control over the church. In Denmark, this policy had been pursued by the kings since the reign of Christian I (1448–81). It had originally been made possible through a close collaboration between the *Curia* and the Danish kings, which circumvented and undermined the power of the local prelates. This understanding between pope and king came to an end during the reign of Frederik I, when, in 1526, the traditional contacts with Rome were suspended. Nothing changed, however, with regard to royal inter-ference in the affairs of the church. Frederik I was, in fact, in a much stronger position than his predecessors with regard to the church, no longer needing to placate and bribe members of the *Curia*. Thus, Christian III continued to reinforce a well-established royal policy towards the church, the only difference being that the change from a Catholic to a Lutheran confession served to harness such policies further. In this respect, developments in Denmark fit neatly into the German model of the Protestant territorial state under princely control.

The theoretical foundation for the new Protestant state was expressed in the ceremonies and speeches at Christian III's coronation in August 1537. Previously, the coronation had been a grand ecclesiastical occasion, where the Catholic archbishop had annointed the king, who through the ceremony achieved a degree of holiness which placed him in an intermediary position between clergy and laity. As such, he was dressed like a deacon and given the eucharist in both forms at the coronation. He was, in effect, annointed like the kings of the Old Testament. Considering Luther's doctrine of the total separation of the two kingdoms (spiritual and temporal), the coronation of Christian III, performed by Johannes Bugenhagen, looks distinctly odd. The Catholic ritual was maintained and only a few evangelical changes were added. Bugenhagen, who had not received episcopal ordination, annointed the king. The climax of the ceremony was announced by a fanfare of trumpets and a hymn sung by Bugenhagen and twelve ministers, upon which the king, sword in hand, read the text for the day, promising to use both the sword and the gospel for the benefit of the people. This ceremony can hardly have reminded the congregation in Our Lady's Church in Copenhagen of Luther's doctrine of the separation of the two kingdoms.

Instead, it was Philipp Melanchthon's concept of the two kingdoms which was expressed at the coronation in Copenhagen. Melanchthon combined the duty of love, which Luther demanded from the prince, with his view of the prince as obliged to help his subjects to salvation. Melanchthon did not derive his ideas about the prince's role within the church from the idea of 'the priesthood of all believers', but from the lay character of ecclesiastical arrangements. For Melanchthon, the Christian prince was the principal member of the church (*praecipuum membrum ecclesiae*) and his main task was to be the keeper of both the tablets of the Law of Moses (*custos utriusque tabulae*). The prince was, in other words, obliged to promote true Christian worship and to guarantee the existence of a just society. His primary obligation, however, was the introduction and preservation of true Christian worship (*cura religionis*). He was to be a father to his people (*pater Patria*) and provide an example to his subjects. Accordingly the great Old Testament priest-kings were shining examples to the evangelical princes. Melanchthon, who was solidly rooted in Christian humanism, had taken over this patriarchal religious concept of the role of the prince from Erasmus. The ultimate goal was, of course, the creation of the 'Christian state' where prince and subjects were united by the 'common good' (*publica utilitas*). Foreign policy, legislation and taxation were to be governed by this principle, and the prince was obliged to educate his subjects with this goal in mind. Many of these aspirations found expression during the coronation ceremony in 1536.

Furthermore, the same principles are in evidence in the royal prefaces to the Danish Church Ordinance 1537/9 and the Church Ordinance for Schleswig and Holstein (1542). Here the King, in Bugenhagen's formulation, stated that he as prince was responsible for the church and that he drew his right and obligation to reform it from his position as 'keeper of the two tablets of the Laws of Moses'. Christian III declared, referring to Old Testament kings and judges (Isaiah 49.3; Ps. 45.13; Rom. 13), that he was obliged to re-create true Christian worship. Lay authority, he stated, 'shall lead Christianity spiritually with the word of God and temporally with nourishment and all good things'.

That Christian III also controlled the church firmly, can be seen from the way visitations within the new Lutheran church were conducted. They took place on the authority of the king and were carried out jointly by the superintendents and the king's local, noble administrators. Christian III refused to appoint an evangelical 'archbishop' (superintendent-general) which was requested by the evangelical clergy. Furthermore, the king tied the clergy closely to the crown by demanding an oath of obligation in connection with appointments. Finally, Christian III also retained full control of the finances of the church, not to mention ecclesiastical legislation and discipline in the post-Reformation church.[22]

The imprisonment of the Catholic bishops had been the central element in the abolition of the Catholic church. Their replacements, the Lutheran bishops, who initially according to the German example were labelled superintendents, were only to concern themselves with the preaching of the gospel. They should supervise ministers and congregations and preach personally in the cathedral towns where they resided.

---

[22] For Luther's letter to Christian III, dated Wittenberg 2 December 1536, see *Martin Luthers Werke. Kritische Gesamtausgabe Briefwechsel*, VII, Weimar 1940, Briefe 7, 604; see also M. Schwarz Lausten, 'Christian III und die deutschen Reformatoren', *Archive für Reformationsgeschichte*, 66 (1975), 17–108 and Lausten, 'Weltliche Obrigkeit', 91–107.

Furthermore, they should serve as the king's theological advisors and supervise the new system of education and social welfare. The traditional diocesan division was maintained and nearly all Catholic parish priests continued to function within the new Lutheran church. It fell to the new superintendents to train and re-educate them – a difficult and often strenuous task. The new Lutheran bishops, however, differed from their Catholic predecessors in that they were salaried employees of the crown.

It was consistent with Christian III's church policy that the cathedral chapters continued. In order to make sure that they did not remain unreformed bastions of Catholicism, an evangelical lecturer was employed within each chapter. The canons, however, kept their benefices and were still expected to perform their devotional activities. Bugenhagen wrote an evangelical manual specifically for the chapters. Later, as we shall see below, the chapters were given an important task within the legal system. The numerous altar-priests, 'eternal vicariates', who had been needed for the reading of requiem masses, were now redundant. But even in their case, the government acted with tolerance and consideration. They were allowed to enjoy their income for life, and only when they died could donors' families, who had the necessary documentation, reclaim the donations. The larger rural monasteries were treated similarly to the chapters. They now fell directly under the supervision of the king and Council, while individual monks were free to leave. However, those brethren who wanted to stay still had to wear the habit, to obey the abbot, and convert to Lutheranism. As in the chapters each of the monasteries had to employ an evangelical lecturer. In administrative terms, the practice already commenced in the later Middle Ages of giving the monasteries, as fiefs of the crown, either to the abbot or to a member of the nobility, was continued.

This lenient policy did not apply to the mendicant orders. All their monasteries were closed and handed over to the relevant magistracies, while those monks who would not convert were banished. Exceptions were only made for brethren who were old and frail. They were allowed to remain and receive food and lodgings until they died.

Education, which had been the responsibility of the Catholic church, fell to lay authority in post-Reformation Denmark. The king had new rules and regulations drawn up and market towns were ordered to found and fund schools, but the role of the church and tradition proved impossible to eliminate. Thus paragraphs dealing with education were included in the Church Ordinance, which in effect became the educational law in Denmark. Likewise, the inspection and supervision of the schools was carried out jointly by the superintendents/bishops and the royal administrators, recruited from the nobility.

The university did not lose its ecclesiastical character after the Reformation, in spite of it becoming the responsibility of the state. It only changed confession, administration and curriculum. As in so much else, it was Johannes Bugenhagen who was the driving force behind these changes. The University of Copenhagen was modelled on Wittenberg. The Lutheran bishop of Zealand also became professor of theology, while the university continued to celebrate its special events in Our Lady's Church.

Before the Reformation, the rationale for charity and poor relief had been centred around the Catholic church's teaching on good works as being meritorious. Through such acts the donor improved his or her prospects of salvation, especially if the recipient was one of the many holy orders whose prayers and charitable deeds were considered particularly beneficial to mankind. After the Reformation, charity and poor relief became the responsibility of local, lay authority. Nevertheless, its rationale remained religious, even if the theological justification shifted. Now charity was considered a general obligation of all true Christians as an expression of neighbourly love. That everyone would be rewarded or punished by God according to the charity shown towards the poor, was the way Peder Palladius (1503–60), the first Lutheran bishop of Zealand, phrased it. It was a complex position, which was difficult to comprehend for many lay people and the new system of poor relief did not function smoothly from the start. Recent research, however, has demonstrated that in general the poor were no worse off after the Reformation than before.

Following the German example, a poor chest was established in each diocese. Donations and property and income from dissolved Catholic confraternities were incorporated in this common chest. The responsibility for creating the chest fell to the superintendents who, together with the royal administrators, were responsible for its administration, appointing the men who would take ongoing responsibility for the chest. The population was encouraged to give generously to the poor, while the government attempted to limit begging. Those who were capable of working were excluded. Beggars had to obtain special certificates from local government which were issued on the recommendation of the ministers.

Hospitals were to be founded in all market towns. The king demanded that the local magistracies bore the responsibility and guaranteed that the funds which had hitherto been used by the Catholic church for similar purposes were retained for the new foundations. It was stipulated that principals and deacons had to be chosen carefully, that the superintendents/bishops were to supervise the hospitals and that the local clergy were obliged to visit the patients several times a week.[23]

It was of paramount importance to Christian III to seek to re-establish law and order and a general conception of justice as quickly as possible following the disruptions of the civil war and the introduction of the Reformation. The abolition of canon law had left a legal vacuum, which the king attempted to fill in the first years of his reign by acting as a travelling supreme court covering the whole country. A sentence from April 1537 shows that in cases of adultery, Roman law, the 'Carolina' of Emperor Charles V, as recommended by Melanchthon, was now in use. Roman law became increasingly influential in the years to come. After some initial hesitation, special courts to deal with matrimonial cases were created, one in each diocese, consisting of the royal administrator and some local, learned clergy, often recruited from the cathedral chapters. These courts met for quarterly sessions. The first Danish matrimonial law was not issued until 1582, but it then continued to constitute the legal basis well into the twentieth century.

Considerable uncertainty, however, remained about how to deal with economic crimes which previously had been covered by canon law. The issue of interest was particularly problematic. Christian III was inclined to follow Luther's ban on interest, but he realised that it was commercially impossible and accepted Melanchthon's advice of a 5 per cent maximum rate of interest. Higher rates were considered to be usury and were severely punished. A remnant of the king's original dislike of any form of interest can possibly be found in his instruction to the clergy to warn their congregations that the taking of interest was sinful.[24]

Personally Christian III was a pious Christian, firmly anchored in Lutheranism. His daily life was characterised by a series of services,

23 *Kirkeordinansen 1537/39*, 202–10 (for schools); 216–18 (for poor relief) and Lausten, *Peder Palladius*, 174–85 (for poor relief). For the university, see W. Norvin, *Københavns Universitet i Reformationens og Ortodoksiens Tidsalder*, II, Copenhagen 1940, 9–70 (*Fundatio et ordinatio vniuersalis schole Haffniensis*, 10 January 1539), Lausten, 'Die Universität Kopenhagen', 99–113; L. Grane, 'Teaching the People. The Education of the Clergy and the Instruction of the People in the Danish Reformation Church', in Grane, *Die dänische Reformation*, 164–84; and M. Schwarz Lausten, 'Københavns Universitet 1536–1588', in L. Grane (ed.), *Københavns Universitet 1479–1979*, I, Copenhagen 1991, 79–167.
24 O. Fenger, 'Reformationen og den danske ret', in H. J. Frederiksen (ed.), Reformationsperspektiver *Acta Jutlandica*, 62, 3, Aarhus 1987, 80–99 and T. Dahlerup, 'Sin, Crime, Punishment and Absolution', in Grane, *Die dänische Reformation*, 277–88.

prayers, hymns and sermons. The king occasionally preached himself and took considerable interest in the theological debates of the day. Throughout his life he corresponded regularly with Luther, Melanchthon and Bugenhagen, as well as some of the other Wittenberg reformers, all of whom he greatly admired. He studied the theological literature which the Wittenbergers forwarded to him, demonstrating a preference for Luther's commentary on the Galatians. However, Christian III took a dim view of any public theological debate. He wanted total uniformity in doctrine and ceremony and acted quickly to stamp out heterodoxy.

In spite of his personal commitment to Lutheranism, Christian III's foreign policy was dictated by *realpolitik*. Undoubtedly, such a policy was necessitated by the economic problems the king faced as a result of the recent civil war and the dynastic problems created by the deposed king, Christian II, who remained imprisoned in Denmark. Such considerations help to explain why Christian III accepted a peace treaty with the emperor, Charles V, in Speyer in 1544. This treaty formed the cornerstone of a series of political initiatives which worked against the interests of the German evangelical princes. In order to secure peace and security, Christian III refused to assist the evangelical princes in the Schmalkaldic War (1546–7) while seeking to establish dynastic contacts with the Habsburgs and other Catholic rulers in Germany. The king even attempted to have members of his family appointed to some of the princely Catholic bishoprics.[25]

From 1536, as opposed to the evangelical preachers who had introduced the Reformation, Christian III emphasised that the Danish church was theologically firmly anchored in Lutheranism as espoused in Wittenberg. The Church Ordinance 1537/9 stressed that ministers should own copies of Luther's *Postill* and Melanchthon's *Apology* (presumably also *Confessio Augustana*) and his *Loci communes*, plus a manual which could interpret Luther's *Smaller Catechism*, Melanchthon's *Instruction for the Visitors in Saxony* and, of course, the Bible. Together Luther and Melanchthon constituted doctrinal authority, while their theological differences were conveniently ignored. Peder Palladius, who had studied for six years in Wittenberg under Luther, became the first Lutheran bishop of Zealand. As the leading professor of theology at the university, he resided in Copenhagen and became the most prominent Danish theologian of the age. His more than fifty books, treatises and lectures demonstrated the influence of Melanchthon, even if more Lutheran views are in

[25] M. Schwarz Lausten, *Religion og Politik. Studier i Christian d. 3.'s forhold til det tyske rige i tiden 1544–1559*, Copenhagen 1977 and Lausten, 'Christian III', 151–82.

evidence, as in his concept of the eucharist. A similar theological orientation can be found in other leaders of the young Lutheran church in Denmark, such as Niels Palladius, the brother of Peder, who served as superintendent/bishop of Lund from 1552 to 1560, and the evangelical preacher, Hans Tausen, who became bishop of Ribe in 1542.

The population noticed the Reformation through the changed role of the minister and through the changes in the service and ceremonies. Gradually Lutheran rectories came into existence and a transformation of the role and the cure of ministers took place. Services were now held in the vernacular, with sermons and communally sung hymns as the central elements, while the eucharist was received in both forms. At the same time, the new bishops were trying hard to eradicate old Catholic beliefs, such as saints, indulgences, purgatory and the use of the rosary. An excellent example of how they went about their tasks can be seen from the *Visitation Book* written by Peder Palladius in the 1540s. Here the leading superintendent described his experiences. Through simple, often allegorical language, Palladius tried to explain the new Lutheran faith to the peasantry in Zealand, deliberately excluding all theological terminology. Clearly, an impressive pedagogical mind was at work behind the tolerance, sense of humour, use of anecdotes and the creative language which characterises his work. It was intended to inspire the people to live godly and responsible lives. But Palladius had considerable understanding for the tough and toilsome life of the peasant and urged the parish people to feast and even to have a drop too much occasionally, celebrating the arrival of 'the shining day of the gospel'.[26] Undoubtedly the success of the Danish Reformation owes a great deal to enlightened and flexible Lutheran theologians and church leaders such as Palladius. He himself has provided us with invaluable information about how the new Lutheran teachings were introduced in the countryside through his *Visitation Book*.

[26] *Kirkeordinansen 1537/39*, 158–60, 230; L. Jacobsen (ed.), *Peder Palladius' Danske Skrifter*, I–V, Copenhagen 1911–25; M. Schwarz Lausten, *Biskop Niels Palladius*, Copenhagen 1968; Lausten, *Peder Palladius*. See also J. Ertner, *Peder Palladius' lutherske Teologi*, Copenhagen 1989; M. Christensen, *Hans Tausen*, Copenhagen 1942; Hans Tausen, *Postil*, I–II, ed. B. Kornerup, Copenhagen 1934 and Grane, 'Teaching the People', 164 84.

CHAPTER 3

The early Reformation in Sweden and Finland, c. 1520–1560

E. I. Kouri

The Reformation in Sweden and Finland has often been described as a peaceful transition from a universal, albeit corrupt, Catholic church to a pure, princely-led national church, but this idealistic picture is not entirely credible. In fact, the evangelical movement made a curiously hesitant beginning in the first generation of reformers.[1] The preconditions for the reception of Protestantism within, as well as without, Germany differed significantly, because of the pluriformity of the religious, political, social and educational landscape. However, although the shape and progress of the individual evangelical movements in the various countries were moulded by local circumstances and pressures, the early Reformation never degenerated into parochialism. For all the regional and national variations, the national/territorial Reformations remained part of the same movement.

Christianity had been brought to Sweden gradually. When Ansgar, the monk sent to the north by the emperor in 829, became archbishop of Hamburg-Bremen, he became the religious leader of the whole Nordic missionary area.[2] Three centuries later, in the first document relating to the church and Finland, a letter from Pope Alexander III sent in 1171 to the Swedish leaders, the state of Christianity in Finland is described as precarious. The federal relationship which is reported to have existed between Sweden and Finland at this time made it possible for missionaries to promote Christianity in Finland. Consequently, at the beginning of the next century (1209), Pope Innocent III confirmed a Finnish bishopric, which he described as *novella plantatio*, to be under the

---

[1] See O. P. Grell, 'Scandinavia', in A. Pettegree (ed.), *The Early Reformation in Europe*, Cambridge 1992, 118.

[2] W. Trillmich (ed.), *Rimberti Vita Anskari – Rimbert, Ansgars Leben*. Ausgewählte Quellen zur deutschen Geschichte des Mittelalters, XI, Darmstadt 1978, 1–13. See also B. Sawyer, P. Sawyer and I. Wood (eds.), *The Christianization of Scandinavia*, Borås 1987.

jurisdiction of the archbishop of Uppsala.[3] Some years later the Catholic church was firmly established in Sweden and Finland. The Holy See paid special attention to Finland which was seen as the western bulwark against Orthodox Russia.[4]

In spite of their remote location, Sweden and Finland did not remain isolated from the events which shook the foundations of the Catholic church in the late Middle Ages. Even if the church had only been properly established there at the beginning of the thirteenth century, it had begun to encounter growing criticism in Sweden around 1500, and in Finland people were complaining about the bureaucracy and corruption of the ecclesiastical authorities.[5]

In Sweden and Finland the decadence of the church was not as conspicuous as in the south, but the church found its political and social status challenged during the Sture period. Sten Sture the Elder, while regent (1470–1503), tried to restrict the political power of the bishops, as well as their economic resources.[6] The ensuing confrontation led to his deposition by the Council (*Riksrådet*) led by the archbishop. His defeat, however, did not prevent his successor, Svante Sture (1504–12), from pursuing identical policies. The archbishop and his supporters continued to promote the traditional policies of the church, which considered a joint government of the ecclesiastical and lay aristocracies as best for the country. This was an ideal they considered best realised within the framework of the Scandinavian Union.[7]

Created in 1397, the Union of the three Scandinavian Kingdoms, which had been dominated by Denmark, was on the verge of collapse by the beginning of the sixteenth century. Furthermore, the fate of the Union became closely associated with the impact of the Reformation in Scandinavia.[8] Relations between church and state were already strained

---

[3] K. Pirinen, 'Suomen lähetysalueen kirkollinen järjestäminen', in *Novella Plantatio*. Suomen Kirkkohistoriallinen Seura (= SKHS), LVI, Helsinki 1955, 42–81; T. Nyberg, *Die Kirche in Skandinavien. Mitteleuropäischer und englischer Einfluss im 11. und 12. Jahrhundert*. Beiträge zur Geschichte und Quellenkunde des Mittelalters, x, Sigmaringen 1986, 75–6.

[4] E. Christiansen, *The Northern Crusades. The Baltic and the Catholic Frontier 1100–1525*, London 1980, 178–9.

[5] K. Pirinen, *Turun tuomikapituli keskiajan lopulla*, SKSH, LVIII, Helsinki 1956, 410–18.

[6] See K.-G. Lundholm, *Sten Sture den äldre och stormännen*, Bibliotheca Historica Lundensis, III, Lund 1956, 111–14, and S. U. Palme, *Sten Sture den äldre*, 2nd edn., Stockholm 1968.

[7] K. B. Westman, *Reformationens genombrottsår i Sverige*, Stockholm 1918, 121–3.

[8] See E. Lönnroth, *Sverige och Kalmarunionen 1397–1457*, Göteborg 1934, 10–341; G. Carlsson, *Medeltidens nordiska unionstanke*. Det Levande Förflutna, VIII, Stockholm 1945, 52–111; I. Markussen, 'De nordiske unioner 1380–1523' in *Omstridte spørgsmål i Nordens historie, IV. Reviderte urgaver av avhandlingerne i bind I om de nordiske unioner 1380–1523 og den dansk-norske forbindelse 1536–1814*. Foreningen Nordens Historiske Publikasjoner, V, 1973, 7–39; P. Enemark, *Fra Kalmarbrev til Stockholms blodbad. Den nordiske Trestatsunions epoke 1397–1521*, Copenhagen 1979, 17–147.

when, in 1515, the young and inexperienced Gustav Trolle, whose father had vied with Sten Sture the Younger for the regency in 1512, was elected archbishop. The situation deteriorated and matters came to a head in 1517, when the Swedish parliament decided to remove Gustav Trolle from office.[9] This split in the Swedish leadership encouraged the Danish king, Christian II, who was trying to revive the Union, to invade Sweden. He captured Stockholm; Sten Sture was mortally wounded and Christian II, with the blessing of Archbishop Trolle, organised a massacre of members of the Swedish lay and ecclesiastical aristocracy who were considered to be opposed to his rule. Hardly had Christian II returned to Denmark before a rebellion lead by Gustav Vasa broke out in Sweden. By August 1521 Gustav Vasa had conquered most of the country and was elected regent.[10]

Towns have long been recognised as the nurseries of the evangelical movements. A fair proportion of their inhabitants were not only literate, but also politically aware, while towns, as centres of trade and communication, served to spread the message of the reformers. In German cities, the transition which saw the emergence of evangelical, popular movements had been accomplished by the mid-1520s.[11] The popular element in the Reformation of Sweden and Finland was negligible. Although economic and cultural contacts with Germany are important in explaining the dissemination of evangelical ideas in Sweden and Finland, the recipient societies were too different to aspire to anything like the German urban Reformation. The size of most Swedish and Finnish towns, including Stockholm with its large German population, simply excluded them from playing a role similar to that of the much larger towns and cities in Germany.

Evangelical ideas first reached Stockholm in 1522, where they appear to have been spread by visiting German merchants. Simultaneously, some of the German mercenaries sent by Lübeck to assist Gustav Vasa in his rebellion against Christian II, appear to have disseminated evangelical ideas in Söderköping.[12] A couple of years later the large and influential German population in Stockholm had been won over to the evangelical faith. In 1524 they recruited an evangelical minister, Nicholas

[9] See G. Westin, *Riksföreståndaren och makten. Politiska utveklingslinger i Sverige 1512–1517*. Skrifter utgivna av kungliga vetenskaps-societeten i Lund, LII, Lund 1957.
[10] C. Weibull, 'Gustaf Trolle, Christian II, och Stockholms Blodbad' in *Scandia*, 31 (1965), 1–54; P. G. Lindhardt, *Skandinavische Kirchengeschichte seit dem 16. Jahrhundert*. Die Kirche in ihrer Geschichte, III, Göttingen 1982, 276–7.
[11] H. R. Schmidt, *Reichstädte, Reich und Reformation*, Stuttgart 1986, 130–40.
[12] Westman, *Reformationens genombrottsår*, 148.

Stecker, who had been born in Luther's home town, Eisleben, and studied in Wittenberg, and who eventually became German secretary to Gustav Vasa. The Swedish population of Stockholm, however, was somewhat slower in embracing the new evangelical ideas.[13]

Only Stockholm and a few towns along the Swedish and Finnish coasts gradually developed some popular support for the Reformation. Whereas it has recently been demonstrated that evangelical ideas could find a receptive audience in the German countryside,[14] there was no popular backing for Protestantism among the Swedish peasantry who militantly tried to defend the old church through several rebellions.

When Gustav Vasa was elected king at the parliament which met in Strängnäs in the summer of 1523, Christian II had already gone into exile in the Netherlands after his deposition by the Danish Council. Mutual fear of the exiled king, Christian II, and rivalry with the Hanseatic cities led by Lübeck, did not serve to unite the new kings of Denmark and Sweden, Frederik I and Gustav Vasa. Apart from a meeting between the two in Malmø in 1524, where Frederik I abandoned his claim to the crown of Sweden and the leadership of the Union, the two rulers differed substantially in their attitude to the new evangelical ideas. Thus the early Reformation of the two countries developed differently and largely independently.[15]

In Sweden and Finland, as elsewhere, the progress of the Reformation depended on the complex political changes known as the emergence of the nation state. Hitherto natural alliances and international co-operations had given way to the needs and demands of smaller groups, often defined by a common language, for whom the strengthening of the territorial state became a central aim. This struggle for sovereignty also meant that the state tried to bring the internationalist Catholic church under local lay control; a policy for which evangelical theology provided a much-needed justification.[16]

The beginning of evangelical preaching in Sweden coincided with Danish efforts to renew the Union with the help of members of the Swedish aristocracy and Archbishop Gustav Trolle. Thus, from the very

---

[13] H. Holmquist, *Svenska Kyrkans Historia*, III, Stockholm 1933, 98, 104–6.

[14] T. Scott, 'The Common People in the German Reformation', in *Historical Journal*, 34 (1991), 183–91. See also R. W. Scribner, 'The Reformation and the Religion of the Common People', in H. G. Guggisberg and G. G. Krodel (eds.), *Die Reformation in Deutschland und Europa: Interpretationen und Debatten*, Gütersloh 1993, 221–41.

[15] Grell, 'Scandinavia', 94–119.

[16] T. Lyby, *Vi Evangeliske. Studier over Samspillet mellem Udenrigspolitik og Kirkepolitik på Frederik I.s Tid*, Aarhus 1993, 456–7.

beginning, the national struggle for freedom became linked with the effort to diminish the power of the Catholic church in Sweden. A practical consequence of this policy can be seen in the crown's support for the evangelical party. During the final stages of Gustav Vasa's rebellion, all efforts were concentrated on liberating the country while religious matters took second place. After the victory over the Danes and their allies, however, Gustav Vasa turned his attention to ecclesiastical matters, where new appointments to the vacant episcopal sees took priority. By the time Christian II fled Denmark all the archepiscopal sees were vacant in Scandinavia. The ecclesiastical situation in Sweden and Finland was particularly chaotic. The archbishop of Uppsala, Gustav Trolle, had fled the country, the bishops of Strängnäs and Skara had been executed while the dioceses of Åbo/Turku and Västerås had been vacant since 1522. Furthermore, the bishop of Växjö was old and frail, and only the energetic bishop of Linköping, Hans Brask, was left to defend Catholicism and *libertas ecclesiae*.[17]

Gustav Vasa used this opportunity to weaken the Catholic church by direct interference in the election of the new bishops. He sought to have candidates elected who were politically close to him or to the old Sture party. Initially, he tried to enlist the support of the *Curia* for episcopal candidates who would specifically serve the interests of the realm. When this was rejected by Rome, he drifted towards a new church policy which aimed at creating a national church.[18]

Finland remained under the control of Christian II's supporters while this evangelical re-orientation of Swedish church policy began. When Gustav Vasa gained control over Finland in 1523, a new bishop was appointed to the vacant see of St Henry in Åbo/Turku (named after the Englishman, Henry, who was the first missionary bishop in Finland, and who was murdered by a Finnish peasant). The previous bishop, Arvid Kurki, who, like a number of his predecessors, had received his MA in Paris, drowned in 1522 in the Gulf of Bothnia, trying to escape the Danes. Shortly before his unfortunate death he had been elected archbishop of Uppsala in place of the pro-Union, Christian II supporter, Gustav Trolle. Kurki's successor in Åbo/Turku, Erik Svensson (1523–7), had been Gustav Vasa's chancellor.[19]

---

[17] See chapter 4 and H. Schück, *Ecclesiae Lincopensis. Studier om Linköpingskyrkan under medeltiden och Gustav Vasa*, Stockholm 1959, 145–57.

[18] See chapter 4.

[19] K. Pirinen, 'Keskiajan ja uskonpuhdistuskauden tuomiokapituli 1276–1604', in *Turun tuomiokapituli 1276–1976*, Turku 1976, 49–50, 58.

The Finnish church had enjoyed the same privileged status in society as the Swedish church during the Middle Ages. Its leaders had studied at foreign universities and its wealth was considerable.[20] The prelates exercised both ecclesiastical and temporal power and traditionally played an important role in the realm's *Ostpolitik*. As a Catholic bishopric, the Finnish church belonged to the church-province of Uppsala, but it also maintained direct contacts with the *Curia*. It was only after the Reformation that it became fully incorporated into the Swedish church. That Finnish church leaders tried to manage their affairs independently is probably best explained by medieval episcopal particularism.[21]

When Gustav Vasa realised that he could not count on the unqualified support of the Catholic clergy for his policies, he started to promote representatives of the evangelical movement. At Strängnäs, in 1523, he made the acquaintance of two men, Laurentius Andreae and Olaus Petri, who were to play an important part in the evangelical movement in Sweden until the early 1530s. In 1523 Andreae became Gustav Vasa's secretary and in 1524 Olaus Petri was given the influential position of clerk and preacher to the city of Stockholm. Olaus Petri, Sweden's reformer, was born in Örebro in 1493. In 1516 he matriculated at the University of Wittenberg, where he personally experienced the new evangelical teachings of Luther. Three years later he graduated in Wittenberg and returned to his home country, where he became secretary to the bishop of Strängnäs.[22]

The Swedish church had successfully defended the Catholic ideal of *libertas ecclesiae*: the doctrine that the church had distinct privileges regarding property and income which were protected by ecclesiastical jurisdiction based on canon law. The aristocratic struggle for power within the Scandinavian Union had greatly assisted the church in realising this ideal, even if, by the beginning of the sixteenth century, the church found itself increasingly under fire. Thus, during the Sture period, the government tried to strengthen its control over the church,

---

[20] A. I. Lehtinen, 'Suomalaisia teologeja Sorbonnen kollegion kirjastossa', *Opusculum*, 7 (1987), 147–88.
[21] Pirinen, *Turun tuomiokapituli keskiajan lopulla*, 363–409; E. Anthoni, *Finlands medeltida frälse och 1500-talsadel*. Skrifter utgivna av Svenska Litteratursällskapet i Finland, CDXLII, Helsingfors 1970, 189–94.
[22] See R. Murray, *Olaus Petri*, Stockholm 1952; see also Olaus Petri in *SBL*. For Laurentius Andreae, see *SBL*. See also chapter 4.

but it was not until the reign of Gustav Vasa that relations between church and state changed radically.[23]

In Germany the Reformation had ceased to be a purely religious matter by 1520. Likewise, the rulers of a number of European countries were quick to grasp the political and economic implications inherent in evangelical theology. Gustav Vasa, who was not a particularly religious man, was conspicuously uneasy with the finer points of doctrine of the new faith. His church policy was determined primarily by the wealth of the Catholic church rather than Luther's teachings. Yet it was Luther who had provided him with the theological rationale for crushing the church's political power and confiscating its superfluous riches.[24]

Following the protracted war of independence, the crown badly needed money and support from the church. It was for this purpose that Laurentius Andreae outlined a new church policy. In February 1524 he drafted his well-known letter to the monks in Vadstena. This document has traditionally been seen as the first evangelical writing in Sweden. Here Laurentius Andreae attacked the medieval definition of the church and stated that the church was no more, and no less, than the community of believers. Consequently, the property of the church belonged to the people for whose benefit it could be used. Andreae also took the opportunity to recommend Luther's writings to the monks in Vadstena. Two years later the confiscation of part of the tithes was defended by the crown, referring to the fact that it was better to take from the rich church than from poor citizens. This was a popularist argument which could not fail to appeal to a broad sector of society.[25]

By the mid-1520s Stockholm had become the centre of the evangelical movement in Sweden. Furthermore, it was around this time that Gustav Vasa realised that he could use the evangelical movement for his own political ends. While in February 1524 the magistracy in Stockholm promised to punish all those who were calumniating the new faith, Gustav Vasa attacked priests and monks, accusing them of living at the crown's expense. At the same time he gave his consent to the guiding principle behind Laurentius Andreae's political ideas: that political, as

[23] S. Kjöllerström, 'Kyrkan och den världsliga överheten under senmedeltid och reformation', in C.-G. Andrén (ed.), *Reformationen i Norden. Kontinuitet och förnyelse*, Lund 1970, 87–9; C. G. Andrae, *Kyrkan och frälse i Sverige under äldre medeltid*. Studia Historica Upsaliensia, IV, Uppsala 1960, 146–71.

[24] See for instance P. G. Lindhardt, 'Luther und Skandinavien', in *Luther und die Theologie der Gegenwart*, Göttingen 1980, 134. See also E. Wolgast, 'Einführung der Reformation als politische Entscheidung', in Guggisberg and Krodel (eds.), *Die Reformation in Deutschland und Europa*, 470–8.

[25] I. Montgomery, 'Den Svenska Religionspolitiken', in I. Brohed (ed.), *Reformationens konsolidering i de nordiska länderna 1540–1610*, Oslo 1990, 120–1.

well as religious quarrels among all subjects should be resolved in parliament. During the subsequent parliament of Västerås, in 1525, Gustav Vasa received an oath of allegiance from the estates.[26]

The evangelical movement in Sweden could not, of course, function without a vernacular, evangelical literature. From the very beginning the reformers concentrated on propagating the new faith through the printing press. In July 1525, on the initiative of Laurentius Andreae, the elected archbishop of Uppsala, Johannes Magnus, sent a circular to all cathedral chapters and monasteries regarding the translation of the New Testament into Swedish. The latter was published the following year and is, according to modern scholarship, a translation produced by a team of scholars. Laurentius Andreae and Olaus Petri, however, played the central roles in organising the whole enterprise and in drafting the preface. The principal sources for this translation of the New Testament were the Latin translation of Erasmus and, to a lesser extent, the Vulgate. In addition, the 1524 Danish translation of the New Testament was used as well as Luther's translation and some pre-Lutheran, Low German versions.[27]

The Reformation in Germany had become a forceful, popular movement by the mid-1520s, and the city Reformation had taken institutional form in a number of South German towns and cities, such as Nuremberg and Strasburg. News about the dramatic developments in Franconia quickly reached Sweden via Prussia. At the Diet of Nuremberg in the spring of 1524, the confessional fronts had hardened and an attempt to find a political solution to the urgent problem created by the growing evangelical movement through a national council of the German church failed. It was this ambition to find a solution to the religious confrontation which made Margrave Casimir of Brandenburg-Ansbach ask Lutheran and Catholic theologians to draft answers to twenty-three disputed questions. In response, the leading reformer of Nuremberg, Andreas Osiander, together with colleagues, wrote the *Ansbacher Ratschlag*. Parts of it were published in 1525 and debated during the crucial disputation which took place in that year.[28]

The situation in Sweden in the mid-1520s was not dissimilar to that in Germany. Evidently prompted by events there, Gustav Vasa was

[26] R. Murray, *Stockholms kyrkostyrelse intill 1630-talets mitt.* Samlingar och studier till svenska kyrkans historia, xx, Lund 1949, 35–52.

[27] K. Evers, *Studien zu den Vorlagen des schwedischen Neuen Testaments vom Jahre 1526*, Göteborger Germanistische Forschungen, xxvi, Göteborg 1984, 178–82, 188–9.

[28] See G. Vogler, *Nürnberg 1524–1525. Studien zur Geschichte der reformatorischen und sozialen Bewegungen in der Reichstadt*, Berlin 1982.

planning a national synod. Towards the end of 1526 he asked both religious parties to explain their views regarding the ten central disputed questions, which were similar to those to be found in Osiander's *Ratschlag*. When Peder Galle, the canon in the chapter of Uppsala, provided the Catholic response in writing, Olaus Petri decided to print the evangelical principles. However, he interrupted this work in order to respond to the polemical attack on Luther by the learned, Danish Carmelite theologian, Paulus Helie. Olaus Petri published his answer to Helie in March 1527 while his response to Galle followed two months later.[29]

Early on, the Swedish reformers, like their German counterparts, understood the value of the printing press for dissemination of evangelical ideas. They were greatly assisted by Gustav Vasa, who, in 1526, closed down the Catholic press in Linköping and moved the print works, which had been under the control of the chapter in Uppsala, to Stockholm. From then on all printing presses in Sweden were under evangelical control. Accordingly, Olaus Petri published his first evangelical pamphlet in 1526, where he described Man's road to salvation as prescribed by the Bible. This was partly a translation of Luther's *Betbüchlein* of 1522, but Petri also made use of the works of other German reformers, especially those of Martin Bucer, Johannes Bugenhagen and Urbanus Rhegius.[30]

The religious issues emerged again at the parliament which met in Västerås in June 1527. This parliament had been summoned in order to find a solution to the financial difficulties of the government and it resulted in the statute of Västerås, which led to the confiscation by the crown of all 'superfluous' church property and the end of the church's legal and political privileges. Furthermore, the nobility was given leave to recover all property donated by their families to the church since 1454. Due to the Catholic and conservative position of the Council and the peasantry, the king avoided making any radical changes in religion. Thus the question of relations with Rome was passed over in silence, while the authority of the bishops in all ecclesiastical matters was retained. Parliament, however, emphasised that the word of God was to be preached 'purely' in Sweden. Following the pattern from Germany, a disputation was arranged between Olaus Petri and Peder Galle.[31]

The actual religious alterations made in Västerås were minimal;

[29] See Olaus Petri in *SBL*.
[30] Holmquist, *Svenska Kyrkan*, III, 132–40.
[31] L. Weibull, 'Västerås rigsdag 1527', in *Stockholms blodbad och andra kritiska undersökningar*, Stockholm 1965, 184–224; Montgomery, 'Den svenska religionspolitiken', 121–2.

and as in Prussia, the bishops were given responsibility for putting them into practice.[32] Of far greater significance, however, were the decisions relating to the church's economic position, which made it possible for Gustav Vasa to initiate the policies which ultimately doubled his revenues.

It was this obsession with securing a solid financial foundation for the crown which came to characterise the reign of Gustav Vasa. As a domain state, Sweden's main problem was to transform the crown's income, which was paid in minerals and agricultural produce, into hard cash. Consequently forceful attempts at centralisation, direct administration and transition to a monetary economy became the characteristics of the king's economic policies.[33] It is illustrative of the extent to which Gustav Vasa was prepared to disregard traditional values and the church, if they did not further his financial and administrative aims, that he was prepared to have beautiful, ancient ecclesiastical parchment manuscripts torn up and used for covers of his bailiffs' account books.

Like a number of European rulers, Gustav Vasa initially appears to have favoured a religious solution which would have seen the creation of a reformist national church within the framework of the Catholic church. Accordingly, until the parliament of Västerås in 1527, his church policy was concerned with economic and administrative matters. His disinclination to make any religious changes was undoubtedly based on sound *realpolitik*. He had, after all, as recently as the spring of 1527, just managed to defeat the first major peasant rebellion, the Daljunkern's revolt, directed against his reign.[34]

Traditionally, within Swedish Reformation scholarship, special importance has been attached to the decisions of the parliament of Västerås in 1527, but detailed research into the implementation of the decisions has been lacking. However, if the diocese of Linköping was typical then the decisions of Västerås were slow to be implemented.[35] A sign of the stubborn resistance in Sweden towards the new religious doctrines can be seen in the writings of Olaus Petri on clerical marriage and his attacks on monasticism which were published in 1528. Petri sharply criticised the mendicant orders who constituted the main Catholic bulwark against

[32] Å. Andrén, 'Reformatiokyrkorna och den andliga domsrätten' in *Reformationen i Norden. Kontinuitet och förnyelse*, 98.

[33] E. Ladewig Petersen, 'Office and Offence. Crisis and Structural Tranformation in Seventeenth Century Scandinavia II. Profit from Grant: Sweden and Denmark 1560–1660' in *Scandinavian Journal of History*, 18 (1993), 126–7.

[34] Weibull, *Västerås rigsdag 1527'*, 221.

[35] See H. Schück, *Ecclesiae Lincopensis*, 535–74.

the evangelical preachers in the towns. That year he also published a book of sermons, together with Laurentius Andreae, which, in the main, was a translation of a collection of Luther's sermons published in 1526. However, in order not to antagonise 'the weak', Petri and Andreae promised their readers, in the 1528 preface, that they would soon publish another collection of sermons which would appeal to a wider audience; something they eventually did two years later.[36]

In the Reformation period an evangelical minister/theologian was primarily a preacher. It was thought that *res et verba*, correct doctrine and the proper ability to express oneself, were what constituted a real preacher. Olaus Petri was instrumental, through his writings, in bringing about a gradual transformation of the liturgy and the acceptance of services in the vernacular in Sweden. In 1531 he published the Swedish mass, but he also worked more energetically than anyone else to promote evangelical preaching in Sweden. The son of a blacksmith, he is alleged to have favoured the saying that just as the blacksmith is supposed to forge, so a clergyman's task is to preach.[37]

The preaching and the writings of the reformers obviously furthered the progress of the early evangelical movement. There appears to have been a remarkable agreement on doctrine among the leading Swedish and Finnish reformers. Only among the less educated preachers and among the radical German preachers in Stockholm can a growing theological diversity be detected. In this respect developments in Sweden corresponded to those in Germany.[38] Compared with Germany, however, fervent anti-clericalism and militant evangelical preaching were less conspicuous, even if the early Reformation preaching in Sweden and Finland still carried an implicit anti-Catholic message.[39]

---

[36] See Olaus Petri in *SBL*.

[37] H. B. Hammar, 'Reformationstidens predikan i Sverige', in *Reformationen i Norden. Kontinuitet och förnyelse*, 264.

[38] For the debate about the nature of evangelical preaching in Germany, see B. Moeller, 'Was wurde in der Frühzeit der Reformation in den deutschen Städten gepredigt?' *Archiv für Reformationsgeschichte*, 75 (1984), 176–93; cf. S Karant-Nunn, 'What was preached in German Cities in the Early Years of the Reformation?', in P. N. Bebb and S. Marshall (eds.), *The Process of Change in Early Modern Europe*, Athens, Ohio 1988, 149–63. See also A. Pettegree, 'The early Reformation in Europe: a German Affair or an International Movement?', in A. Pettegree, *The Early Reformation in Europe*, Cambridge 1992, 15–16.

[39] H. Cohn, 'Reformatorische Bewegung und Antiklerikalismus in Deutschland und England' in W. J. Mommsen, P. Alter and R. W. Scribner (eds.), *Stadtbürgertum und Adel in der Reformation*, Stuttgart 1979, 309–25; R. W. Scribner, 'Anticlericalism and the German Reformation' in R. W. Scribner, *Popular Culture and Popular Movements in Germany*, London 1987, 243–56. See also J. M. Stayer, 'Anticlericalism. A Model for a Coherent Interpretation of the Reformation', in Guggisberg and Krodel (eds.), *Die Reformation in Deutschland und Europa*, 39–47.

At the coronation of Gustav Vasa in January 1528, Laurentius Andreae took the theological position, which he had originally advocated in his famous letter to the monastery of Vadstena in 1524, a step further by fully identifying the church with the people. In his coronation sermon, Olaus Petri reminded the king of his responsibilities as *adiutor, nutricius* and *defensor ecclesiae*. Olaus's views on state and church were strongly influenced by Luther, but in separating the true believers from the rest he was inspired by Martin Bucer of Strasburg and the Franconian reformers. However, in stressing that even rulers are bound by the laws of the country, he is solidly anchored within medieval Swedish legal tradition.[40]

Thus far Gustav Vasa and his advisors had managed to avoid committing themselves to any definite religious position. By 1529, however, it had become evident that this approach was untenable and a national synod met in Örebro in February in order to try to find a solution to the religious question. A compromise was reached, which was what Gustav Vasa wanted, but it satisfied no one and could be positively interpreted by Catholics as well as Protestants.[41] It only served to antagonise the hardline evangelicals and disturbances immediately broke out in Stockholm among the influential German population. Olaus Petri was accused of having surrendered to the Catholics. The well-known radical, German preachers, Tileman and Melchior Hoffmann, were particularly hostile.[42]

Meanwhile, in the spirit of the compromise negotiated in Örebro, Olaus Petri took the opportunity to publish a liturgical manual in Swedish. It was mainly a translation of the Catholic Latin Manual, but German evangelical influences can also be identified. Referring once more to 'the weak', he argued for the preservation of all ceremonies which were not expressly against the Bible.[43]

The politico-religious developments in Stockholm were of the greatest importance to the Protestant cause in Sweden. As late as May 1529 the town council had decided to allow the use of both the Latin and Swedish mass, but by August the following year only mass in the vernacular was

---

[40] C. Gardemeister, *Den suveräne Guden. En studie i Olavus Petris teologi*. Studia Theologica Lundensia, XLIII, Lund 1989, 85–90. For the political thinking of Olaus Petri and Laurentius Andreae, see E. I. Kouri, 'Statsmaktstänkandet i början av nya tiden', in E. I. Kouri, *Historiankirjoitus, politiikka, uskonto – Historiography, Politics, Religion*. Studia Historica Jyväskyläensia, XLII, Jyväskylä 1990, 262–8. See also N. K. Andersen, 'The Reformation in Scandinavia and the Baltic', in *The Reformation 1520–1559*. The New Cambridge Modern History, II, Cambridge 1990, 158–9.
[41] See chapter 4.
[42] Holmquist, *Svenska Kyrkan*, III, 141 and 194.
[43] See Olaus Petri in *SBL*.

permitted, while the clergy was ordered to obey the instructions of Olaus Petri and Laurentius Andreae. Stockholm had in effect become an evangelical city. Strängnäs became the first town to follow the example of Stockholm and introduced vernacular services in 1532. The religious innovations in Stockholm, however, met with widespread protest. Faced with a growing number of complaints, Gustav Vasa rejected all suggestions of royal involvement in the changes, emphasising that they had been introduced by the people.[44]

In Germany the evangelical movement provided the common man with a new consciousness and a political platform which allowed grievances against clerical abuses to be given a sharper focus. This new confidence in applying evangelical teachings to special complaints, not to mention the more general search for social justice, is in evidence in the Peasants' War.[45] Contrary to what happened in Germany, popular rebellions and upheavals in Finland and Sweden, particularly in the countryside, were nearly all concerned with the preservation of the 'old religion'. Only three months after the synod of Örebro, a Catholic revolt, Västgötaherrarnas' rebellion, broke out in southwest Sweden. The rebels, who were recruited from a broad spectrum of society, accused Gustav Vasa of having introduced an unchristian regime by expelling bishops and priests and installing heretics who introduced new doctrines. The king only managed to contain the danger by promising to retain the *status quo* in religion. Undoubtedly, the Catholic rebels had been encouraged to take action by recent developments in Germany, where the Diet of Speyer had called a halt to further evangelical reforms and secularisation of church property.[46] Furthermore, the rebels would have been encouraged by the growing split between Gustav Vasa and Lübeck, caused by the king's attempt to undermine the commercial monopoly he had been forced to grant the Hanseatic cities of the Baltic in 1523, by allowing the Dutch to trade with Sweden. Thus the Hansa was actively supporting rebellion in southwest Sweden in the spring of 1529.[47]

Some of the rebel leaders fled the country in May 1529, and a month later Gustav Vasa summoned the lay estates to a parliament in Strängnäs. Here he gave a speech, written by Laurentius Andreae, which sought to allay the religious worries of the common people. He took the

[44] See Laurentius Andreae in *SBL*.
[45] See T. Scott and R. W. Scribner, *The German Peasants' War. A History in Documents*, London 1991.
[46] S. Kjöllerström, 'Västgötaherrarnas uppror', *Scandia*, 29 (1963), 89–90.
[47] S. Lundkvist, *Gustav Vasa och Europa*. Studia Historica Upsaliensia, II, Uppsala 1960, 64–5.

opportunity to emphasise the decisions taken in Västerås in 1527, where it had been decided that the word of God should be preached 'purely'.[48]

During the 1520s, relations between the king and the reformers remained close and confidential. Gustav Vasa often relied on their advice, even in matters of state. Andreae, in particular, played an important part within the administration. The Västgötaherrarnas' rebellion, however, signalled the end of Laurentius Andreae's career within the government of Gustav Vasa. The rebels had singled Andreae out for criticism. They saw him as the architect of Gustav Vasa's anti-monastic policies in particular. The king, who may gradually have begun to doubt Andreae's judgements, eventually decided to remove him, not least because he had become a focus for the dissatisfaction of the Catholic peasantry. Furthermore, at the parliament in Strängnäs in 1529, Laurentius Andreae had argued that the changes in religion had not been introduced on the king's orders, but had been made to please God, whose laws even the king had to obey. In a letter to the exiled bishop, Hans Brask, written in the king's name in 1529, Andreae argued that the decisions taken in Västerås in 1527 were part of Swedish law.[49]

Similar hostility towards Olaus Petri was also increasingly expressed, not least because of his prominent position as the kingdom's leading evangelical writer. It was during 1529 that Gustav Vasa realised that the risks of being closely associated with the reformers had become greater than the possible gains, and a widening gap between royal aspirations and those of Petri and Andreae can be detected. From then on the king became more cautious and was unwilling to make any changes to doctrine or ritual. The influence of the reformers gradually diminished.[50]

In the early 1530s it became obvious that the ideas of the evangelical reformers no longer corresponded with those of Gustav Vasa. In 1531 Laurentius Andreae lost his seat on the Council and his chancellorship was given to Olaus Petri. By November 1532 Andreae had been removed from virtually all political influence; within a year Petri experienced a similar fate. Andreae was also marginalised ecclesiastically when he lost the two archdeaconries of Strängnäs and Uppsala in 1534. His isolation appears to have been almost complete and his name does not

---

[48] Holmquist, *Svenska Kyrkan*, III, 198–9.
[49] S. Kjöllerström, *Gustav Vasa, klockskatten och brytning med Lübeck*. Scripta minora regiae societatis humaniorum litterarum Lundensis, II–III, (1969–70), Lund 1970, 24–45.
[50] See Olaus Petri in *SBL*.

re-appear in the sources until 1539/40. The reasons for the downfall of the reformers were political, as much as ideological. Their replacement within government was the reformist, Kristoffer Andersson, who provided greater scope for Gustav Vasa's *realpolitik*. Thus, for instance, the payment of tithes to the crown was justified in 1534 with a reference to Swedish law, as well as *lex divina*.[51]

The historical episcopate, *successio apostolica*, was preserved in Sweden and the Catholic bishops were allowed to continue in office. The humanist orientation of most of the bishops, who were heavily dependent on the king, made them amenable to changes in ceremonies. The appointment in 1531 of a new archbishop of Uppsala was a momentous event for the Swedish church. The chosen candidate, Laurentius Petri, brother of Olaus, and promoted by Andreae, was a cautious member of the evangelical party. The immediate occasion for his promotion was the approaching marriage of Gustav to Catherine of Saxony-Lauenburg, including her coronation as queen of Sweden.[52]

The new archbishop had studied in Wittenberg, notably under Melanchthon, whose humanist, educational and pedagogical ideas appealed to him. However, Laurentius Petri's Protestantism appears to have been closer to that of Luther and his brother than Melanchthon. His interests in practical ecclesiastical matters and ritual were inspired by Johannes Bugenhagen and another Wittenberg reformer, Johannes Brenz. However, Laurentius Petri's views were probably closest to those of the English reformer, Thomas Cranmer, who, like him, had to deal with an almost tyrannical ruler.[53]

Meanwhile Gustav Vasa maintained his cautious church policy. In 1533 he forbade the new archbishop to make any further ecclesiastical reforms without royal consent. That year, Laurentius Petri drafted a commentary to the Västerås documents, which shows his independent thinking about the relations between state and church. He defended the government's confiscation of church property, but suggested that the funds collected should be used to support students and the poor. This shows that the submission of the Swedish and Finnish church to lay government was not as complete as has often been claimed. In accordance with Melanchthon, Petri stated that the king should not be seen as

[51] Å. Andrén, 'Reformationskyrkorna och den andliga domsrätten', in *Reformationen i Norden. Kontinuitet och förnyelse*, 104.
[52] See chapter 4 and S. Kjöllerström, 'Gustav Vasa und die Bischofsweihe (1523–1531)', in *Für Kirche und Recht. Festschrift für Johannes Heckel*, Cologne 1959, 180–3.
[53] See Laurentius Petri in *SBL*.

dominus religionis, but rather as *praecipuum membrum ecclesiae*, and that the church should remain independent in spiritual matters.[54]

As stated above, Sweden, and to an even greater extent Finland, witnessed a princely Reformation with very limited popular involvement. Step by step the Catholic church-province of Uppsala became the national Swedish church, independent of any foreign authorities. In the early 1530s it still had room for Lutheranism, Christian humanism and reformist Catholicism. It gradually developed in a Lutheran direction, but within it there remained more Catholic elements than in any other Lutheran church.[55]

The Reformation in Finland followed the developments in Sweden to a great extent, but it had its own special character. The actual reform work was carried out by young Finnish theologians who had become acquainted with the new religion during their studies at foreign – predominantly German – universities. The first Lutheran canon and later archdeacon in Åbo/Turku, Pietari Särkilahti, was the son of a mayor of Åbo/Turku. He had studied for some years in Rostock, Louvain and probably Wittenberg. In 1524 he returned to his native country and until his untimely death in 1529 he exerted considerable influence over the younger priests.[56] Furthermore, Olaus Petri's activities in Stockholm, as well as the close connections between the German population there and in Åbo/Turku, Viborg/Viipuri and the Baltic cities, where the Reformation had taken hold in the mid-1520s, helped the new faith to spread in Finland.[57]

The principle that the word of God had to be preached to people in their mother tongue, and that they should be given the opportunity to read it in the vernacular, helped to create and nourish new written languages in remote and obscure parts of Europe. Literature published during the Reformation in Swedish, and particularly in Finnish, was mainly written for ecclesiastical purposes. This was a significant cultural achievement of lasting importance. In Sweden the leading author in this field was, of course, Olaus Petri. *The Manual* (1529) and *The Mass* (1531) were predominantly his work. In addition, he wrote a number of other

[54] *Ibid.*
[55] K. Pirinen, *Keskiaika ja uskonpuhdistuksen aika*. Suomen kirkon historia, I, Porvoo 1991, 277.
[56] S. Heininen (ed.), *Paulus Juusten, Catalogus et ordinaria succesio episcoporum Finlandensium*. SKHS, CXLII, Pieksämäki 1988, 88; K. Pirinen, *Turun tuomiokapituli uskonpuhdistuksen murroksessa*. SKHS, LXII, Helsinki 1962, 20–2 and 45–8.
[57] O. D. Schalin, 'Hava Wiborg och Nyland utgjort en tidig härd för reformationen', *Tidskrift för kyrkomusik och svenskt gudstjänstliv* (1936), 109–13.

works, for example a *Collection of Sermons*, a *Swedish Chronicle* and *Rules for Judges*, and he even compiled a Swedish–Latin dictionary.[58]

Olaus Petri was influenced by the teachings of Luther, and to a lesser extent by Melanchthon. In his legal writings a Melanchthonian element is conspicuous. Contemporary German humanism also left its mark on Petri's thinking, while inspiration from southern Germany, Nuremberg, Württemberg and Strasburg is traceable.[59]

There is no doubt about Luther's pre-eminent significance for the first generation of Swedish and Finnish reformers. However, as in the case of Olaus Petri, Luther was by no means the only influence, and from the 1530s he seems to have been superseded by other reformers. In addition, all the leading Swedish and Finnish reformers, with the exception of Laurentius Andreae, had studied in Wittenberg where they had met Luther. However, the Luther whom Olaus Petri knew was a different man from the Luther the Finnish reformer, Mikael Agricola, encountered some twenty years later.[60]

The translation of Luther's works demonstrate his influence in Scandinavia. The Danish translations with twenty-eight editions and nineteen titles take second place only to the Dutch translations, while there was only one Swedish and one Finnish translation in Luther's lifetime – in both cases his *Small Catechism*. This work had become an essential tool for a programme of Christian education throughout evangelical Europe. In the translations there is a preference for catechismal works and sermons over political and polemical writings.[61]

Besides Luther and Melanchthon, the Swedish reformers drew on the South German reformers. As we have seen, Olaus Petri, in drafting his pamphlet on the way to Man's salvation in 1526, used Luther, Bucer, Bugenhagen and Rhegius as sources. The first part of his work on the word of God and human commands and laws, published two years later, was a free translation of Osiander's *Ansbacher Ratschlag*. In another treatise he published in 1529, Petri again made use of Osiander's ideas. Osiander's metaphysical and speculative mysticism can be clearly traced in the hymn he wrote in the mid-1530s. It is also worth noticing that, for

[58] B. Hesselman (ed.), *Samlade skrifter av Olavus Petri*, 4 vols., Uppsala 1914–17; S. Lindroth, *Svensk Lärdomshistoria*, I, Stockholm 1975, 233–43. For Olaus Petri as historian, see G. T. Westin, 'Ty der som sant är vill jag ju gärna skrivna. Olaus Petri om historikerns problem och uppgift', in *Studier i äldre historia tilläggande Herman Schück 5/4 1985*, Stockholm 1985, 181–93.

[59] S. Ingebrand, *Olavus Petris reformatoriska åskadning*. Studia Doctrinae Christianae Upsaliensia, I, Uppsala 1964, 345–6.

[60] B. Ahlberg, 'Luther i Norden', in *Reformationen i Norden. Kontinuitet och förnyelse*, 37–8.

[61] B. Moeller, 'Luther in Europe: His Works in Translation, 1517–1546', in E. I. Kouri and T. Scott (eds.), *Politics and Society in Reformation Europe*, London 1987, 236.

example, the Swedish prayer book of 1544, which was reprinted more than ten times, was heavily influenced by a prayer book published in Nuremberg in 1536 and by Johannes Brenz's prayer book of 1538.[62]

It has been stated that Sweden and Finland became a cultural province of Germany because of the Reformation.[63] It seems that books published on the Continent, in particular in Germany, quickly found their way to the northern periphery. German booksellers visited Scandinavian towns and native printers ordered books from abroad. It is also important to remember that those who had studied abroad brought books back with them on their return – many of them on theology.[64] Thus, when evangelical literature and its impact on Scandinavia is discussed, this direct influence from the centres of Protestantism should not be overlooked. The number of people able to read books published in foreign languages was, of course, limited, but among the nobility, the middle class and even the peasantry there were many who could read the writings of the native reformers. Illiteracy as such was not a hindrance, as long as there was, at least, one person in the household who could read. Furthermore, in various social groups special readers were employed.[65] The evidence does not allow us to present a comprehensive and detailed analysis of the impact of evangelical literature in Sweden and Finland, but it cannot have been insignificant, even if the editions were small and the book prices high.

The reformers thought that education would advance the Protestant cause by banishing ignorance and implanting knowledge of the truth. Schools were still controlled by the church, and although it lost its traditional monopoly on higher education, it retained a considerable influence on Swedish schooling. Gustav Vasa, for his part, did not value higher education, but he believed that the parishes should have clergymen and the crown civil servants who were able to read, write and count. It caused some tension when he ordered a number of secondary school pupils to leave school prematurely to take up positions within local and central administration. The Swedish and Finnish reformers proved

---

62 M. Lindström, 'Olavus Petri och Andreas Osiander', *Svensk Teologisk Kvartalskrift*, 17 (1941), 206–25; see also Holmquist, *Svenska Kyrkan*, III, 153, 155, 159, 174, 185–6, and 237–8. For the Swedish prayer book, see S. Estborn, *Evangeliska svenska bönböcker under reformationstidevarvet. Med en inledande översikt över medeltidens och reformationstidens evangeliska tyska bönlitteratur*, Lund 1929, 120–44.

63 Lindroth, *Svensk Lärdomshistoria*, 118.

64 J. Vallinkoski, *The History of the University Library at Turku*, I, Helsingin yliopiston kirjaston julk., XXI, Helsinki 1948, 78–9, 81.

65 M. G. Scholz, *Zur Hörerfunktion in der Literatur des Spätmittelalters und der frühen Neuzeit. Theorien und Modelle zur Rezeption literarischer Werke*, Stuttgart 1975, 143–5; G. Frühsorge, *Die Begründung der väterlichen Gesellschaft in der europäischen eoconomica christiana*. Stuttgart 1978, 110–23.

more hostile to pagan rites and magic practices than the Catholic clergy. Statutes criminalising the use of magic were enacted, but their observance appears to have been inconsistent. There were, it is true, witches, but there were as yet no real witch-hunts.[66]

The shift of Gustav Vasa's church policy in a more cautious direction can be partly explained by the rebellions of the late 1520s and early 1530s, and by the latest developments abroad. In 1531, for example, the so-called 'church bell revolt' broke out in Sweden. This rebellion, which was not put down until 1533, was brought about by royal confiscation of church bells. The fundamental cause of the uprising, however, was a new tax levied to pay back part of Lübeck's loan to the government. The growing political and commercial importance of the Baltic Sea increased the interest of the major powers in the region. The danger of the internal disturbances being used by foreign potentates was ever present.[67]

In Denmark a Catholic reaction followed the death of Frederik I in 1533.[68] Again, the more social and radical tendencies of the evangelical movements in Germany, not least the recent Reformation in Lübeck, may have fuelled Gustav Vasa's suspicions with regard to the loyalty of the evangelical leaders in Sweden. Furthermore, in 1536, a conspiracy was discovered to blow up the king with gunpowder and hand over Stockholm to the Hansa. Among the conspirators were the master of the royal mint and several of the German merchants. Vagrant and sometimes radical German preachers had helped to spread Protestantism among the German residents, especially among the leading merchants.[69]

In 1533, without warning, Gustav Vasa abrogated the treaty with Lübeck which had granted the city considerable trading privileges in Sweden and Finland. When Lübeck attacked Sweden in the following year, Gustav entered into a defensive alliance with Duke Christian of Schleswig and Holstein who was shortly to succeed his father as king of Denmark and Norway.[70] As a result of the 1534–6 war, Sweden freed herself from the disadvantageous trade concessions granted to Lübeck in the 1520s and the rest of her debt to the city. This favourable outcome and the rapidly improving financial situation of the crown gave Gustav

---

[66] M. Nenonen, *Noituus, taikuus ja noitavainot.* Historiallisia tutkimuksia, CLXV, Helsinki 1992, 431–3; and chapter 7.
[67] Kjöllerström, *Gustav Vasa, klockskatten och brytning med Lübeck,* 40.
[68] Grell, 'Scandinavia', 111 and chapter 4.
[69] K. B. Westman, 'Reformation och Revolution', *Uppsala Universitets Årsskrift,* 7, 8 (1941), 24–5.
[70] See chapter 2.

Vasa increased power, which was soon to be reflected in his church policies.[71]

The political situation of the Swedish church started to change gradually in the wake of the peace treaty with Lübeck in 1536. In the same year the Reformation was officially introduced in Denmark and Norway. At the synod held in Uppsala it was decided that the evangelical mass and manual should be introduced throughout the country, while celibacy was officially abolished. Gustav Vasa gave his silent consent and the break with the Catholic church was complete. The Swedish church had now become a national evangelical church, but it was not until the Succession Parliament held in Västerås in 1544 that Sweden was officially pronounced an evangelical kingdom. However, the crown and not the bishops were made responsible for ecclesiastical customs and practices.[72]

The fact that in the late 1530s Gustav Vasa took a more positive interest in the efforts to change the Swedish church in an evangelical direction was partly due to his ambition to join the Schmalkaldic League. In 1538 Denmark was accepted as a member, while the Swedish application was rejected. This can be partly explained by the strained political relations between the two countries. Rumours also circulated in Germany about close contacts between Gustav Vasa and the emperor. In early 1541 Sweden again tried, with the support of Luther, to become a member of the League, but once more she was unsuccessful.[73] Sweden became a more reliable partner in the eyes of German Protestants when she concluded a peace treaty with Denmark in September 1541. Soon the Lutheran states of Scandinavia – with their close economic, dynastic, political and religious ties with some of the Protestant ruling houses in Germany – were seen as potential allies by their fellow Protestants abroad.

By then an important change had taken place in Sweden. In 1540 Gustav Vasa's church policy had begun to resemble that of the German territorial princes. Having tired of the independent tendencies of the Swedish reformers, he recruited the former Habsburg councillor, Conrad von Pyhy, as his chancellor. On the recommendation of Luther

[71] E. I. Kouri, 'Die diplomatisch-politischen Beziehungen zwischen den Protestanten in Deutschland und Schweden 1525–1547', in Kouri, *Historiography, Politics, Religion*, 186–8.

[72] Holmquist, *Svenska Kyrkan*, III, 305–9; M. Roberts, 'On Aristocratic Constitutionalism in Swedish History, 1520–1720', in M. Roberts, *Essays in Swedish History*, London 1967, 19–20; Å. Andrén, 'Reformationskyrkornas gudtjänstliv', in *Reformationen i Norden. Kontinuitet och förnyelse*, 169–70.

[73] For Luther's role, see *Martin Luthers Werke. Kritische Gesamtausgabe, Briefwechsel*, IX, Weimar 1941, 426–35.

and Melanchthon, the Pomeranian theologian, Georg Norman, was invited to Sweden to advise Gustav Vasa on church affairs. This so-called 'German period' lasted from 1539 to 1544. The newcomers brought with them from Germany a new political ideology, which emphasised the power of the ruler and his control over a territorial state church.[74] The king's power was further magnified by the increasing financial resources of the crown. The balance of power between Gustav Vasa and his subjects, not to mention between him and the reformers, started to tilt in his favour.

During 1539 Gustav Vasa repeatedly attacked Laurentius Andreae and Olaus Petri for failing to teach obedience towards secular authority. The tensions culminated at the parliament in Örebro in December 1539, where the king took the necessary measures to secure full royal control over the Swedish church. New instructions were issued and the Swedish and Finnish churches finally experienced a princely Reformation in church government. The tensions between the king and the reformers had a long history and can be documented in various ways. Olaus Petri, for example, interpreted the sign in the sky over Stockholm in 1535 as an omen of the trials endured by the country because of the sins of its rulers.[75] In 1539 he published a sermon maintaining that God sends famine, pestilence and war to all those who despise His commands. Since, according to Petri, the present rulers, unlike their predecessors, did not deal with the offenders, the task fell to the preachers.

In Örebro legal proceedings were instituted against Laurentius Andreae and Olaus Petri. They were impeached and held responsible for almost every failed royal policy and all the revolts against Gustav Vasa. They were also accused of having had contacts with politically unreliable elements among the burghers of Stockholm. Olaus Petri was said to have known about the conspiracy of 1536 to kill the king and was accused of having labelled him a tyrant. The downfall of the reformers was part of a general shift in Gustav Vasa's church policy, and the legal proceedings which ensued were primarily a political action to neutralise them and their supporters. Although they were condemned to death in January 1540, the reformers were immediately pardoned by Gustav Vasa. Having had their wings clipped they remained useful to the king and the

[74] I. Svalenius, *Georg Norman. En biografisk studie*, Lund 1937; and I. Svalenius, *Gustav Vasa*, 2nd edn., Lund 1963, 169–71.
[75] H. Sandblad, *De eskatologiska föreställningarna i Sverige under reformationen och motreformationen*, Lychnos-bibliotek, v, Stockholm 1942, 65–72.

following year, together with Pyhy and Norman, who had passed the death sentence over them, they were actively involved in introducing the new reforms of church government. Until his death in April 1552 Laurentius Andreae lived quietly in Strängnäs, while in 1542 Olaus Petri was appointed school inspector in Stockholm, only to be given the rectorship there the following year. To the end of his life, however, he continued to criticise Gustav Vasa in his sermons.[76]

Luther's influence on the introduction of the Reformation in Denmark and Sweden differed significantly. His friend and collaborator, Johannes Bugenhagen, personally supervised the drafting of the new Danish Church Order, regularly consulting Luther, and the establishment of the Lutheran state church in 1537. In Sweden it took much longer to reach a normative, evangelical codification of ecclesiastical law. Bugenhagen's Swedish counterpart, the Melanchthonian Georg Norman, drafted a Church Ordinance in 1540, but it was never completed. In it Norman repeatedly referred to the later edition of Melanchthon's *Loci*, but not once did he mention Luther.[77]

A parliament was summoned in 1544 to meet in Västerås partly in order to deal with the most serious of the revolts of Gustav Vasa's reign which had broken out in southern Sweden. As so often before, the revolt was caused mainly by economic and social grievances, but Catholic priests used the opportunity to try to have the old faith re-introduced. Even the emperor and other foreign potentates demonstrated an alarming interest in this rebellion.[78] All this made clear to Gustav Vasa that a complete break with Catholicism and the establishment of a hereditary national monarchy was in the interest of the crown.

Meanwhile, in Finland the Reformation had advanced in a more peaceful manner. When, in 1527, the frustrated Erik Svensson had obtained permission to resign his bishopric, a pious Dominican Catholic reformist, Mårten Skytte (1528–50), was appointed as *electus* to the see of Åbo/Turku. It was Skytte's decision to send talented young Finnish students to Wittenberg in the early 1530s which had far-reaching importance for the Reformation in Finland. The first of them returned in 1536. It was these scholars who introduced the Reformation to the Finnish

---

[76] H. Lundström (ed.), 'Handlingar från rättergången med Olaus Petri och Laurentius Andreae i Orebro 1539–1540', *Kyrkohistorisk Årsskrift* (1909), 64–70, and 73–82.

[77] For Norman's draft, *Articuli ordinantiae*, see O. Ahnfeldt (ed.), 'Bidrag till svenska kyrkans historia under 16:e århundert', *Lunds Universitets Årsskrift*, 30 (1895), 12–25; S. Kjöllerström, 'Visitatio Gustaviana. Ett otryckt dokument av Georg Norman', *Kyrkohistorisk Årsskrift*, 31 (1930), 196–8.

[78] Kouri, 'Die diplomatisch-politischen Beziehungen', 196–211.

people.[79] Personally Skytte represented traditional Catholic piety, but he opposed neither the new evangelical ceremonies and customs nor the crown's reduction of church property. In Finland services in the vernacular were introduced around 1537. It was then that the Finnish service transformed the royal Reformation into a Finnish Reformation. Simultaneously the Reformation took a sharp evangelical turn. The monasteries, for instance, were closed and their property was confiscated.[80]

After a fumbling start, uniformity in doctrine and ceremonies was recognised to be in the interest of the realm. State and church, however, tried to achieve this objective in different ways. The church acknowledged the king as *praecipuum membrum ecclesiae* and as *custos utriusque tabulae*, but it wanted the right to define doctrine.[81] This caused tension, not only between church and state, but also within the church. Generally speaking, confessionalism was not very conspicuous. In the early Reformation period the Swedish and Finnish reformers thought that the scriptures were the only necessary guiding principle. Accordingly, there was no need for additional confessional definitions. Archbishop Laurentius Petri's first proposal for an evangelical Church Ordinance in 1547 was rejected by the king. The second proposal, made in 1561, did not meet with immediate approval either. It was not until ten years later that this proposal was ratified by the parliament of Stockholm.[82] In Denmark the *Confessio Augustana* was formally accepted in 1569,[83] but in Sweden and Finland it was not until 1593, supplemented with the three creeds of the early church, that it became normative.

The reformers strove to create an orderly Christian society. Soon the magnitude of the task of educating a 'truly' Christian people became clear. Important for this purpose was the printing press established in

---

[79] Pirinen, *Turun tuomiokapituli uskonpuhdistuksen murroksessa*, 71–8. For Finnish students in Wittenberg, see S. Heininen, *Die finnischen Studenten in Wittenberg 1531–1552*, Schriften der Luther-Agricola-Gesellschaft, A XIX, Helsinki 1980.

[80] J.Knuutila, 'Strävan efter liturgisk uniformitet i Finland 1537–1614', in *Reformationens konsolidering i de nordiska länderna 1540–1610*, 351–72, especially 368–9.

[81] Here the Swedish church allied itself closely with Melanchthon, see especially P. Melanchthon, *Philippi Melanchthonis Opera Quae Supersunt Omnia. Corpus Reformatorum* (C. G. Bretschneider et al., eds.), 28 vols., Halle 1834–60, XVI, 420–1 and *Corpus Reformatorum*, XXI, 31–2 and 983–1015; see also Kouri, 'Statsmaktstänkandet', 242–4.

[82] E. Färnström, *Om källorna till 1571 års kyrkoordning särskilt med hänsyn till tyska kyrkoordningar*, Uppsala 1935; S. Kjöllerström, *Svenska förarbeten till kyrkoordningen av år 1571*. Samlingar och Studier till Svenska Kyrkans Historia, II, Stockholm 1940. For Laurentius Petri's theological development, see I. Montgomery, *Värjöstånd och lärostånd. Religion och politik i meningsutbrytet mellan kungamakt och prästerskapet i Sverige 1593–1608*. Studia Historico-ecclesiastica Upsaliensia, XXII, Uppsala 1972, 23–6.

[83] See below chapter 5.

Stockholm in 1543. During that year Mikael Agricola's ABC book was published in Finnish which included a translation of Luther's *Small Catechism*. During the next thirty years about one hundred evangelical writings were printed in Stockholm.[84]

After the deaths of Laurentius Andreae, Georg Norman and Olaus Petri in the early 1550s, Archbishop Laurentius Petri became the leading figure in the Swedish church. In the *rabies theologorum* about the finer points of doctrine he maintained a middle course. Petri had already played a leading role in organising and translating the Swedish Bible of 1541, while in the following decade he was active in publishing important pastoral works, such as the hymn book of 1553, and two years later a book of sermons, in two parts. The sermons were freely translated from the works of Luther and Veit Dietrich and were moderate in tone. Later, in 1557 he wrote the first Swedish book on temperance and in 1559 a tract on Christian family life.[85]

Meanwhile in Finland it took four years before a successor to Bishop Mårten Skytte, who had died in 1550, was found. Then, however, no fewer than two bishops were appointed, because Gustav Vasa had decided to divide the country into two bishoprics. Mikael Agricola was elected to the see of Åbo/Turku, and Paavali Juusten to the newly created see of Viborg/Viipuri in eastern Finland.[86] The king went even further, demoting the new leaders of the Finnish church to *ordinarien*, i.e. to the equivalent of superintendents in Germany.[87]

Mikael Agricola was one of the young men upon whom Särkilahti's preaching had made a profound impression in the late 1520s. He was born around 1510 on the southern coast of Finland, and after attending school in Viborg/Viipuri he arrived in Åbo/Turku in 1528, where he later became Bishop Skytte's secretary. In 1536 he left for Wittenberg, where he listened to Luther's lectures on Genesis and Melanchthon's on Demosthenes, Euripides, Socrates and Aristotle's *Ethics*.[88] Three years later, having received his MA, he returned to Finland in the company of Georg Norman. In Åbo/Turku he became headmaster of the Latin school and nine years later an assistant to Skytte. After Skytte's death he

[84] See I. Collijn, *Sveriges bibliografi intill år 1600*, II, Uppsala 1927–31.
[85] Holmquist, *Svenska Kyrkan*, III, 288–95 and 349–51; for Laurentius Petri, see also *SBL*.
[86] S. Kjöllerström, *Kräkla och mitra. En undersökning om biskopsvigningar i Sverige under reformationstidevarvet*. Biblioteca Theologiae Practicae, XIX, Lund 1965, 26 and 34–5; A. Läntinen, 'Viipurin hiippa-kunnan perustamisvaiheet', *Historiallinen Aikakauskirja* (1982), 195–8.
[87] S.-E. Brodd, 'Superintendenturen som erstättning för och komplement till biskopsämbetet i svenska kyrkan 1539–1631', in *Reformationens konsolidering i de nordiska länderna 1540–1610*, 211–12.
[88] Heininen, *Die finnischen Studenten*, 47–51.

succeeded to the post, but did not receive the full title of bishop until 1554. In the following year war broke out between Sweden and Russia. This forced Gustav Vasa to spend far more time in Finland while Agricola became increasingly involved in the diplomatic negotiations between the two countries. In 1557 he was sent to Moscow as a peace negotiator and on his way back he fell ill and died on the Karelian Isthmus.[89]

Mikael Agricola is known not only as Finland's reformer, but also as the father of Finnish literature. He could rightly be characterised as the *praeceptor Finlandiae*. The first work to appear in Finnish was his above-mentioned ABC book, published in 1543. The following year his biblical prayer book was printed. This large manual of almost 900 pages, which contains material from the Bible, the church Fathers, medieval authors and reformers, was the only one of its kind in Scandinavia.[90]

As a young man in Wittenberg, Agricola had started to translate the New Testament into Finnish, and he continued this work on his return to Åbo/Turku. His translation of the New Testament was published in 1548. In addition to the Greek text published by Erasmus, he used Erasmus's Latin translation, the Vulgate, Luther's Bible, the Swedish New Testament of 1526 and Gustav Vasa's Bible of 1541. About a quarter of the Old Testament – the Psalter and parts of the Books of the Prophets – was published in 1551–2. It had been translated by Agricola, assisted by a group of scholars. Over and above the texts, all the translations contain commentaries and summaries, which were incorporated in prefaces to individual sections or books from the Bible, in headings of the different chapters and in short notices in the margins of the text. The prefaces to the gospels were translated from Erasmus's Latin New Testament, while those for the other books of the New Testament were adopted from Luther's Bible, with the exception of Luther's critical preface to Revelation, which he translated from the Swedish Bible. Agricola translated the summaries of the Psalms from the works of Luther's colleagues, Veit Dietrich and Georg Major, while the summaries of the Books of the

[89] J. Gummerus, *Michael Agricola, der Reformator Finnlands. Sein Leben und Werk*. Schriften der Luther-Agricola-Gesellschaft, II, Helsinki 1941; S. Heininen, *Nuori Mikael Agricola*. Suomi CXX:3, Helsinki 1976; V. Tarkiainen and K. Tarkiainen, *Mikael Agricola. Suomen uskonpuhdistaja*, Keuruu 1985, 27–121. For the struggle for control over the Baltic region in the mid-1550s, see S. Lundkvist, 'The European Powers and Sweden in the Reign of Gustav Vasa', in E. I. Kouri and T. Scott (eds.), *Politics and Society*, 513–14.

[90] *Mikael Agricolan teokset*, 3 vols., Porvoo 1931. For the prayer book, see J. Gummerus (ed.), *Mikael Agricolan Rukouskirja ja sen lähteet*. SKHS, XLIV: 1–3, Helsinki 1941–55.

Prophets are from Veit Dietrich and Johannes Bugenhagen. Agricola also translated the mass and the manual from Swedish in 1549.[91]

Agricola's substantial literary output consists mainly of translations of Latin, German and Swedish writings, but it also reflects his cautious reforming activities and his personal thoughts. Agricola was not a radical reformer, but rather a Melanchthonian traditionalist. In liturgical questions, for example, he was old fashioned and the situation in Finland gave him no reason to attack the Catholic church aggressively. His reverent attitude towards tradition can be seen from his affection for late medieval piety and the eucharist. However, he stressed the importance of catechetic instruction, and was of the opinion that the first duty of a priest was to teach. His tolerant attitude towards various forms of religious life and doctrines makes him a typical representative of Finnish religious thinking in the early Reformation period.[92]

When Gustav Vasa died in 1560, Sweden was confronted with a number of difficult national and international problems. He had remained firmly in control of the church until the end, but the lack of any firm doctrinal foundation for the new evangelical church was to cause serious difficulties during the reigns of his sons. They, unlike their father, were well educated and interested in theological questions. Each of them, however, wanted to shape the church according to his own preferences, which served to unsettle the church for decades.

In the Reformation period, the Swedish and Finnish clergy, as one of the four estates of the realm, had a relatively strong political position. In parliament they took part in the political debate, while the other estates considered them to be the experts in religious matters. This was not always easy for the king to accept. In 1554–7 Gustav Vasa tried to diminish the power and influence of the clergy, in particular that of the bishops. He did so by splitting up the old established bishoprics and personally appointing the new bishops. Thus, as we have seen, Finland was divided into two bishoprics in 1554.

Gustav Vasa's sons, however, seem to have found it difficult to decide whether or not to maintain this practice. Mikael Agricola always tried to avoid getting involved in any of the political disputes of his time, a policy which was not continued by his successor, Petrus Follingius (1556–63)

---

[91] S. Heininen, 'Mikael Agricola eksegeettinä', *Suomalaisen eksegetiikan ja orientalistiikan juuria.* SKHS, CLXI, Helsinki 1993, 9 and 15–25. For Agricola's prefaces, see I. Fredrikson, *Studier i Mikael Agricolas bibliska företal,* Umeå 1985.

[92] Pirinen, *Keskiaika ja uskonpuhdistuksen aika,* 288 and 291–4; Tarkiainen and Tarkiainen, *Mikael Agricola,* 248–92.

from Linköping. The latter immediately involved himself in the quarrels between Gustav Vasa's sons, King Erik XIV and Johan, duke of Finland. Johan, who had married a sister of the Polish king, had begun to conduct an independent foreign policy with the support of Follingius.[93] Consequently, Erik intervened and conquered the castle of Åbo/Turku, using the opportunity to remove Follingius from his post. After Follingius' dismissal the king transferred Paavali Juusten from Viborg/Viipuri to Åbo/Turku (1563–75). To the see of Viborg/Viipuri he appointed Knuut Johanneksenpoika (Canutus Johannis), who, however, died the following year.[94] It was not until 1569 that a new bishop was elected for Viborg/Viipuri. He was Eerik Härkäpää (1569–78), who had received his MA in Wittenberg. Theologically, these men, like many Swedish and Finnish theologians of the period, moved gradually from traditional Philippism towards a mild, Melanchthonian orthodoxy.[95]

Politically and socially, as well as religiously and culturally, the Reformation proved a crucial period of transition for Sweden and Finland. Not all the consequences were positive: unlike in Denmark, it heralded a period of cultural decline. This was, of course, partly due to the desperately shrinking economic resources of the church which, to a greater extent than in a number of other countries, had been the mainstay of learning. Communications with the Catholic centres of learning became infrequent or were disrupted altogether. Clergymen with a university education became rarer and scholarly connections were limited to Protestant German universities, above all to Wittenberg and later Rostock.[96] On the other hand a rapidly increasing number of vernacular ecclesiastical writings were published, which became the basis of Swedish and Finnish literature. On the political level too, contacts and co-operation increased with Protestant Europe, and with Germany in particular.[97]

[93] W. Tham, *Den svenska utrikespolitikens historia*, 1:2, Stockholm 1960, 27–9.
[94] M. Parvio, *Paavali Juusten ja hänen messunsa. Liturgianhistoriallinen tutkimus.* Suomi, CXXII:3, Helsinki 1978, 14.
[95] J. Paarma, *Hiippakuntahallinto Suomessa 1554–1694.* SKHS, CXVI, Pieksämäki 1980, 151–3.
[96] O. Hartvig, *Album Academiae Vitebergensis*, II, Halis 1894; A. Hofmeister, *Die matrikel der Universität Rostock*, II, Rostock 1891; L. Daae, *Matrikel over Nordiska Studerende ved fremmede Universiteter*, I, Christiania 1885; K. G. Leinberg, *Finske studerande vid utrikes universiteter före 1640*, Helsingfors 1896; S. Göransson, *De svenska studieresorna och religiösa kontrollen från reformationstiden till frihetstiden.* Uppsala Universitetets Årsskrift, VIII, Uppsala 1951, 1–16; C. Callmer, *Svenska studenter i Wittenberg.* Skrifter utgivna av Personhistoriska Samfundet, XVII, Stockholm 1976. For the Finnish situation, see especially J. Nuorteva, *Finländarnas utrikes studiegång före grundläggandet av Åbo Akademin 1313–1640*, forthcoming 1994.
[97] E. I. Kouri, 'For True Faith or National Interest? Queen Elizabeth I and the Protestant Powers' in Kouri and Scott (eds.), *Politics and Society*, 419–22.

After the introduction of the Reformation, the social composition of the clergy changed: an ecclesiastical career, which had already become considerably less attractive to the nobility in Sweden and Finland towards the end of the fifteenth century, was no longer to be seriously considered by members of this class. The end of clerical celibacy led to great changes too. Through the married clergy, a special parsonage culture gradually developed which was to influence the material and spiritual life in Sweden and Finland in a highly significant and lasting fashion. The reformers paid special attention to nurturing a new kind of evangelical clergyman, who was supposed to be not only well educated, but also morally blameless. His work was 'to study, preach, and pray'. The reality, however, did not always correspond to such high ideals, and the clergy was constantly faced with accusations of drunkenness and greed.[98]

The social status of the clergy declined. Similarly, the status of the church in society altered. Administratively and financially it became ever more dependent on the crown, which could use its right to appoint, and its control over economic matters, to influence the church's decisions. In spite of that it never came fully under the control of the state: historical episcopacy, theologically trained clergy and ancient Swedish and Finnish self-government at parish level helped the church to retain its own profile. Gustav Vasa's disinclination to make any changes in liturgy and ceremonies, at least during the early Reformation period, also served to encourage a *de facto* independence; it may even have been a royal acknowledgement of this. However, in spite of all its shortcomings, a territorial church with a genuine Lutheran flavour was established in Sweden and Finland in the reign of Gustav Vasa. Neither later doctrinal fluctuations nor his successors' political vagaries were able to change this course decisively.

[98] Pirinen, *Keskiaika ja uskonpuhdistuksen aika*, 362–4.

CHAPTER 4

The Catholic church and its leadership

Ole Peter Grell

The Catholic church in Scandinavia disappeared within two decades of the beginning of evangelical preaching in these countries. The late medieval church in the Nordic countries was beset with problems similar to those in the rest of Europe. There was growing princely and papal interference in local church affairs, and increased involvement by bishops in predominantly lay, political and economic activities. This was often to the detriment of the church's religious obligation which, after all, should have been primary. Even taking this into consideration, however, the speed of this collapse is remarkable.

To some extent it may well have been this perceived weakness, or failure to resist the Reformation which accounts for the scant interest taken in the Catholic church and its leaders by scholars of Scandinavian Reformation history.[1] Of greater significance, however, is the fact that most Scandinavian Reformation history has been written from a Protestant perspective which retrospectively has viewed the victory of Protestantism as a more or less obvious outcome, confronted as it was with what is seen to have been a morally corrupt and politically inept Catholic church.[2] This is a view which has served to underline that there is little need to take a closer look at the Catholic church and its leadership in sixteenth-century Scandinavia.

This conveniently simplistic view of the church and its leadership on the eve of the Reformation, characterised by decay, lack of piety and proper worship, has not been restricted to Scandinavian Reformation

---

[1] Apart from a number of biographies of individual Catholic bishops of the Reformation era, only two geographically limited studies, of the archbishopric of Lund and the bishopric of Linköping, have been published, see G. Johannesson, *Den Skånska Krykan och Reformationen*, Lund 1947 and H. chück, *Ecclesia Lincopensis. Studier om Linköpingskyrkan under Medeltiden och Gustav Vasa*, Stockholm 1959. The only work which lays claim to study the Catholic leadership in Denmark in the Reformation years offers little more than a biography of three of the bishops, see P. G. Lindhardt, *Nederlagets Mænd. Det katolske bispevældes sidste dage i Danmark*, Copenhagen 1968.

[2] For an example of this bias, see Lindhardt, *Nederlagets Mænd*, 167.

history. Recently, however, its validity as an explanation for the European Reformation has been seriously challenged by a number of scholars.[3] Accordingly, this chapter intends to provide a re-assessment of the Catholic church in Denmark, Norway and Sweden in the period immediately before and during the Reformation, while trying to appraise the problems it was confronted with and its attempts to tackle them.

The Catholic church in Denmark, led by the archbishop of Lund and consisting of eight bishoprics (including Schleswig), was the wealthiest of the Scandinavian church-provinces, followed by the Swedish church led by the archbishop of Uppsala and divided into six bishoprics (including Åbo/Turku in Finland). The Norwegian church was considerably poorer than its neighbours and consisted of only five dioceses, including the archbishopric of Trondheim.[4]

Within the Scandinavian countries monasticism was by far the strongest in Denmark. here the traditional orders, as well as the mendicant orders, were better represented and the monasteries were wealthier. However, even in Denmark recruitment had proved difficult for most orders in the decades leading up to the Reformation and several monasteries were close to dissolution well before the emergence of the evangelical movement. Furthermore, well in advance of the Reformation an increasing number of monasteries had come under the control and management of the lay nobility.

As was the case in the rest of Europe in general and Germany in particular, the three scandinavian church-provinces had witnessed increased royal and papal interference in church affairs during the fifteenth century. By the beginning of the 1520s the situation in Scandinavia, however, appears to have been unusually grim. This is evident from the first public letter issued in December 1522 by the rebellious members of the Danish Council and other members of the nobility, only a few months before King Christian II was finally deposed. The rebels list the damage to the holy church and her personnel as their primary reason for rebelling, stating that:

---

[3] See among others, J. Bossy, *Christianity in the West 1400–1700*, Oxford 1985 and E. Cameron, *The European Reformation*, Oxford 1991, especially 2–37.

[4] The eight Danish bishoprics were, besides the archbishopric of Lund, those of Roskilde, Odense, Børglum, Aarhus, Viborg, Ribe and Schleswig. The Swedish church consisted of the archbishopric of Uppsala and the bishprics of Linköping, Skara, Strängnäs, Västerås, Växjö and Åbo in Finland. The five Norwegian bishoprics were the archbishopric of Trondheim and those of Bergen, Oslo, Stavanger and Hamar, see *Kulturhistorisk Leksikon for Nordisk Middelalder*, I, Copenhagen.

the holy church and her personnel are troubled and have lost their freedom, privileges, property and treasures against all Christian faith and justice; her prelates are taken by their throats without sentence, against justice and the Christian faith, imprisoned and never given justice; Masses, services and everything which belongs to God is destroyed; heretics, who have abandoned the holy Christian faith, lure us away from the holy Christian faith through their Lutheran writings and roguishness, misrepresenting everything which belongs to the eternal God. Unfortunately, we are daily faced with the fact that there are no archbishops in these three kingdoms, Denmark, Sweden and Norway who should preside over the holy Christian faith next to our holy father, the pope; furthermore, the Västerås, Skara and Åbo castles, farms, property, and churches belonging to the church and priests in these dioceses are ruled by other tyrants, clerks and laymen...[5]

Apart from the general accusations against Christian II of having interfered with and deliberately weakened the Catholic church and promoted 'Lutheranism', the letter more specifically implies that the king was to blame for the fact that all three Scandinavian provinces were without archbishops, and that a substantial number of dioceses remained without bishops (more than half the Norwegian and half the Swedish).[6] If not the whole truth, these accusations certainly contained enough substance to make them stick. Furthermore, they offer a reasonable point of departure for a closer inspection of the Catholic church and its leadership in Denmark, Norway and Sweden during the Reformation era.

DENMARK

The Danish archbishopric of Lund had been in total disarray since the death of Archbishop Birger Gunnersen in December 1519. Gunnersen had been an unusual encumbent, coming from a lower-middle-class rather than a noble background. He had fiercely defended the privileges of his see and chapter, especially against encroachments on church property by an often hostile, local nobility.[7] In order to exercise its right to elect a successor, the chapter in Lund had quickly proceeded to elect one of their own, the canon, Aage Sparre. Sparre, who was a member of the local nobility, however, failed to gain the royal support necessary in order to receive papal confirmation. Instead, King Christian II wanted the chapter to elect one of his loyal servants, the secretary Jørgen Skodborg, a commoner, whose background and career was similar to the

[5] See C. Paludan-Müller, *De første Konger af den Oldenborgske Slægt*, Copenhagen 1874, 442–3.
[6] See footnote 4.
[7] See the description by the Erasmian, Paulus Helie, in *Skibykrøniken*, ed. A. Heise, Copenhagen 1967, 61.

recently deceased archbishop. The chapter in Lund eventually bowed to royal pressure, even if Aage Sparre only withdrew under protest, and duly elected Skodborg in January 1520 (its second election in less than two months). In these circumstances Skodborg's confirmation from Rome should only have been a formality. Unfortunately for him, however, Christian II had consented to the decisions of the Fifth Lateran Council which had assembled in 1512 and been dissolved in 1517, shortly before Luther began his campaign against indulgences. Thus, the king had accepted full papal supremacy over the church and its councils, unbound by any concordats. Accordingly, Leo X had already reserved the right to appoint the next incumbent to the see of Lund well in advance of the vacancy. Consequently, when news of Gunnersen's death reached Rome the archbishopric of Lund was immediately reserved for Cardinal De Cesis, who demanded the considerable sum of 6,000 guilders in order to relinquish his rights.

Before Skodborg was able to start negotiations with the cardinal he had fallen out with his royal benefactor. Christian II had wanted Skodborg to return to the crown the strategically important island of Bornholm in the Baltic, plus several fiefs in Scania, which had been given to the archbishopric in the later Middle Ages. This was rejected outright by the elected archbishop and the chapter. Finding his wishes obstructed, the king decided to promote the candidature of yet another, and more amenable royal servant, Didrik Slagheck.[8] Slagheck, who was the illegitimate son of a priest in Münster in Germany, had been in the retinue of the papal legate, Johannes Angelus Arcimboldus, who had arrived in Scandinavia in 1517 to sell indulgences for Pope Leo X. It was information coming from him which had led Christian II to take action against Arcimboldus, when, in 1518, the King confiscated what the legate had collected for the pope in Sweden.

By 1519 Slagheck had formally entered royal service and in 1520 he was made dean of the chapter in Roskilde. That year he accompanied the king on the military campaign in Sweden which resulted in the re-conquest of that kingdom and the execution in November of more than eighty members of the Swedish aristocracy, including the bishops of Skara and Strängnäs. Slagheck appears to have played a significant part

---

[8] Skodborg appears to have had the support of Christian II until the summer of 1521. In August 1521 Emperor Charles V, Christian II's brother-in-law, supported his candidature at the *Curia*, see A. Krarup and J. Lindbæk (eds.), *Acta Pontificium Danica, 1316–1536*, V–VII, Copenhagen 1913–43, VI, no. 4798.

in formulating the policy behind these executions and the king's Swedish policy in general and was rewarded with the vacant bishopric of Skara.[9]

Some time within the next six months Slagheck must have been elected archbishop of Lund. Thus for the second time in less than eighteen months the king forced the chapter to reverse its decision and accept a candidate of his choice.[10] Slagheck was consecrated on 25 November 1521, but by then his involvement in the executions in Stockholm and the subsequent failed regency in Sweden, which he had shared with another two men of the cloth, Gustav Trolle, archbishop of Uppsala, and Jens Andersen Beldenak, bishop of Odense, had taken on ominous significance. Christian II had found himself under growing pressure from the *Curia* to provide an acceptable· explanation, and to allocate responsibility, for the unfortunate happenings in Sweden. The arrival of the papal nuncio, the Franciscan, Franciscus de Potentia, in Copenhagen in the autumn of 1521, only emphasised the pressing need to find a solution to this problem. For a while the king seems to have dithered between making Jens Andersen Beldenak, the bishop of Odense, rather than Didrik Slagheck responsible for the Swedish events. Eventually he opted for Slagheck who, as a foreign careerist of dubious ability, must have seemed the less costly choice of scapegoat. Consequently, two months after his consecration, Didrik Slagheck was executed in Copenhagen. In February 1522, only a month after Slagheck's execution, the chapter in Lund, on the king's suggestion, elected Johan Weze, another German in royal service. His occupancy of the archbishopric lasted only a year. In April 1523 he accompanied his mentor, Christian II, into exile in the Netherlands. By then no less than four candidates, including De Cesis whose claim had reverted on Slagheck's death, and Sparre, whom the chapter considered the only freely elected archbishop, could lay claim to the archbishopric due to interference from the deposed king and the *Curia*.[11]

The subsequent election of Christian II's uncle, Duke Frederik of Schleswig and Holstein, as king of Denmark promised immediate improvements for the church and the archbishopric. The Catholic bishops, who were all members of the Danish Council (*Rigsrådet*), had evidently learned their lesson and they made sure that a number of paragraphs were included in Frederik I's coronation charter to protect the privileges of the church. The first ten paragraphs deal exclusively with the church

[9] See *Skibykrøniken*, 67–70.
[10] *Acta Pontificium Danica*, VI, nos. 4874–80. The papal confirmation of Slagheck is dated 12 July 1521.
[11] See Johannesson, *Den Skånska Kyrkan*, 23–61.

and its privileges. Apart from the second paragraph which obliged King Frederik I to fight the 'Lutheran heresy' the most significant paragraphs were the fourth and fifth, which not only secured the nobility a future monopoly on the bishoprics, but also guaranteed that no foreigners or servants of the *Curia* could be appointed to any prelacy in Denmark. Instead, all future recruits for such jobs had to be found within the native nobility or among Danes who were learned doctors in either theology or canon law.[12] Evidently the Danish bishops, supported by their lay colleagues in the Council, were hoping to create a national and aristocratically led Catholic church on a par with the Catholic church in France.

At the time of Frederik I's accession, all the Danish bishops, apart from the bishop of Odense, Jens Andersen Beldenak, who was the son of a shoemaker, were recruited from the nobility. Even if it has been shown that during the fifteenth century prelacies within the Danish church were increasingly filled with members of the lower nobility/gentry who often used their appointments to raise themselves and their families socially, or in some cases even by individuals from non-noble backgrounds who had risen through royal service,[13] this was no longer the case by the beginning of the sixteenth century. On the eve of the Reformation the Danish bishops, with one exception, were of a distinctly aristocratic nature.

Considering the close family ties which existed between the bishops and the majority of the lay members of the Council, it is surprising that the bishops found it necessary to engineer a declaration by the Council in June 1524 expressing allegiance to the pope and the Catholic church and promising resistance to the Lutheran heresy.[14] After all, these were promises the new king, Frederik I, had made only the previous year. Apart from being worried about the reliability of the king's promises, and the threat from the evangelical propaganda which Christian II, who had recently turned Protestant, was actively producing abroad, the bishops may well have had doubts about the religious commitment and reliability of their friends and relatives within the aristocracy.

If Aage Sparre had nurtured high hopes of receiving support from the

---

12 Coronation charter in *Aarsberetninger fra Geheimearchivet*, II, (Copenhagen 1856–60), 65–79, see especially 71.
13 See T. Dahlerup, 'Danmark', in *Den nordiske Adel i Senmiddelalderen. Struktur, funktioner og internordiske relationer. Rapporter til det nordiske historikermøde i København 1971, 9–12 august*, Copenhagen 1971, 45–80. See also N. Lund and K. Hørby, *Dansk Socialhistorie, Samfundet i vikingetid og middelalder 800–1500*, II, Copenhagen 1980, 260–1.
14 C. F. Allen, *De tre nordiske Rigers Historie under Hans. Christiern den Anden, Frederik den Første, Gustav Vasa, Grevefeiden, 1497–1536*, 5 vols, Copenhagen 1864–72, IV, part II, 355–7.

new king for his claim on the archbishopric, developments over the next couple of years must have disappointed him. By the autumn of 1523, Frederik I had already begun to use his main competitor, Jørgen Skodborg, who now resided in Rome, for various diplomatic tasks at the *Curia*. Sparre's exposed position as *electus* was further in evidence during the spring of 1525 when Christian II's last major adherent in Denmark, Søren Norby, who controlled the island of Gotland in the Baltic, led a major peasant rebellion in Scania. The inability of the local nobility to suppress the rebellion was a serious blow to Sparre's claim to leadership of the Danish church, but the siding with the rebels of one of his canons, Christiern Pedersen, whose writings and translations of Luther were later to play an important part in the Danish Reformation, not to mention a considerable number of local priests, cannot but have seriously undermined Sparre's position.

At the parliament (*Herredag*) which met in May 1525 in Kolding, Frederik I complained about the nobility's inability to deal with the rebellion in Scania and expressed concern over the growing conflict between prelates, nobility, burghers and peasants. The Council responded by acknowledging that the lack of an able man as archbishop of Lund had been to the detriment of the kingdom. They stated that king and Council ought presently to provide the cathedral in Lund with a qualified man and not allow the holy church to be treated in a way which evoked the wrath of God and ruined the kingdom's inhabitants.[15] If not the religious, then certainly the political arguments would have convinced Frederik I. Accordingly, it is no coincidence that it is during this period that Frederik I finally decided to seek confirmation in Rome for a new archbishop in Lund and that the candidate turned out to be the only other local candidate, Skodborg. However, by January 1526 when Skodborg had finally received papal confirmation and consecration,[16] Frederik I had already committed himself to a cautious, evangelical church policy and no longer had any use for a properly consecrated Catholic archbishop.

That Frederik I had become increasingly evangelical in the spring of 1525 is evident from the Diet of Schleswig and Holstein which met in Rendsburg in May. The Catholic church in the duchies under the leadership of the bishop of Schleswig, Gottschalk Ahlefeldt, found itself increasingly isolated from its traditional supporters among the local nobility, while finding it difficult to defend the rights and privileges of the

---

[15] For the Council's statement, see *Nye Danske Magazin*, vols. 1–6, Copenhagen 1794–1836, 5, 44.
[16] See *Acta Pontificium Danica*, VI, nos. 4995, 5012–16 and 5022.

church. Faced with complaints from family and friends among the nobility over the use of excommunication in debt cases involving the church, and the practice of priests charging the sick and dying for the administration of extreme unction, not to mention the employment of 'unlearned' priests who had no knowledge of the gospel and only 'preached fables', the Catholic church and its leader in the duchies were on the defensive. They had to promise to redress these shortcomings and to guarantee that in future the gospel would be preached purely and in the vernacular. The church also had to shoulder a greater part of the increased tax burden necessitated by the military threat of an invasion from Christian II. In return, Frederik I and the nobility promised only that God and the saints would not be allowed to be derided and that bishops and prelates would not be allowed to be smeared or blamed, on the guarantee that the church should continue to receive its traditional income such as tithes.[17] By 1525 the Catholic church in the duchies looked increasingly politically isolated while facing mounting social and religious dissatisfaction from the population in general.

That members of the nobility in Denmark demonstrated similar hostility to the church during the parliament which met a few months later in Copenhagen is mentioned in a letter the bishop of Oslo, Hans Reff, sent to Olav Engelbriktsson, the Norwegian archbishop. Here Reff pointed out that the younger members of the Danish nobility in particular had intended to undermine the church by laying their hands on its property. These plans had only been halted by the timely intervention of the bishop of Roskilde, Lage Urne, and the bishop of Aarhus, Ove Bille.[18]

The Catholic church in Denmark managed to weather this attack on its social and economic position considerably better than in the duchies, but the signs for the future were ominous for the church. In Denmark, as well as in Schleswig and Holstein, the accumulation of ecclesiastical property and land was a major cause for a growing anti-clericalism, not only among the nobility, but also among the burghers in the major towns and cities.[19] This hostility was further fuelled by the increased taxation

[17] For the negotiations of the diet, see W. Leverkus (ed.), 'Berichte über die Schleswig-Holsteinischen Landtage von 1525, 1526, 1533, 1540', in *Archiv für Staats- und Kirchengeschichte der Herzogthümer Schleswig, Holstein, Lauenburg* ... 1840, 453ff. See also O. P. Grell, 'Scandinavia', in A. Pettegree (ed.), *The early Reformation in Europe*, Cambridge 1992, 99.

[18] For this letter, see N. J. Ekdahl (ed.), *Christiern IIs Arkiv*, III, Stockholm 1836, 968–85, especially 976.

[19] For the cities, see O. P. Grell, 'The Emergence of Two Cities: The Reformation of Malmø and Copenhagen', in L. Grane and K. Hørby (eds.), *Die dänische Reformation vor ihrem internationalen Hintergrund*, Göttingen 1990, 130–2.

necessitated by the threat of an invasion from Christian II. The growing tax burden following the accession of Frederik I added pressure to a feudal system already under severe strain, and caused a growing number of disturbances among the peasants, not only in Scania, as shown above, but also in Jutland. The nobility wanted the church to shoulder a larger share of the expenses. The fact that most of the bishops were relatives appears to have had little, if any, significance for them. Considering that the church controlled around a third of all arable land, and that the bishops were wealthier than most of the lay aristocracy, it was a request which could hardly be ignored.[20]

That it was in the politico-economic sphere that the Catholic church first faced trouble is underlined by the negotiations at the next diet of the duchies held in Kiel in February 1526. This time Bishop Gottschalk Ahlefeldt complained that 'the martinist sect' had inspired the population to refuse to pay tithes and other duties in spite of the promises the church had received the previous year in Rendsburg. Evidently neither the nobility nor Frederik I had done anything to alleviate the population's unwillingness to pay tithes and other regular fees to the church. The peasantry may well have been encouraged in their refusal to pay by their noble lords, as was later the case in Jutland, especially the unpopular third of the tithes which went to the bishops. It is, however, significant that the prelates in the duchies were primarily concerned with the economic rather than the religious consequences of the teachings of the growing evangelical movement.

The political weakness of the Catholic church in the duchies is emphasised by the agreement, forced on the prelates, to defray most of the costs of Frederik I's renewed armament against Christian II without any promise from the diet to suppress the evangelical movement, or from the duke to stop issuing letters of protection to evangelical preachers, or even to hinder the increased tendency of the clergy to marry.[21]

The church in Denmark faced similar difficulties with Frederik I and the nobility, as can be seen from the negotiations at the parliament which met in Odense in November 1526. By February 1526, Frederik I had already indicated a commitment to the evangelical side by having his daughter, Dorothea, betrothed to the recent Protestant convert, Duke

---

[20] See K. Erslev, *Konge og Lensmand i det 16. Aarhundrede*, Copenhagen 1879, 96–110 and S. A. Hansen, *Adelsvældens Grundlag*, Copenhagen 1964, 76–8.

[21] For the diet, see H. V. Gregersen, *Reformationen i Sønderjylland*, Aabenraa 1986, 76–9; for peasant disturbances see A. Heise, 'Bondeopløb i Jylland i Kong Frederik den Førstes Tid', *Historisk Tidsskrift*, 4, V (1875–7), 269–332, especially 291.

Albrecht of Prussia. The Danish prelates opposed the marriage, but appear to have had little or no backing from their noble colleagues within the Council. Frederik I seems only to have added spite to injury when he began eating meat on Fridays in connection with Dorothea's departure for Prussia in June 1526.[22]

Meanwhile, the king had, as mentioned above, also found it necessary to change his stance on the appointment of a new archbishop in Lund. His interest in having the papally confirmed and consecrated archbishop, Jørgen Skodborg, instated in Lund had waned dramatically during the second half of 1525. That their prospects of getting a properly confirmed archbishop in Lund were no longer the best was quickly realised by the Danish prelates, whose most senior member, Lage Urne, in May 1526 requested Aage Sparre, whom he no longer felt able to address as *electus*, to vacate his see in the interest of the church for the properly consecrated Skodborg. Sparre, however, disregarded the request from the bishop of Roskilde and remained in Lund.[23]

Faced with the threat of an impending invasion from Christian II, Frederik I needed an incumbent in Lund whose loyalty could not be questioned (Skodborg was a former secretary to Christian II) and who would not be in a position to offer strong opposition to the evangelical changes in church policy the king undoubtedly was contemplating by 1526. These aspirations would have been further encouraged by the outcome of the Diet of Speyer, which offered the German princes the legal pretext for introducing new evangelical territorial churches. The result was that in august 1526 Sparre received a letter, signed by the king and fifteen lay members of the Council, guaranteeing him the right to occupy the see until the king and Council decided whether he or Skodborg was the properly elected archbishop. Furthermore, in case the king and Council found for Skodborg, Sparre was allowed to retain the archbishopric until Skodborg had reimbursed him the 3,000 guilders he had just furnished for the defence of Scania. In this connection Sparre and the see were promised full protection against the possible use of excommunication by Rome. In order to retain the archbishopric, Sparre had in effect acted as a schismatic. By providing Frederik I with a 'loan' of 1,000 guilders and donating smaller sums to the councillors closest to the king, Sparre secured his position further. Consequently, Frederik I

---

[22] For the prelates' opposition to the marriage, see T. C. Lyby, *Vi Evangeliske. Studier over Samspillet mellem Udenrigspolitik og Kirkepolitik på Frederik I's Tid*, Aarhus 1993, 135 and 424; see also Grell, 'The Emergence of Two Cities', 133.
[23] Johannesson, *Den Skånska Kyrkan*, 40.

wrote to the *Curia* supporting his confirmation. However, Sparre can hardly have expected a positive reaction from Rome, having in effect bought the see from the king, thereby preventing the papally confirmed archbishop from being enthroned.[24] The fact that none of the bishops on the Council signed the letter is indicative of Sparre's isolation within the Danish church by the end of 1526. His occupancy of the archbishopric was perceived to be a serious danger to the church by three of the leading bishops, Ove Bille, Stygge Krumpen and Lage Urne, who all urged him to vacate the see for Jørgen Skodborg during the early months of 1527.[25]

Undoubtedly the recent events at the parliament which had met in Odense during November and December 1526 must have made the three bishops realise that the need for action was urgent. Once more, under pressure from family and friends among the nobility, the prelates had been forced to agree to pay a considerable proportion of the new taxes. It is evident that the lay nobility was becoming increasingly anti-clerical, not only because of the wealth of the church, but also because of the prelates' attempts to reinforce and expand their spiritual income, especially among the peasantry, in order to recover some of the vast sums they had to find for the defence of the realm. This added further tension to a feudal system already close to breaking point.

The bishops were forced to accept the demand, originally brought forward in 1525, that in future property donated by or bought from the nobility should not remain with the church, but was to be inherited by members of their families, i.e. returned to the lay nobility. This was the only way to ensure that their lay colleagues on the Council promised to protect the rights and privileges of the church.

It was also decided that the fees traditionally paid to Rome in connection with confirmation of bishops and other major clergy should now go to the king, if Frederik I was able to reach an agreement with the *Curia*. This decision in effect was a considerable step towards establishing a national church under royal control. Less than a month after the Odense meeting Frederik I appointed the dean of the cathedral in Viborg, Knud Henriksen Gyldenstjerne, co-adjutor and eventual successor to the bishop of Odense, Jens Andersen Beldenak. Gyldenstjerne, a loyal servant of the king who had been one of only two clerics to sign the letter

[24] Johannesson, *Den Skånska Kyrkan*, 42–4; for Frederik I's letter to Rome supporting Sparre's candidature, see *Acta Pontificium Danica*, VI, no. 5026.
[25] See Heise, 'Bondeopløb', 305–6, note 2.

which gave Sparre permission to retain the archbishopric in August 1526, promised in accordance with the recent decision in Odense to pay the king the same amount of money that had hitherto been paid to Rome when he succeeded the present incumbent.

For the prelates it must have been a deeply worrying development. It was similar developments which had led some of them to be among the instigators of the rebellion against Christian II in 1523. No wonder the leading bishops wanted Aage Sparre to vacate the archbishopric for the papally confirmed Skodborg. Without a properly consecrated archbishop in Lund and with the prospect of being cut off from Rome, the Catholic church in Denmark was in a perilous state. That the bishops were right to worry is confirmed by the fact that the correspondence and contact with Rome was almost completely halted from 1526.[26]

Thus far, however, the leaders of the Catholic church appear to have seen their problems as being primarily of a political and economic nature. 'Lutherans' and their heretical teachings had been noted, as we have seen, as early as 1522 and in Frederik I's coronation charter in 1523; and they were also mentioned during the parliament of 1526. A couple of the bishops had by then already taken action against individual evangelical preachers active within their sees. Ove Bille had issued a letter to the magistracy in the town in Jutland where Simon Skåning had begun preaching in the spring of 1526 and Lage Urne had later that year prevented the later reformer of Malmø, Claus Mortensen, from preaching in Copenhagen. Obviously the two bishops had been determined to enforce their jurisdiction, rather than trying to tackle the evangelical teachings of these men.[27] This may well have been a natural concern for the Danish bishops, many of whom had studied canon law at the universities of Cologne, Greifswald and Rostock, as pointed out by a number of Danish church historians, but more importantly, maintaining

---

[26] For the parliament of 1526, see *Nye Danske Magazin*, 5, 99–212; see also C. Paludan-Müller, 'Herredagene i Odense 1526 og 1527', in *Kongelige Videnskabernes Selskabs Skrifter*, Series 5, Historisk og Philosofisk Afdeling IIB, Copenhagen 1857, 292–4; for Gyldenstjerne's letter of subjection dated 10 January 1527, see F. Münter, *Den Danske Reformationshistorie*, 2 vols., Copenhagen 1802, I, 541–3 and 538–40. The contact between the Danish church and Rome seems to have been excellent until 1526; thus more than 800 documents and letters exist for the period 1513–26, whereas only sixty documents and letters exist for the following period 1527–36 and most of these are directed to Christian II and his exiled followers, see *Acta Pontificium Danica*, VI. Identical results have been achieved by P. Ingesman, 'Danmark og Pavestolen i Senmiddelalderen' in P. Ingesman and J. W. Jensen (eds.), *Danmark i Senmiddelalderen*, Aarhus 1994. See also Lyby, *Vi Evangeliske*, 48.

[27] For Claus Mortensen, see Grell, 'Two Cities', 135–6. Bishop Ove Bille's letter against Simon Skåning is printed in *Danske Magazin*, I, Copenhagen 1794, 216–17.

their jurisdiction must have been the central issue for the bishops, since this provided them with the foundation necessary simply to dismiss the teachings of the evangelical preachers without any need of entering into a theological debate.

The prelates' attempt to stop Frederik I from using individual letters of protection for the evangelical preachers failed during the meeting in Odense. The king issued at least two letters in 1526 to the reformers of Viborg – in October to Hans Tausen and in December during parliament to Jørgen Jensen Sadolin.[28] The prelates' insistence in 1526 that those who wanted to preach either in German or Danish should obtain permission from the bishops, confirms that they were still trying to control the situation through their jurisdiction. Whether or not the added clause that these preachers should 'preach the word of God' can be interpreted as a move by the prelates towards a more Erasmian and humanist Catholic position, which in Denmark had a forceful exponent in the Carmelite friar, Paulus Helie, as originally claimed by J. O. Andersen, is questionable. The bishops might well have considered this vague clause a necessary concession to gain the support of their lay colleagues on the Council and to convince the king to abstain from the continued use of his letters of protection.[29]

Furthermore, the parliament in Odense took place less than six months after Paulus Helie, preaching to the court in Copenhagen, had been ridiculed by Frederik I's courtiers for promoting a programme of limited humanist reform of the church. The time for reform from within the church had clearly passed, as developments in Schleswig/Holstein under Frederik's son, Duke Christian, and in Jutland, especially in Viborg, had already demonstrated.[30] Accordingly, when the bishops in Jutland, Stygge Krumpen, Ove Bille, Jørgen Friis and Iver Munk finally felt the need to tackle the evangelical movement theologically, they sought assistance from abroad, from two well-known mainstream Catholic controversialists and not locally from Paulus Helie. Considering Helie's involvement in the prelates' campaign against Christian II, it is significant that the bishops preferred to seek the support of Luther's antagonist, Johannes Eck, and another famous German theologian, Johannes Cochlæus. In the spring of 1527 they unsuccessfully invited Eck

---

[28] For Tausen and Sadolin, see Grell, 'Scandinavia', 105–6.
[29] For Frederik I's use of letters of protection, see O. P. Grell, 'Herredagen 1527', *Kirkehistoriske Samlinger*, 1978, 69–88.
[30] See Grell, 'Scandinavia', 98–106.

and Cochlæus to Denmark in order to preach and write against the 'perfidious heretics' in Jutland.[31]

By then another parliament had been called to meet in Odense in August 1527 and the prospects for the leaders of the Danish church looked increasingly grim. Politically isolated within the Council and economically weakened by the large sums they were forced to find for the defence of the realm, the prelates now had to tackle not only a rapidly growing evangelical movement in the major towns of Jutland, but also to confront an increasingly rebellious peasantry who resisted the church's attempt to maximise its spiritual income. Thus the economic and political pressure brought to bear on the prelates from at least 1525 by the king and the lay aristocracy, had forced the bishops to collect types of spiritual income which had not hitherto been enforced in order to indemnify the church. Undoubtedly many of the rebellious peasants in Jutland were encouraged in their refusal to pay such fees by their noble landlords, such as the king's evangelical chancellor, Mogens Gøye.

In his report to Frederik I of April 1527, Gøye points out that the peasants argue that neither God's law nor the law of the land obliges them to pay these fees, while stressing their loyalty to the king. Likewise, it is Gøye who informs Frederik I of the peasants' complaints about the shortage of priests in the countryside, where districts consisting of between fourteen and sixteen parishes were left with only two or three priests. By 1527 anti-clericalism was growing among the peasantry. It was primarily directed against the bishops who were seen as greedy and failing in their primary obligation to provide the population with priests and regular church services. This hostility was aggravated by the bishops' seizure of chalices and church bells from the local parish churches, in order to provide the king with the promised funds and materials for his armaments. The local population took particular exception to such acts.[32] Furthermore, they held the prelates responsible for these actions forced upon the church by the king and the Council.

When the parliament met once more in Odense in August the Catholic leadership would have been worried as much by the domestic situation as by developments abroad. They knew that princely,

<hr />

[31] A copy of this letter is preserved among Ove Bille's papers, The Royal Library, Copenhagen, Ny kgl. Saml. 1301e, 2, vol I, dated 14 June 1527. It was first printed in P. Terpager, *Ripæ Cimbricæ*, Copenhagen 1736, 553–62 and wrongly dated 19 May 1527.
[32] See Heise, 'Bondeopløb', 287–93.

territorial Lutheran churches were in the process of being established in Germany and had been informed of the decisions of the Swedish parliament which had met a couple of months earlier in Västerås, removing all vestiges of economic and political power from the Catholic church in Sweden.

It is evident from the negotiations which took place in Odense that the growing insurrection among the peasantry in Jutland was by now directed against the church and the prelates in particular. The bishops defended themselves by arguing that they were merely the first target for an insurrection, which, inspired by the politico-evangelical propaganda of Christian II, wanted to disrupt the whole of society. Once more, however, they found themselves isolated from their lay colleagues. The nobility's support came at a price, even if the prelates pointed out that for the first time in generations they were all recruited from the aristocracy. As in 1526, another demand raised in 1525 by the lay nobility eventually had to be accepted by the leaders of the church: fines imposed on peasants at church courts should in future revert to their feudal lords. Considering what had just happened in Sweden, the cost of the nobility's support might have been considerably higher. The church managed to retain its traditional jurisdiction and most of its rights in theory, if not necessarily in practice.

Frederik I refused to stop his continued use of letters of protection for evangelical preachers, while only promising to prevent the physical attacks on members of the mendicant orders who found themselves on the religious front line in towns where the evangelical movement was gaining ground. The bishops, on the other hand, had to promise to provide more and better priests for the parishes and remedy other ecclesiastical shortcomings. A general political and religious consensus was, however, easily reached on the politico-evangelical propaganda produced by Christian II and his helpers abroad and smuggled into the kingdom. A ban against the import of such books was issued which also included Luther's, *Ob Kriegsleute auch ijnn seligen Stande sein künden*, which had attacked the rebellion against Christian II (1526).[33]

Considering the difficulties the church was confronted with in the summer of 1527, the prelates did not do badly. Faced not only with lack of support from family and friends within the aristocracy, but often direct

---

[33] For the negotiations during the parliament of 1527, see *Nye Danske Magazin*, 5, 215ff and 288ff. For the decisions, see K. Erslev and W. Mollerup (eds.), *Kong Frederik I's danske Registranter*, Copenhagen 1881/2, 132ff. For the prohibition against the import of Luther's, *Ob Kriegsleute ...* see Allen, *De tre nordiske Riger*, IV, part II, 457–8.

hostility, and the machinations of an increasingly evangelical monarch who constantly chipped away at their jurisdiction, not to mention a growing anti-clericalism from below, the prelates managed to defend their and the church's position better than could have been expected.

Disappointed with their inability to force king and Council to provide real support for their cause, the prelates must have decided to continue down the avenue already taken the previous year by bishops Lage Urne in Roskilde and Ove Bille in Aarhus, tackling the evangelical movement within their individual sees. Lage Urne appears to have been particularly successful in rooting out the embryonic evangelical movement in Copenhagen, not least because of his determined action and the respect he was able to command.[34] In Viborg, where the evangelical movement by 1527 was well in control, the local bishop, Jørgen Friis, failed disastrously when he attempted to arrest the leading evangelical preacher, Hans Tausen. Most likely his attempt took place in the autumn of 1527 prior to the intervention of the bishop of Odense, Jens Andersen Beldenak. The letters Beldenak wrote to the magistracies of the towns of Aalborg and Viborg, both within the see of Viborg, are unusual in that they are the only examples we have from this period of a bishop intervening outside his own bishopric. However, considering the strength of the evangelical movement in Viborg and the low standing of its bishop, Jørgen Friis, it is not surprising that the other bishops felt that something had to be done.[35]

The letter to Viborg in particular has in recent research been seen as proof that at least some of the Danish bishops were trying to promote some form of Christian humanism by 1527. There is, however, little if anything in the letter to support this claim. Instead, Jens Andersen Beldenak argues forcefully for the traditional authority of the church, the Fathers, and the validity of the *Vulgata*. Mistakenly, the conciliarism he expresses has been seen as proof of his Christian humanism. However, he probably shared his conciliarist position with all his episcopal colleagues. It had already been aired by Ove Bille in his above-mentioned letter from the previous year and again at the recent parliament in Odense. Furthermore, it had in this vague form been a commonly held

---

[34] See Grell, 'The Emergence', 135–45. See also the articles on Bille and Urne in *Dansk Biografisk Leksikon* (Danish Dictionary of National Biography) 3rd edn., henceforth *DBL*.

[35] For Friis, see *DBL*.

belief in most of Catholic Europe since the height of the church councils in the fifteenth century.[36]

That some of the Catholic bishops should have moved towards an Erasmian position identical to that of the Carmelite, Paulus Helie, by the second half of the 1520s, as some scholars will have it, cannot have been the case. This view has been based on the fact that in 1526 the prelates had employed Helie to provide an attack on the introduction by Hans Mikkelsen, prefacing Christian II's recently commissioned translation of Luther's New Testament. But Helie was used repeatedly by the Danish bishops for the defence of the church, especially by Ove Bille and Lage Urne, who were both 'old-fashioned' Catholics. The bishops, who were not specifically trained to deal with theological questions, and faced difficulties in recruiting German assistance, clearly found him a useful ally for specific tasks. He himself ploughed a lonely intellectual furrow, desperately trying to counter the negative effects of his own humanist teachings at the university while watching his most talented pupils and fellow Carmelites become prominent evangelical leaders, such as Christian Skrock, Peder Laurentsen and Frants Vormordsen. Likewise, his antagonism to most of the prelates and the way they administered the church is in evidence in most of his writings, from his chronicle (*Skibykrøniken*) to the unpublished attack on Peder Laudentsen's *Malmøbook* from 1530 which had been specifically commissioned by the bishop.[37]

Jens Andersen Beldenak's attempt to bring a halt to the evangelical movement in Viborg failed, while a personal intervention in Malmø a year later by Aage Sparre, the elected archbishop in Lund, proved successful. With the threat of a possible heresy trial involving the magistracy and backed by the armed escort of the local Catholic nobility, Sparre was able to force the magistracy in Malmø to send their evangelical preachers into exile.[38]

In spite of Sparre's temporary success in Malmø the prelates saw the

[36] Jens Andersen Beldenak's letter is reproduced in the answer written by Hans Tausen, see H. F. Rørdam (ed.) *Smaaskrifter af Hans Tausen*. Copenhagen 1870, XII–XIV and 23–94, especially 69–70 and 82; for Ove Bille's letter, see footnote 31 above. For examples of the general influence of conciliarism, see J. A. F. Thomson, *Popes and Princes 1417–1517: Politics and Piety in the Late Medieval Church*, London 1980, 25–8. For some recent examples of the misinterpretation of Jens Andersen Beldenak's letter, see Lindhardt, *Nederlagets Mænd*, 109–10 and P. Jacobsen, 'Jens Andersen Beldenak', in *Kirkehistoriske Samlinger*, 1992, 45–70, especially 63.
[37] For Helie, see *DBL*; for *Skibykrøniken*, where only Bishop Lage Urne is given a relatively positive treatment, see A. Heise (ed.), *Skibykrøniken*, Copenhagen 1967; for Helie's response to Peder Laurentsen's *Malmøbook*, see M. Kristensen and N. K. Andersen (eds.), *Skrifter af Paulus Helie*, 7 vols., Copenhagen 1932–48, III, 57–284.
[38] See O. P. Grell, 'The City of Malmø and the Danish Reformation', in *Archiv für Reformationsgeschichte*, 79 (1988), 311–40, especially 319–20.

church's position deteriorate further towards the end of this decade. They found it increasingly difficult to get the peasantry to pay tithes and other fees, especially in Jutland. Meanwhile, in the towns and cities the mendicant orders came under direct attack. Thus, between 1528 and 1532 three-quarters of the twenty-eight Franciscan monasteries in Denmark disappeared. Often they were forced to close after violent incidents perpetrated by local magistracies.[39] The same magistracies were simultaneously supporting the evangelical movement which was by now growing rapidly in the economically important towns and cities along the Sound. These developments were strongly supported by the king who from 1528 made increasing use of his patronage to church benefices to secure the appointment of evangelical ministers.[40]

It is something of a paradox that the observant mendicant orders, as well as the Carmelites, who constituted the theological backbone of the Danish church on the eve of the Reformation, indirectly contributed so much to the demise of the Catholic church. On a par with Germany, the Dominicans in particular had, well in advance of the start of evangelical preaching, prepared the ground for the Reformation by giving sermons which underlined the importance of personal faith and piety, attacking empty rites and often emphasising a social dimension, such as the unequal distribution of wealth.[41]

But the Danish church also suffered other, directly self-inflicted damage in the decades leading up to the Reformation. As in Germany, the increased sale of indulgences by the papacy from 1500 onwards had been particularly damaging. According to Paulus Helie, the harm was not only done by the papal legate, Arcimboldus, who had arrived in Denmark in 1517, the year Luther published his ninety-five theses against indulgences. The damage to the popular standing of the church had already commenced through earlier sales of indulgences, such as that of 1502, which had officially been intended to raise money for a crusade against the Turks.[42]

In addition, the increasing number of dispensations given by the papacy to canons at the Danish cathedrals in particular, allowing them to hold incompatible ecclesiastical positions, often without having

---

[39] See H. Heilesen (ed.), *Krøniken om Gråbrødrenes fordrivelse fra deres Klostre i Danmark*, Copenhagen 1967. For the continuous difficulties for the church in collecting tithes and other fees in Jutland, see *Nye Danske Magazin*, 5, 310–14.

[40] 'Lybyy, *Vi Evangeliske*, 438–9.

[41] See A. Riising, *Danmarks middelalderlige Prædiken*, Copenhagen 1969 and E. Ladewig Petersen, 'Preaching in Medieval Denmark', in *Medieval Scandinavia*, III, Odense 1974.

[42] *Skibykrøniken*, 43 and 55.

received the required ordinations, not to mention permissions for non-residency, all served to give the impression of a church prepared to bend its own rules and regulations at pleasure. This picture of moral decay was enhanced in the minds of laymen by the open disregard for celibacy shown by the clergy. Among the most notorious cases was that of Bishop Stygge Krumpen, who lived with a married noblewoman, Elsebeth Gyldenstierne, at the monastery in Børglum.[43]

Furthermore, by the summer of 1529 the Catholic hierarchy had been severely weakened through the death of Bishop Lage Urne and the retirement of the ageing Jens Andersen Beldenak, bishop of Odense. Beldenak had been assisted by his successor, Knud Henriksen Gyldenstjerne, for nearly three years. Realising the potential damage to the church by allowing an unconfirmed candidate to take control of the bishopric, Beldenak and the chapter had a clause included in the letter of resignation, pointing out that the pope's confirmation ought to have been obtained.[44]

The breach of episcopal unity within the church, which had occurred with Aage Sparre's permission from the king and Council to retain the archbishopric in August 1526, widened not only with the appointment of Gyldenstjerne, but also with the confirmation by the king and Council of Joachim Rønnow as the elected bishop of Roskilde. Rønnow had to promise that he would not interfere with preachers who preached the word of God, nor try to prevent priests and monks from marrying. As in 1526, the bishops refused to be party to these decisions and only one, the bishop of Børglum, Stygge Krumpen, signed the letter confirming Rønnow as bishop of Roskilde.[45] The consequences of these appointments were quickly to be felt. In 1529 Hans Tausen, on Frederik I's instigation, moved from Viborg to Copenhagen, adding extra impetus to the evangelical movement there, while the whole of Funen had become evangelical by 1532, by which time Glydenstjerne had already made the other Viborg reformer, Jørgen Jensen Sadolin, his assistant.[46]

The end of 1529 saw further ominous developments for the prelates, when decrees were issued by Frederik I for a parliament to meet in Copenhagen the following July. The intention was clearly that a final

---

[43] For the dispensations, see *Acta Pontificium Danica*, VI. For Stygge Krumpen, see *DBL*.

[44] C. Paludan-Müller, *Jens Andersen Beldenak*, 2nd edition, Copenhagen 1837, 139.

[45] See Münter, *Reformationshistorie*, II, 701–5, for Rønnow's letter of subjection to king and Council. See also H. Knudsen, *Joachim Rønnow*, Copenhagen 1840, 32–4. For Stygge Krumpen, see *DBL* and H. Gregersen, *Stygge Krumpen*, Frederikshavn 1979.

[46] Grell, 'Scandinavia', 109 and L. Helveg, *Den danske Kirkes Historie indtil Reformationen*, Copenhagen 1870, part 2, 921–4.

solution to the religious strife had to be reached in Copenhagen. None of the bishops can have been in doubt that the king intended some form of Reformation after a public debate between the two sides, following the already well-known pattern from Germany. The prelates recruited as much qualified theological support as they could muster. Apart from the local talent of Paulus Helie and several members of the cathedral chapters, two German theologians from the University of Cologne were enticed to come to Denmark to defend the church.

However, the bishops must have breathed a sigh of relief when, during the spring of 1530, developments abroad forced a change of the agenda for the forthcoming parliament. As so often before, it was the threat of an imminent invasion from Christian II, who had now returned to the Catholic fold and been reconciled with his brother-in-law, Emperor Charles V, which brought about the change. The defence of the country became top priority for the meeting. Once more considerable sums had to be found, and the king, as well as the lay nobility, needed the Catholic leaders, not least for their unquestionable loyalty, but also for their ability to contribute large parts of the taxes and loans necessitated by the military threat. In return the prelates wanted renewed guarantees that the privileges and jurisdiction of the church would be fully protected in future, pointing out that the promises made to the church at the parliament in Odense in 1527 had all been broken.

While some sort of unofficial religious debate took place between the Catholic and evangelical parties in Copenhagen in the form of an exchange of letters, the prelates must have realised that there was little if any chance of real support for the church from the king and the lay aristocracy, and that only circumstances beyond their control had given them a stay of execution. That the traditional rights of the church remained seriously threatened can be seen from the royal charter given to all major towns, which permitted the magistracies to employ evangelical ministers.[47]

A feeling of despair must have characterised the Catholic camp during the last three years of Frederik I's reign. The best they could hope for was to be able to fight a rearguard action which would delay the progress of the evangelical movement and the dismantling of the Catholic church. Any hopes of a restitution of the church to its former power and glory must have seemed remote. Consequently, in 1531 the now elderly bishop of Ribe, Iver Munk, who, in 1526, had actively defended the church

---

[47] For the parliament of 1530, see *Danske Magazin*, 6 series in 6 vols., Copenhagen 1745–52 and 1842–1928. Series 4, VI, 12–16 and Grell, 'The City of Malmø', 323–4.

against the evangelical encroachments of Frederik I's son, Duke Christian, retired, but only after having secured the bishopric for his nephew, Oluf Munk.[48] Likewise in 1532, the elected archbishop, Aage Sparre, who for years had been prepared to sacrifice the needs of the church to his own interests by holding on to the see of Lund, and who by 1529 had given up all attempts of obtaining confirmation from Rome, finally decided to resign. This was in order to make room for the dean of the chapter, Torben Bille. Like Gyldenstjerne and Rønnow, the other post-1526 *electi*, Oluf Munk and Torben Bille were obliged to sign letters of subjection to Frederik I. Bille promised to promote evangelical teaching in general and specifically not to hinder the Reformation in Malmø and the other evangelical towns in Scania.[49]

From the Catholic church's point of view, the retirement of elderly prelates who had tired of the struggle, must have been less serious than the activities of the papally confirmed bishop of Børglum, Stygge Krumpen. From the summer of 1529, Krumpen had demonstrated an increasing willingness to compromise the Catholic position in order to placate the king and his evangelical councillors. This stance, however, cannot be interpreted as a move towards a more humanist/Erasmian position on Krumpen's part, as seen by some scholars. There is in fact hardly any indication of such a change in the surviving documents and it ought rather to be interpreted as a piece of *realpolitik*. On a par with his recognition of Rønnow's appointment in 1529, it all served to protect and secure his political position.[50]

The death of Frederik I in April 1533, however, provided the prelates and their supporters within the lay aristocracy with the opportunity they needed to avoid the gradual demolition of the Catholic church and the introduction of a full Reformation. The Catholics used the opportunity to full effect and the bishops were among the prime movers in the decision of the parliament, which met in June, to postpone the election of a new king until the following year. Only a few days after the beginning of parliament news had reached them of the decisions taken at the diet of the duchies in Kiel. Frederik's evangelical son, Duke Christian, had been chosen to succeed his father and the prelates had been forced to accept

[48] For Iver and Oluf Munk, see *DBL*; see also Grell, 'Scandinavia', 100–1.

[49] Grell, 'The City of Malmø', 325; for Oluf Munk's letter of subjection, see Peder Laurentsen, *Malmøbogen*, ed. H. F. Rørdam, Copenhagen 1864, LXXIII–IV. For Sparre's attempts to receive papal confirmation, see *Acta Pontificium Danica*, VI, no. 4940.

[50] For the humanist interpretation, see J. O. Andersen on Krumpen in *DBL* and Lindhardt, *Nederlagets Mænd*, 137; for the more convincing view of Stygge Krumpen as a competent *realpolitiker*, see Gregersen, *Stygge Krumpen*, 41–2.

that the third of the tithes which they had traditionally received was no longer to be paid. Furthermore, the bishop of Schleswig, Gottschalk Ahlefeldt, had been forced to allow evangelical services to take place in Schleswig cathedral. Consequently, Ahlefeldt had sent a letter to the elected archbishop in Lund, Torben Bille, pointing out that the survival of the Catholic church in Schleswig was now totally dependent on developments in Denmark.[51] The letter must have confirmed the Danish prelates' intention to avoid the election of Duke Christian as their new king for as long as possible.

To fill the vacuum, the Council took over the administration of the realm on a regional basis until further notice. The meeting also guaranteed the continuation of the Catholic church in Denmark as a national church under episcopal control, but outside papal influence. It was decided that in future only preachers licenced by the bishops would be allowed to preach. The elected bishop of Zealand, Joachim Rønnow, led the Catholic party by initiating a trial by the Council of the prominent evangelical preacher, Hans Tausen, while parliament was still in session. Tausen was accused of having slandered the bishops, especially Rønnow, of having preached without episcopal permission, and of holding heretical views of the eucharist. Tausen was found guilty and considering the accusations given a relatively mild sentence: banishment from the sees of Scania and Zealand and a ban against preaching without episcopal licence. The leniency of the sentence probably owed a great deal to the existence within the Council of an influential evangelical minority. However, even this sentence proved impossible to execute, not least because of the strong opposition it attracted from the citizens of Copenhagen. Accordingly, Tausen was allowed to continue his evangelical activities in the city, promising only to obey the bishop and to avoid anti-Catholic polemics.[52]

The elected archbishop, Torben Bille, supported by the predominantly Catholic, lay aristocracy of Scania, acted more determinedly against the evangelical movement in his see. He commenced by tackling the preachers in the smaller towns, finally taking action against the city of Malmø in early 1534, when he had the evangelical preachers outlawed through the high court. Considering the important role of Malmø and

[51] See Grell, 'The City of Malmø', 326–7 and H. V. Gregersen, *Reformationen i Sønderjylland*, Aabenraa 1986, 178–81. See also O. P. Grell, 'Scandinavia', in R. W. Scribner (ed.), *The Reformation in National Context*, Cambridge, 1994, 111–29.

[52] For Tausen, see *DBL*; see A. Heise, 'Herredagen i Kjøbenhavn i 1533', *Historisk Tidsskrift*, Series 4, 3 (1872–3), 222–517, especially 436–78. See als *Skibykrøniken*, 161–5.

Copenhagen in the rebellion which ensued, the attempts of the bishops and especially those of Torben Bille and his colleagues among the lay aristocracy in Scania to reinstate the Catholic church to its former position of power were to a large extent responsible for the civil war which followed.[53] Furthermore, the bishops appear to have been contemplating renewing the links with Rome in the wake of the parliament in Copenhagen. Letters to have Joachim Rønnow and Torben Bille confirmed by the pope were drafted and, in the case of Oluf Munk, successfully forwarded to Rome.[54] A Catholic revival was imminent, but the outbreak of the civil war in the spring of 1534 was to destroy these prospects. The rebellion of Malmø and Copenhagen, strongly supported by Lübeck, forced the bishops and their supporters among the aristocracy to elect Duke Christian as king in the summer of 1534. They must have hoped to be able to elect Duke Christian in their own time. He was, after all, the only possible candidate if the personal union between Denmark and Norway and the duchies was to be maintained. The bishops must have hoped to do this from a position of strength where they could dictate some, if not most, of the conditions of future church policy. Instead they were forced to elect the new king in great haste and from a position of weakness, having to rely on his military and political strength for their own survival.

It was as the leader of a victorious army that Duke Christian, now King Christian III, made his entry into Copenhagen on 6 August 1536. Six days later the Catholic bishops paid the price for their actions in 1533 when they were all imprisoned. The bishops were accused of having caused the civil war, and even if Christian III and his advisors had briefly contemplated the imprisonment of all the members of the Danish Council who had been involved in the decisions in 1533, they alone were held responsible. Simultaneously, all episcopal castles and estates were taken over by the crown. The lay Catholic members of the Council were neutralised when they were forced to sign letters of subjection in which they accepted that in future bishops should be excluded from the Council and from all political influence, while also promising not to hinder the preaching of 'the pure word of God'.

When parliament met in Copenhagen in October the bishops were publicly accused of having been responsible for the previous years' disasters. A comprehensive document had been drawn up by the king, providing detailed accusations against each of them. By far the most

---

[53] See Grell, 'The Emergence', *passim* and 'The City of Malmø', 327–8.
[54] *Acta Pontificium Danica*, VI, nos. 5065, 5066, 5069, 5075, 5077–8, 5080–5; see also Lindhardt, *Nederlagets Mænd*, 149–50.

damning and comprehensive accusations were raised against the elected bishop of Roskilde, Joachim Rønnow, and the bishop of Børglum, Stygge Krumpen. That these two became the prime target for Christian III's anger had less to do with their brand of Catholicism than with their political undertakings during the civil war. Rønnow and Krumpen were in many ways closely connected and shared the same political outlook. Krumpen, as shown above, had been the only bishop prepared to support Rønnow's appointment by Frederik I. The two men had un-doubtedly been prominent among those within the Council who had pushed hard for the postponement of the election of a new king in 1533. Similarly, neither appears to have been particularly worried about the religious/theological consequences of the evangelical movement, as long as the traditional power and jurisdiction of the bishops could be pre-served, and both had worked hard to strengthen episcopal control within their sees following the death of Frederik I. It is no coincidence that when the bishops were released, after having signed similar letters of subjection to those of their lay colleagues, Stygge Krumpen was the last to be freed in June 1542, nearly four years after the others, while Joachim Rønnow died in prison in 1544.[55]

Thus, it was the crown which benefited most, both politically and economically, from the demise of the bishops and the Catholic church, but to see their fall as engineered solely by Christian III and his German advisors would be wrong. A majority of the Danish nobility had, at least since the mid-1520s, wanted a politically and economically weaker church. Together with the crown they had brought increasing political and economic pressure to bear on the church during the reign of Frederik I in order to pay the escalating costs of confronting the threat from the exiled king, Christian II. They had little hesitation in joining hands with Christian III in 1536. It was, after all, not the king, but the leaders of the nobility, who first placed the responsibility for the decisions in 1533 solely on the bishops' shoulders. Well in advance of the bishops' arrest on 12 August, the nobility had washed their hands of responsibility for the civil war and assigned the blame to the bishop.[56]

The religious and ecclesiastical transformation which had taken place in Denmark in less than two decades is illustrated by the two coronations in 1524 of Frederik I and in 1537 of his son, Christian III. In 1524 the

[55] For the imprisonment and accusations against the bishops, see H. F. Rørdam, *Monumenta Historicæ Danicæ*, I, Copenhagen 1873, 133–256. See also K. Hørby, *Reformationens indførelse i Danmark*, Copenhagen 1968.
[56] Hansen, *Adelsvældens Grundlag*, 81. The nobility published a pamphlet entitled: *Antwort vnd Entschuldigung ...* on 3 July 1536 in which they placed the responsibility squarely on the bishops, see Johannesson, *Den Skånska Kyrkan*, 348.

ceremony had been conducted by the only consecrated Catholic archbishop available in Scandinavia, Gustav Trolle of Uppsala, while in 1537 it was performed by Luther's collaborator, Johannes Bugenhagen.

The Catholic bishops accepted their fate quietly. Ove Bille continued to use the title of bishop, but like his colleagues he appears to have had no difficulty settling down to an existence as a noble and feudal lord. Not surprisingly the former bishops proved successful administrators and landowners; they had, after all, plenty of experience. Some, like Knud Henriksen Gyldenstjerne, belonged to the wealthier section of the aristocracy by the time they died. A couple, Jørgen Friis and Oluf Munk, were even re-appointed to the Council as lay members. Flexibility clearly characterised the new order and two Catholic prelates, the abbots Henrik Tornekrands and Eskild Thomesen, retained their seats on the Council in spite of parliament's decision in 1536 that only laymen should serve in future.

The Catholic church was abolished in 1536/7, but Catholic ceremonies and traditions continued to exist, while Catholic clerics survived within the major monasteries and cathedral chapters, especially in Roskilde and Lund, where they actively promoted their faith well into the 1550s.[57] The Catholic bishops and their church had suffered defeat in 1536, but not without a fight. The bishops had tenaciously resisted the attempts of the king and the nobility to diminish their power during the reign of Frederik I. That the battle was predominantly fought in the legal and political spheres is hardly surprising. These were exactly the areas where the bishops found themselves under attack from the king and the aristocracy. The prelates may have lacked both the energy and ability to take up the religious/theological challenge posed by the evangelical party, but that was mainly a challenge from below and the bishops must have perceived it to have been less dangerous than that coming from the king and the nobility. Hindsight, of course, has to some extent proved them wrong, but the evangelical movement would hardly have succeeded without the prior attacks by the king and the lay aristocracy on the church's legal, economic and political position.

NORWAY

While the archbishopric of Lund had been the chief target for royal interference in the Danish church in the decades leading up to the Reformation, the politically weaker Norwegian church witnessed royal

---

[57] See Grell, 'Scandinavia'.

interference at all levels during these years. Since the first decade of the sixteenth century, the crown had actively tried to impose its own candidates on vacant bishoprics in Norway. As a rule these men were Danes who had risen through royal service. Thus in 1506 the chapter in Oslo had been forced to renege on its original election of Torkell Jensson and to accept the royal candidate, the Dane, Anders Mus.[58] In 1521 Mus was forced out of the see of Oslo to make room for another royal servant, Hans Mule, who, however, had not received papal confirmation by the time Christian II fled to the Netherlands.

In 1510, on the death of Archbishop Gaute Ivarsson of Trondheim, the chapter had elected the canon, Jon Krabbe, as his successor only to find the election nullified when Pope Julius II, on royal recommendation, confirmed Erik Valkendorf, the chancellor of the later king, Christian II, as archbishop of Trondheim. Once appointed, however, not all royal servants remained loyal to the crown, and Valkendorf proved to be very much a case in point. He became a staunch defender of the church's rights and independence. Consequently, Valkendorf came into conflict with his royal mentor and was eventually forced to flee Norway and seek assistance in Rome in the autumn of 1521.[59]

Even if it was royal policy to promote loyal servants, preferably Danes who, as newcomers, were not connected to the Norwegian nobility and therefore considered politically more reliable, it was possible for Norwegians to become bishops too, as can be seen from the case of Magnus Lauritssøn who became bishop of Hamar in 1513. It is, however, significant that until the last months of 1522, when Christian II's political difficulties made him more or less impotent, Norwegians were only given the lesser bishoprics of Hamar, Stavanger and Bergen.

The political difficulties and subsequent flight of Christian II made it possible for the chapter in Trondheim to elect a candidate of their own choice, the dean, Olav Engelbriktsson, who was to become the dominant figure within the Norwegian church in the turbulent years of the Reformation. Similarly, Christian II failed in having his candidate, the Dane, Hans Knudsen, elected to the see of Bergen which had become vacant in 1522 on the death of Bishop Andor Ketilsson. In the changed political climate the chapter felt strong enough to disregard the king's wishes and to elect its own candidate, the archdeacon, Olav Torkelsson.

Undoubtedly, the Norwegian church was in trouble in the autumn of 1522, as indicated by the public letter issued by the Danish rebels in December of that year. Evidently, Christian II carried considerable

[58] See Allen, *De tre nordiske Riger*, I, 435–76. [59] See *ibid.*, II, part II, 86–94.

responsibility for the problems which then surrounded the bishoprics of Trondheim and Oslo, whereas, at most, he can only be accused of having delayed the election of the new bishop of Bergen.

Bearing in mind that Christian II had not only been responsible for the death of the imprisoned bishop, Karl of Hamar, in 1512, while serving as stadtholder, but had also directly interfered in the affairs of the Norwegian church, it is surprising that the Catholic bishops and especially the primate, Olav Engelbriktsson, should decide to tie their cause and that of the church to the exiled king.

The new archbishop certainly appears to have been adept at playing a political game of duplicity from the outset. Following his election, Olav Engelbriktsson had immediately set out for Rome to secure papal recognition. On the outward journey he visited Christian II in exile in the Netherlands and gave him his oath of allegiance; while returning home he passed through Flensburg in Schleswig where he offered Frederik I a similar oath. Together with the Danish nobleman, Vincens Lunge, who through his marriage into one of the leading Norwegian noble families, had obtained a place on the Norwegian Council, Olav Engelbriktsson played a decisive role in the developments in Norway during this period. Vincens Lunge and the archbishop were instrumental in forcing Frederik I to sign a coronation charter for Norway which was nearly identical to the one he had signed the previous year in Denmark. It offered the Norwegian church identical guarantees to that of its Danish sister church. The Norwegian prelates cannot but have been optimistic in 1524. No longer were any of the bishoprics vacant, and for the first time in years the church had just successfully exercised its right to elect the candidates it wanted as archbishop of Trondheim and bishop of Bergen, while the new archbishop had just ordained Hans Mule as bishop of Oslo.

The strength of the Catholic church and its leader, Olav Engelbriktsson, was considerable during the first years of Frederik I's reign. When Bishop Hans Mule was drowned in September 1524, the king attempted to force the chapter to elect his secretary, Iver Kjeldssøn Jul, as their new bishop. The royal candidate, however, stood no chance against the archbishop's choice, Hans Reff, who was duly elected and instated in the spring of 1525. Within Norwegian historiography there has been a tendency to see Olav Engelbriktsson and some of the other bishops, such as Magnus Lauritssøn of Hamar, as exponents of a nationalist policy. There is very little evidence to support such a claim and Engelbriktsson is, in my opinion, better understood as a traditional, Catholic archbishop who wanted to protect the independence of his church at all costs. This was an aim which was best achieved through a policy which coincided with the interests of the Norwegian nobility *vis-à-vis* the crown.[60] Furthermore, this concern explains the archbishop's interest in promoting Hans Reff, a Dane, who had arrived in Trondheim in the retinue of the previous archbishop, Erik Valkendorf. A friendship had clearly developed between Engelbriktsson and Reff while, under Valkendorf's guidance, they had collaborated in the production of the first printed liturgy for the Norwegian church, *Missale Nidrosiense* (1519). Thus Reff was appointed because his loyalties were seen to rest with the church and the archbishop, rather than the king.

It was not until the autumn of 1526 that the evangelical movement began to make some impact in Norway. Initially it appears to have been limited to Bergen where the German Hansa had its base, and it may well have been inspired by itinerant German preachers. We know from the complaint Bishop Olav Torkelsson forwarded to Olav Engelbriktsson that he had been forced to leave the town in order to avoid harassment from Vincens Lunge and *de secta lutheriana*. Lunge, who by 1529 was actively espousing the evangelical cause, may well, with his political flair, have recognised the much stronger orientation of Frederik I and his government towards the evangelicals by 1526 and realised that the time had come for a move in the same direction in Norway. Consequently, the political alliance which had existed between the archbishop and Lunge broke down. In 1529 the conflict between them resulted in open warfare after Lunge had instigated an iconoclastic attack on one of the churches in Bergen and been instrumental in the plundering of the Dominican monastery.

Meanwhile, Frederik I, ignoring the promises made in his coronation charter only to appoint Norwegian noblemen as vassals of the royal fiefs, had placed his loyal Danish supporters in charge of the most strategically important castles. By 1529 the king was prepared to offer support to the evangelical movement when he issued letters of protection to two preachers in Bergen.[61] It is no coincidence that it was during 1529 that Archbishop Olav Engelbriktsson resumed contacts with the exiled king, Christian II. From then on the fate of the Catholic church in Norway

---

60 For an example of this nationalist interpretation, see the article on Olav Engelbriktsson in *Norsk Biografisk Leksikon* (Norwegian Dictionary of National Biography), henceforth *NBL*.

61 See C. F. Wisløff, *Norsk Kirkehistorie*, I, Oslo 1966, 393–7. See also A. C. Bang, *Den norske Kirkes Historie i Reformations-Aarhundredet*, Christiania 1895, and C. Paludan-Müller, *Grevens Feide*, II, Copenhagen 1854, 1–42.

became closely connected with that of Christian II. Finding himself under increasing political pressure from Frederik I and the most prominent representative of the Norwegian nobility, Vincens Lunge, the archbishop needed allies. Sheer desperation must have forced Olav Engelbriktsson to join hands with the exiled king. The archbishop well knew that Christian II was no friend of the church, even if he had recently returned to the Catholic fold, but no other options seem to have been available to Engelbriktsson if a gradual demolition of the church was to be avoided. Consequently, Christian II came to influence developments in Norway to an even greater extent than in the rest of Scandinavia.

Olav Engelbriktsson pretended to be loyal to Frederik I until Christian II finally arrived in Norway in November 1531 with an expeditionary corps from the Netherlands. The archbishop had, however, gradually indicated his views by attending neither the parliament which met in Oslo in 1529 nor the meetings in Copenhagen in 1530 and 1531, while during the summer of 1531 he received and assisted Christian II's emissary, the former archbishop of Uppsala, Gustav Trolle, in his covert activities in Norway. Together with the bishops of Hamar and Oslo, Magnus Lauritssøn and Hans Reff, Olav Engelbriktsson did his utmost to support Christian II with troops, as well as money, during his brief and disastrous campaign in Norway which resulted in the exiled king's imprisonment in Denmark in 1532. Considering that both Engelbriktsson and Lauritssøn stood by Christian II to the end, they escaped lightly from a political venture which might well have destroyed them both, by paying considerable fines.[62]

The death of Frederik I and the attempt by the Catholic bishops and their lay allies in Denmark to initiate a Catholic resurgence was warmly welcomed by the leaders of the Norwegian church. Once more the archbishop of Trondheim nailed his and his church's colours to the mast of Christian II, while his old adversary, Vincens Lunge, quickly opted for Frederik's son, the Lutheran, Christian III. Even when it became increasingly obvious that those espousing the imprisoned king's cause in the civil war in Denmark were fighting a losing battle, the archbishop refused to be swayed. With hindsight it is somewhat ironic that Christian II's Danish supporters fought for the evangelical cause, while his Norwegian allies wanted to preserve the Catholic church.

By the summer of 1535, Olav Engelbriktsson's hope of success appears

---

[62] See A. Heise, *Kristiern den anden i Norge og hans Fængsling*, Copenhagen 1877 and *NBL* for Olav Engelbriktsson, Magnus Laruitssøn and Hans Reff.

to have rested solely on the intervention of the German duke, Frederick of the Palatinate, who had married Christian II's daughter, Dorothea, in May. Having feigned willingness to accept Christian III as king of Norway in September, the archbishop abandoned all caution in January 1536 when, during a meeting of parliament, he had his opponent, Vincens Lunge, killed and several members of the Council imprisoned, including the bishops Hans Reff and Magnus Lauritssøn. His coup, however, failed spectacularly when little support materialised in Norway and the promised troops from Duke Frederick of the Palatinate never arrived. The archbishop held out until April 1537, when he fled to the Netherlands where he died a few months later. His staunchest supporter among the bishops, Magnus Lauritssøn, was imprisoned by Christian III in the summer of 1537 and died in Antvorskov monastery in Denmark in 1542. Bishop Hans Reff, who appears to have been theologically the most flexible of the Norwegian bishops, avoided imprisonment by signing a letter of subjection to Christian III similar to those signed by his Danish colleagues on their release.[63] The timing of the collapse of the Catholic church in Norway was undoubtedly closely related to the developments in Denmark, but considering the continued strength of Catholicism in Norway, where Protestantism had hardly made any real impact by 1537, one cannot help wondering whether or not the Catholic church and its bishops might have been able to survive for longer had their cause not been so closely intertwined with that of Christian II, owing mainly to the political decisions taken by the church's last archbishop.

Christian III certainly wanted to keep the religious changes in Norway to a minimum in order not to antagonise the population. That the king opted for a slow and gradual change in religion, in spite of the new Danish Lutheran Church Order introduced in 1537, can also be seen from the appointment in 1541 of the first superintendent for the now united sees of Oslo and Hamar. The choice fell on Hans Reff who thus became the only properly ordained and confirmed Catholic bishop in Scandinavia to serve in a similar capacity within one of the new Protestant churches.

SWEDEN AND FINLAND

The Catholic church in Sweden and Finland was in a far stronger position than its Scandinavian sister churches on the eve of the Reformation. The Catholic ideal of the independent church – *libertas ecclesiae* –

---

63 For Reff's letter of subjection, see Rørdam, *Monumenta Historiæ Danicæ*, I, 232–3.

had almost been realised in Sweden around 1500. The church was in a powerful position, having managed to maintain its independence of the crown, as well as the *Curia*. This had been achieved, not least, because of the constant struggle for power between the reigning Danish kings and their Swedish supporters on the one hand, and those who supported an independent, 'national' policy on the other. This had made it possible for the church to place itself in a pivotal position between the two parties, constantly courted by the main political forces.

Furthermore, the Swedish church was not generally perceived to have decayed, or to be in a spiritual crisis, to the same extent as the Catholic church in Denmark and Germany towards the end of the Middle Ages. As on the Continent, there was a growing hostility towards the monastic culture in general and towards the mendicant orders in particular, but lay support for the church remained strong at parish level. The reason for this was undoubtedly closely related to the decentralised nature of the Catholic church in Sweden and Finland, where local churches exercised considerable independence, and lay involvement at parish level, especially concerning financial and economic affairs, was significant.[64] This explains the strong and continuous support for Catholicism among the Swedish population throughout the sixteenth century.

The Swedish church also differed in another important aspect from the rest of the Scandinavian churches. It was largely unconnected with aristocratic interests, and apart from its archbishop, Gustav Trolle, all its bishops and prelates were recruited from among the burghers and the lower nobility at the beginning of the sixteenth century.[65]

By December 1522 when the rebellious members of the Danish Council published their above-mentioned public letter, Gustav Vasa's rebellion against Christian II and the Union had already proved successful. In July that year, Gustav Vasa was joined by Hans Brask, the bishop of Linköping, and the only remaining Swedish bishop of any ecclesiastical and political consequence.[66] Brask added significant strength to Gustav Vasa's cause, and the following month Gustav Vasa was elected regent of Sweden.[67]

If the Catholic church in Sweden can be seen to have profited from the political conditions surrounding the Scandinavian Union during the

---

[64] See H. Holmquist, *Svenska Kyrkans Historia*, III, Uppsala 1933, 28–38.

[65] See for instance, H. Schück, *Ecclesia Lincopensis. Studier om Linköpingskyrkan under Medeltiden och Gustav Vasa*, Stockholm 1959, 521–32. For Gustav Trolle, see *DBL*.

[66] For Hans Brask, see *SBL*. Brask was the first influential member of the Swedish Council to join Gustav Vasa.

[67] Schück, *Ecclesia Lincopensis*, 145.

later Middle Ages, then it must be concluded that the collapse of the Union, towards the end of Christian II's reign, would cause it tremendous damage. Among the more than eighty members of the Swedish lay and ecclesiastical aristocracy which Christian II had executed in Stockholm in November 1520 were the bishops of Skara and Strängnäs. Christian II immediately instated two of his henchmen, Didrik Slagheck, later briefly archbishop of Lund, and Jens Andersen Beldenak, bishop of Odense, in these bishoprics. When they, together with the archbishop, Gustav Trolle, fled before Gustav Vasa's advancing army in 1521, three of the seven Swedish sees were vacant.[68] By the summer of 1522 a further two sees had lost their incumbents; Bishop Otto of Västerås, who had been imprisoned by Christian II, died in Stockholm, while Bishop Arvid of Åbo in Finland died while fleeing Christian II's supporter, Søren Norby. Evidently, Christian II bore full responsibility for this decimation of the leadership of the Catholic church in Sweden. Only two bishops remained in place by the autumn of 1522, the elderly and powerless Bishop Ingemar of Växjö and Hans Brask, who was to provide the leadership for the Catholic church in Sweden during some of the most difficult years leading up to the Reformation.

For Gustav Vasa and Hans Brask, it was of paramount importance to fill the vacant bishoprics as quickly as possible in order to strengthen both church and state at this difficult time. Consequently, the two men appear to have co-operated without any significant difficulties until the end of 1522. Since neither Didrik Slagheck nor Jens Andersen Beldenak had received papal confirmation of their elections to the dioceses of Skara and Strängnäs, it proved unproblematic to have new candidates elected. The chapter in Strängnäs elected its dean, Magnus Sommar, a humanist and a strong defender of the conciliarist position, towards the end of 1522, while the chapter in Skara also chose one of its own, the canon, Magnus Haraldsson, around the same time. Early in 1523 the former chancellor of Sten Sture, the prelate, Peder Sunnenväder, who had recently returned from exile, was elected bishop of Västerås. These three bishoprics had proved easy to fill; the archbishopric and the see of Åbo, however, presented serious problems. Åbo remained under the control of Søren Norby who supported the deposed king, Christian II, and it was accordingly left vacant, while the see of Uppsala, which had a properly

---

68 That the diocese of Strängnäs is not mentioned among the vacant Swedish bishoprics in the public letter from the rebellious members of the Danish Council in December 1522, is explained by the rebels' unwillingness to antagonise a possible ally, the bishop of Odense, Jens Andersen Beldenak, who had been given the see of Strängnäs.

elected and consecrated archbishop, Gustav Trolle, who had gone into exile for political reasons, posed a serious dilemma, not least because Trolle continued to have his supporters within the chapter in spite of his close association with Christian II. Gustav Vasa, however, did not hesitate to seize the archbishopric's income and possessions for the use of the crown, while forcing the chapter to elect a successor for Trolle. They elected the dean of Västerås, Master Knut, who was a friend of Peder Sunnenväder, the new bishop there. Master Knut, however, appears to have quietly renounced his position as *electus* some month later, a decision which, in effect, left the diocese of Uppsala without an incumbent.[69]

Gustav Vasa had promised to uphold all the privileges of the Catholic church when elected regent in 1521, and initially he supported Hans Brask in his efforts to get papal recognition for the newly elected bishops. Meanwhile, it was left to Brask to take up the battle with the emerging evangelical movement in Sweden which was gaining ground especially among the resident German population in the coastal towns. During 1522 Brask issued a public letter threatening those who bought or read Luther's works with excommunication. Likewise, he circulated Pope Leo X's bill of January 1521 and the placards of the universities of Cologne and Louvain against Luther among the Swedish clergy and nobility. Brask was strongly supported in his anti-evangelical campaign by the dean in Strängnäs, Olaus Magnus.

Hans Brask, however, was worried not only about the deteriorating religious situation in Sweden, but also about the fact that Gustav Vasa showed little inclination to adhere to his promise to protect the privileges of the church. Instead, the regent had started to press his chosen candidates into most of the important vacant positions in the church, while seizing as much ecclesiastical income as he could lay his hands on, especially from the estates of deceased clergy. In Marsh 1523 Brask wrote a letter to Olaus Magnus's brother, Johannes, who had resided in Rome since 1518, and whose teacher and mentor, Hadrian VI, had recently succeeded Leo X as pope.[70] Here Brask complained about the economic sufferings of the Swedish church and the hostility it encountered from the laity, pointing out the difficulties in defending the clergy's traditional privileges and enforcing the payment of tithes. In the months leading up to the parliament, which met in Strängnäs in June 1523, Hans Brask must have realised that he needed new allies in order to contain the policies of

[69] See Holmquist, *Svenska Kyrkan*, III, 74–6.   [70] For Johannes Magnus, see *SBL*.

Gustav Vasa. Consequently, he became closely associated with the influential aristocrat, Ture Jönsson, who remained a supporter of the Scandinavian Union.

Gustav Vasa was elected king on 6 June 1523 at the parliament of Strängnäs. This meeting officially laid to rest all prospects of a Scandinavian Union, while virulently attacking the exiled archbishop, Gustav Trolle. The time, however, had come for Gustav Vasa to pay some of the bills incurred in connection with his conquest of Sweden which had largely been financed by the Hanseatic cities under the leadership of Lübeck. These cities were granted a virtual monopoly of the trade on Sweden and a promise by the Swedish government to repay them 120,000 marks.[71]

Johannes Magnus, who had been made papal nuncio for Sweden by Hadrian VI with the special commission to combat heresy, returned home while the parliament was meeting. Magnus was treated with the greatest respect by Gustav Vasa and his councillors, who used the opportunity to write to the *Curia*, professing their loyalty to the Catholic cause, but requesting the replacement of the archbishop, Gustav Trolle, with another and 'better' Swede, and asking for permission to introduce ecclesiastical reforms. Furthermore, they made Johannes Magnus's planned campaign against heresy conditional on these requests being granted and on the elected bishops receiving confirmation from the pope. Nothing, however, came of this approach, and when Johannes Magnus began to take action against the evangelicals in the summer of 1523, Gustav Vasa immediately moved to guarantee that the ambitious nuncio delayed or cancelled his plans. The king made sure that the chapter in Uppsala elected Johannes Magnus archbishop. Magnus accepted the election on condition that it received the pope's approval. By putting his personal ambition before providing crucial support for an increasingly embattled Catholic church in Sweden, Johannes Magnus undermined the attempts by Hans Brask and his only supporter among the Swedish episcopal college, Magnus Haraldsson of Skara, to protect the church against the economic/political encroachment of the king on one hand, and the emerging evangelical party on the other.

Shortly after the parliament of Västerås, Stockholm, the last foothold of Christian II in Sweden, surrendered to Gustav Vasa. With no more major military campaigns planned, the king needed to pay off his German mercenaries as quickly as possible. They, however, insisted on

---

[71] Holmquist, *Svenska Kyrkan*, III, 84–8.

payment in silver, refusing to accept the debased Swedish currency. Accordingly, Gustav Vasa was in urgent need of capital. Consequently, it was decided to impose a forced loan on the church. Most of the silver treasures of the cathedrals, major churches and monasteries were confiscated by the crown which only faced protests from two of the bishops, Hans Brask and Magnus Haraldsson. Another likely supporter of Brask's policies, the elected bishop of Västerås, Peder Sunnenväder, who politically might have proved an even more dangerous opponent than the bishops of Linköping and Skara, was neutralised by Gustav Vasa in September, when he was dismissed as *electus*. In his place, the king had elected the elderly canon, Peder Månsson, who resided in Rome. Månsson, alone among all the Swedish bishops elected in the wake of Gustav Vasa's victory in Sweden, managed to obtain papal recognition and confirmation. By now Gustav Vasa had also gained control of Finland, and he made sure that one of his servants, Erik Svensson, was elected to the vacant see of Åbo. Svensson, a flexible Christian humanist, who like most of the bishops Gustav Vasa had elected in the 1520s and 30s favoured a national Catholic church, could easily be goaded and controlled by the crown.

At this stage, Gustav Vasa and his chancellor, Laurentius Andreae, the architect of the Swedish Reformation, still appear to have favoured some form of accommodation with the *Curia*.[72] Letters were written in September and October to Rome requesting confirmation of the elected archbishop and bishops, while asking for the traditional fees payable to Rome – the annates – to be cancelled. The letters professed loyalty and promised to fight heresy, to convert the Lapps and to convince the Russian Orthodox church to become part of the Catholic church, if only the pope would accept the Swedish request. The letters, which were forwarded through Olaus Magnus, who would never again return to Sweden, failed to obtain the acceptance of Pope Clement VII, Hadrian VI's successor. Clement VII only confirmed Peder Månsson as bishop and allowed Johannes Magnus to administer the archbishopric of Uppsala. The pope's answer, which reached Sweden in April 1524, guaranteed that Gustav Vasa carried out his threat of breaking away from Rome and personally taking control of the Swedish church. Thus Sweden broke off its connections with Rome earlier than any other European country.[73]

Gustav Vasa's attempt to circumvent the pope by getting Johannes

---

[72] See Grell, *Scandinavia*', 112–18.   [73] Holmquist, *Svenska Kyrkan*, III, 90–6.

Magnus to confirm the elected bishops, arguing that Magnus, as papal nuncio, was invested with such powers, failed because of Hans Brask's determined intervention. Brask pointed out that whatever powers Johannes Magnus had been invested with as a nuncio were null and void since the death of Pope Hadrian VI who had commissioned him. Once again, Johannes Magnus appears to have played a rather unfortunate part in the political and religious confrontation surrounding the Swedish church. Only Brask's intervention prevented him from playing the obliging part Gustav Vasa had assigned to him. Not surprisingly Johannes Magnus was to offer Hans Brask little if any assistance in his attempt to protect the privileges of the church and to tackle the growing evangelical heresy during the subsequent years.[74]

With the support of only one of his colleagues, Bishop Magnus Haraldsson of Skara, Brask tried to preserve the privileges and doctrines of the Catholic church in Sweden. Firstly, he tried to fight off the king's encroachment on the church's economic and political position. Gustav Vasa had already given notice of his intentions through the famous letter which his evangelical chancellor, Laurentius Andreae, forwarded to the monastery in Vadstena in February 1524. Here he identified the church with the people, arguing that the wealth of the church belonged to the nation.[75] The Catholic prelates found themselves under growing political pressure when, during a Council meeting in the autumn of 1524, their right to hold royal fiefs was seriously questioned. The following year Gustav Vasa went further when it was decided to secularise the monasteries and appropriate that part of the tithes which was to be paid to the parish churches during 1525 for the use of the crown. Bishop Brask, however, pointing to the ancient privileges of the church, managed to prevent the crown from seizing this part of the tithes.

Secondly, Hans Brask did his utmost to suppress the embryonic evangelical movement which was more or less openly encouraged by Gustav Vasa. Here, however, he was spectacularly unsuccessful. He failed to block the king's appointment of the leading evangelical, Olaus Petri, to the important position of minister to the town of Stockholm. His attempt to get the elected archbishop, Johannes Magnus, to introduce the inquisition in Sweden, met with a similar fate. When Brask protested to the king and Johannes Magnus over Olaus Petri's marriage in 1525, Gustav Vasa defended the evangelical minister while the elected archbishop remained silent. Not surprisingly, Brask's correspondence from

[74] See Schück, *Ecclesia Lincopensis*, 147–8.   [75] Grell, 'Scandinavia', 113.

1524 to 1525 is characterised by a growing pessimism.[76] Realising that no support for action against the evangelical movement could be hoped for from central government, Brask tried to prevent 'the Lutheran heresy' from entering his own diocese by issuing a comprehensive letter of condemnation to his clergy. Similarly, he tried to encourage his hesitant colleagues among the clergy to take action by circulating imported anti-Lutheran tracts by, among others, Johannes Cochlæus and the English bishop, John Fisher. Furthermore, together with one of his supporters, the learned canon of Uppsala, Peder Galle, he used the printing press to publish anti-evangelical literature, until Gustav Vasa finally intervened in 1526, moving the Uppsala press to Stockholm and closing down Brask's press in Linköping.[77]

Meanwhile Gustav Vasa had survived the first rebellion against him, driven, as most of those which followed, by a mixture of political, economic and religious grievances. The rebellion, which had started in Dalarna in 1524, was led by a group of dissatisfied Catholic clerics, headed by the deposed bishop of Västerås, Peder Sunnenväder, and Master Knut, the dean of Västerås, who had briefly been the elected archbishop of Uppsala. Undoubtedly these men were in collusion with the Norwegian archbishop, Olav Engelbriktsson, who eventually offered them refuge in February 1525.[78]

The elected archbishop, Johannes Magnus, continued to be a willing tool in the hands of Gustav Vasa and his evangelical chancellor during 1525. He lent his authority to Laurentius Andreae's scheme for a translation into Swedish of the New Testament, much to Hans Brask's despair. In order to facilitate and accelerate the work, it was to be divided between the different chapters and monasteries. Brask expressed his reservations to his clerical friends, Magnus Haraldsson and Peder Galle, and he clearly saw the project as a way of introducing evangelical heresy through the back door. However, by 1526 Johannes Magnus must have realised that his compliant attitude brought no advantages either to him personally or the church. Belatedly, he tried to support the policies pursued by Brask and in March he secretly sought support from his friend, the Norwegian archbishop, Olav Engelbriktsson.[79]

Seen from a Catholic perspective, the political developments in

---

[76] See Holmquist, *Svenska Hyrkan*, III, 100–8, and Schück, *Ecclesia Lincopensis*, 148–9.

[77] See R. Murray, *Olavus Petri*, Stockholm 1952, 28–53 and Holmquist, *Svenska Kyrkan*, III, 112 and 131. For printing, see R. Kick, 'Le Livre et la Réforme dans le royaume de Suède 1526–1571', in J.-F. Gilmont, *La Réforme et le Livre*, Paris 1990, 459–78.

[78] See M. Roberts, *The Early Vasas. A History of Sweden 1523–1611*, Cambridge 1968, 55–6.

[79] See the article on Johannes Magnus in *SBL*.

Sweden were ominous during the first eight months of 1526. The parliament which met in Vadstena had given Gustav Vasa full control over all the Swedish monasteries while another parliament which met in Stockholm in August had witnessed further demands from the king on the finances of the church. This time Gustav Vasa was not satisfied with a loan, but demanded two-thirds of the tithes for 1526, in total contravention of the church's privileges.[80] Undoubtedly the recent Diet of Speyer in Germany, with its positive outcome for the Protestants, had boosted the confidence of Gustav Vasa, who also used the opportunity to have one of the leaders of the rebellion of 1524, the dean, Master Knut, sentenced to death during the parliament which met in Stockholm.

If the sentence was supposed to send a message to the leaders of the church to abstain from further political involvement, it met with some success. Bishop Erik Svensson vacated the see of Åbo and returned to a less exposed existence as dean of Linköping, while Johannes Magnus reverted to his earlier more co-operative mood. A month later, Johannes Magnus gave in and, while on a diplomatic mission to Poland, went into exile, thus becoming the first of a group of refugee Swedish prelates to reside in Danzig.

The undisputed leadership of the Catholic church in Sweden now fell to the bishop of Linköping, Hans Brask, who energetically tried to halt the progress of the evangelical movement. However, faced with the increasingly evangelical policies of the crown, Brask was constantly on the defensive. He was able to register small success such as the expulsion of an evangelical preacher from his own diocese, and he managed to avoid taking part in the religious debate which Gustav Vasa initiated towards the end of 1526. Instead, the king convinced Peder Galle to provide a written answer to the ten questions, later expanded to twelve, which he had directed to Catholics, as well as evangelicals. Rather than the intended religious disputation before king and Council, the affair resulted in the publication of a number of pamphlets.[81] Brask must have realised that he needed to take the initiative in order to prevent Gustav Vasa from totally undermining the church's political and economic position. Claiming to be in poor health, he avoided accepting Gustav Vasa's invitation to spend Christmas at court in Uppsala. Instead he travelled to Västergötland, the stronghold of his aristocratic ally, Ture Jönsson, for a meeting of the leaders of the 'Catholic party'. Here the plans for the political and anti-evangelical rebellion, Daljunkern's revolt,

---

[80] H. Yrwing, *Gustav Vasa, Kröningsfrågan och Västerås Riksdag 1527*, Lund 1956, 49–70.
[81] See Holmquist, *Svenska Kyrkan*, III, 132–4.

which broke out in early 1527, are likely to have been drawn up, even if Hans Brask, his colleague Magnus Haraldsson and Ture Jönsson cannot be directly linked to the subsequent uprising.

Meanwhile Gustav Vasa was demonstrating that he had no intention of upholding the church's traditional privileges. In February 1527 he had the prelate and rebel, Peder Sunnenväder, who had recently been handed over to him by the Norwegians, condemned to death by the lay members of a mixed court. This happened in spite of the protests of Hans Brask and other church leaders, who, being members of the court, argued that the procedure was against canonical law and the privileges of the church. Furthermore, the king had also begun to undermine the jurisdiction of the church by issuing letters of protection to renegade monks and evangelical preachers.[82] Here Gustav Vasa may well have been prompted by the successful use of this expedient in Denmark by Frederik I.

Hans Brask appears to have hoped to be able to use the Daljunkern's revolt as a way of pressing concessions out of Gustav Vasa. A pro-Catholic church policy would be met with the church's political and economic support. Undoubtedly, the king was under severe pressure, with a revolt on his hands, the growing danger of a war with Russia, and Lübeck issuing ultimata for the immediate repayment of the war debts from the early 1520s. However, by the time a parliament met in Västerås in June 1527, the rebellion had run out of steam. Gustav Vasa no longer needed the political support of the church; instead he intended to dismantle the political and economic power of the church. Only the Catholic church possessed the resources from which a financial reconstruction of the kingdom could be engineered.

Twenty lay members of the Council, plus four clerical members, the bishops of Linköping and Västerås and the elected bishops of Skara and Strängnäs, were present at this parliament. Gustav Vasa was escorted by a considerable number of soldiers. This show of strength must have encouraged those who disagreed with the king's policies to take a low profile.[83] The king seems to have suspended the church's traditional privileges immediately. He excluded the clergy led by Hans Brask from the negotiations, eventually presenting the four bishops with a *fait*

---

[82] See *ibid.*, 142–4 and Yrwing, *Gustav Vasa*, 64–70.
[83] Yrwing has argued that the soldiers were only there for the king's personal protection. Considering that the rebellion had already run out of steam by the end of May, the presence of a considerable number of troops cannot be satisfactorily explained as a measure purely dictated by security, *Gustav Vasa*, 86–116.

accompli, which they were compelled to accept. It meant a total demise of the economic and political power of the Catholic church in Sweden. The prelates were to return all their fiefs to the crown, while the church was to hand over that part of its income to the crown which was surplus to maintaining its spiritual obligations. A clause making it possible for the lay nobility to reclaim all properties donated by their families to the church since 1454 must have tempted many a hesitant nobleman to support the king's policies. On Gustav Vasa's insistence, some form of religious debate took place during parliament. Bishop Hans Brask who was strongly opposed to any form of debate appears to have been briefly imprisoned as a consequence of his opposition. Apart from showing the impotence of the Catholic leaders, the debate was intended to demonstrate that the evangelical preachers were only preaching the word of God.[84]

For Brask and his supporters the outcome of the parliament of Västerås was a disaster. The Catholic church had lost all vestiges of power: gone was its economic and political influence and, of course, the church's jurisdiction. Doctrinally the church still remained intact, but the prelates must have seen the writing on the wall after the government had acknowledged that the theology of the evangelical preachers was both orthodox and acceptable.

Gustav Vasa and his advisors did not hesitate to put parliament's decisions into action. The economic beneficiary of the decisions of Västerås was the crown, which had possessed less than 6 per cent of the landed property in Sweden in 1521, as opposed to the church, which then controlled 21 per cent, a figure which by 1560 had grown to more than 28 per cent of the total.[85] Not surprisingly, Hans Brask personally received the toughest treatment by the king of all the bishops, while the chapter in Linköping escaped comparatively lightly. By the autumn of 1527 Brask must have recognised defeat. Consequently, he took the opportunity during a visitation of the island of Gotland, to flee to Danzig where he joined the already exiled prelate, Johannes Magnus.[86]

In connection with the coronation ceremony in Uppsala in January 1528, Gustav Vasa badly needed to have the elected bishops of Skara, Strängnäs and Åbo consecrated, in order to give the ceremony the necessary legitimacy. For this purpose he was able to use the last

---

[84] For the parliament of Västeråas, see L. Weibull, 'Vesteråas riksdag 1527', *Scandia*, 10 (1937), 76–128, Yrwing, *Gustav Vasa*, 86–116 and Schück, *Ecclesia Lincopensis*, 153–5.

[85] For these figures, see J. Rosén, *Svensk Historia*, I, 3rd edition, Stockholm 1969, 314.

[86] See Schück, *Ecclesia Lincopensis*, 535–41.

remaining papally consecrated bishop, the elderly Peder Månsson of Västerås who, under pressure, consecrated Magnus Haraldsson, Magnus Sommar and Mårten Skytte a week prior to the coronation. That Gustav Vasa was not yet prepared to turn his back fully on those who supported the traditional position of the Catholic church in Sweden can be seen from the fact that the coronation was performed by Brask's sole ally within the episcopal college, Magnus Haraldsson of Skara. The occasion, however, was neatly counter-balanced by having the evangelical leader, Olaus Petri, preach the coronation sermon. Some months later it became evident that the king did not trust the conservative bishops, Peder Månsson and Magnus Haraldsson, who were both given reformist assistants to watch over them, while the crown increased its influence within their chapters through new appointments.[87]

The king had successfully curtailed the political and financial influence of the Catholic church and its bishops at Västerås, but so far he had refrained from any doctrinal interference and only insisted on a *de facto* toleration of the evangelical movement. Evidently, he could only hope to maintain such a religious equilibrium for a limited period, since popular dissatisfaction and disturbances were on the increase. The growing need for religious uniformity caused him to convene a national synod in Örebro in February 1529 under the chairmanship of Laurentius Andreae. Very little was achieved, however. the Latin mass was to continue in a slightly modified form, while evangelical services were allowed to co-exist with the traditional Catholic rites. This indecisiveness did not calm the situation. In April 1529 another peasant revolt, the 'Västgötaherrarnas rebellion', broke out, this time in southwest Sweden. Once more the crisis was to a considerable extent brought about by political/economic dissatisfaction, but this time the anti-evangelical element was much more prominent. The rebels complained about the unchristian government and the new Lutheran heresies and on this occasion they were supported by members of the gentry and the nobility, while leadership was provided by the aristocrat, Ture Jönsson and the bishop of Skara, Magnus Haraldsson.[88] It was undoubtedly the most serious of the many rebellions Gustav Vasa had to face during his reign. At the same time it was also the last occasion where a serious attempt was made to revert the king's church policies and preserve the old church.

The loyalty of the Christian humanist prelates, such as Bishop

[87] See Yrwing, *Gustav Vasa*, 117–34 and Holmquist, *Svenska Kyrkan*, III, 160–2.
[88] Grell, 'Scandinavia', 115, and S. Kjöllerström, 'Västgötaherrarnas uppror', *Scandia*, 29 (1963), 1–93.

Magnus Sommar and the dean of Skara and assistant to Magnus Haraldsson, Sven Jacobi, who owed their appointments to the king, proved of paramount importance in this situation. It was their negotiations with the rebels, which took the sting out of the rebellion and caused it to peter out within four weeks. In May the leaders of the rebellion, Bishop Magnus Haraldsson and Ture Jönsson, acknowledged defeat and fled to Danzig, where they joined the other exiled leaders of the church.[89]

At the subsequent parliament which met in Strängnäs in June 1529, Bishop Hans Brask was, probably correctly, portrayed as the real instigator of the rebellion. If nothing else the revolt made Gustav Vasa and his councillors realise that any hope of accommodating the exiled bishops, Hans Brask and Johannes Magnus, was futile, and plans for their depositions and replacements were finally drawn up.[90] Once more within one decade the episcopal college had been severely depleted. Three bishops had gone into exile, leaving the sees of Uppsala, Linköping and Skara vacant, a fourth bishop, Ingemar Petri of Växjö died early in 1530, while Bishop Peder Månsson had in effect been under administration since 1528. This left only two active bishops in place, Magnus Sommar of Strängnäs and Mårten Skytte of Åbo. Thus, by 1530 the government needed to fill four bishoprics. This was made much more urgent by Gustav Vasa's plans to marry Catherine of Saxony-Lauenburg. The presence of a number of bishops at the marriage ceremony and coronation of the queen was considered essential for the sake of legitimacy. It proved least problematic to find new bishops for the dioceses of Linköping and Växjö. The dean of Linköping, Jöns Magni, who had served the king loyally during the recent crisis, succeeded Hans Brask, while the canon, Johannes Boecii, was made bishop of Växjö. Sven Jacobi, however, had some reservations about his election to the see of Skara, which, according to canonical law, could not be considered vacant, but after some hesitation he accepted. However, it proved far more difficult to find a candidate willing to accept the archbishopric of Uppsala. On the suggestion of king and Council, the chapter in Uppsala first elected Mårten Skytte, and when he refused, they chose Sven Jacobi who could not be tempted to accept either. Finally, Laurentius Petri a younger brother of the reformer, Olaus Petri, was elected and accepted in September 1531.

As the 1529 revolt encouraged Gustav Vasa to break off all contact with the exiled, conservative bishops, so it caused him to adopt a far less

---

[89] Kjöllerström, 'Västgötaherrarnas uppror', 43–67.   [90] *Ibid.*, 87–8.

pro-evangelical policy for most of the 1530s. From the autumn of 1529 he moved closer to the views held by the Christian humanist Catholics he had promoted to the bishoprics, especially Sven Jacobi, who became a member of the Council. Likewise, the king also began to offer the church greater protection against the encroachments of the nobility and the royal administrators. It is no coincidence that these policies coincided with the fall from royal favour of the two leading Swedish reformers, Laurentius Andreae and Olaus Petri.[91]

Meanwhile the new, reformist generation of Swedish bishops took the opportunity, while assembling for the royal wedding, to pursue their own agenda. As much as they had proved willing collaborators with the king in the demise of the church's political and economic power, they were, at least theoretically, committed to the defence of the doctrines of the church. The only two consecrated bishops, Magnus Sommar and Peder Månsson, drew up a secret document, probably inspired by the only remaining Catholic stalwart, the canon, Peder Galle, in which they condemned the 'Lutheran heresy' and the changes within the Swedish church, including the approaching consecration of the new archbishop. They then convinced two of the the newly elected bishops, Johannes Boecii and Sven Jacobi, to join them and to promise to seek papal confirmation of their elections at the first possible moment. Only the elected bishop of Linköping, Jöns Magni, did not take part in this affirmation of the traditional, doctrinal and ecclesiastical position of the Swedish church.[92]

However, this document was never acted upon, and the humanist/re-formist, Catholic bishops proved as easy to control and mould for the crown as they had been during the 1520s, when Hans Brask had tried to provide strong leadership. Whether or not the reformists managed to delay the introduction of a full Reformation in Sweden for a generation, until the introduction of the Protestant Church Order in 1571, or only for a decade until 1540, when an evangelical church government was introduced by the Wittenberg theologian, Georg Norman, is debatable. The prominence of the reformist bishops during the 1530s is probably best explained by the need for Gustav Vasa to pursue a middle course in church affairs, which could be presented as truly Catholic to the conservative peasantry, while simultaneously not being perceived as openly hostile by the growing evangelical movement in the towns. Sven Jacobi and his colleagues appear to have served this royal purpose excellently.

[91] Grell, 'Scandinavia', 115.   [92] Holmquist, *Svenska Kyrkan*, III, 216–17.

The exiled bishops in Danzig, Hans Brask, Johannes Magnus and Magnus Haraldsson continued to work for the Catholic cause, not only in Sweden, but in the whole of Scandinavia. Both Johannes and Olaus Magnus were active in prompting the *Curia* to initiate attempts to recatholicise Denmark in the late 1540s and 1550s.[93] Furthermore, the considerable literary output by the two brothers may well be seen as one long campaign to draw Scandinavia in general, and Sweden in particular, to the attention of the leaders of the Counter Reformation in Rome.[94] In this respect the efforts of the exiled Swedish prelates were significant in retaining Counter Reformation interest in Scandinavia throughout the Reformation period.

When Christian II, who had returned to Catholicism in 1530, began his military campaign to regain his Scandinavian kingdoms in 1531, the Swedish population was not only urged by the exiled archbishop of Uppsala, Gustav Trolle, to receive him as their rightful king, but also by one of the exiles in Danzig, bishop Magnus Haraldsson, who had recently sworn him loyalty. Johannes Magnus, on the other hand, stayed clear of political adventurism and remained loyal to Gustav Vasa, while Hans Brask appears to have been close to supporting Christian II.[95]

A couple of years later, following the death of Frederik I, when the leaders of the Danish church were trying to initiate a Catholic revival, Johannes Magnus approached his Danish colleagues, asking for their help in restoring the exiles to their sees in Sweden. He was brushed off by the Danish bishops, who pointed out to him that the misfortunes of the Swedish prelates were of their own making. In contrast to them, the Danes relied on their superior birth and noble family and friends. Seen at the time, the Danish prelates' interpretation of the predicament of the Swedish bishops must have rung true. Three years later, however, when the Danish bishops found themselves imprisoned by Christian III, while the Swedish exiles in Danzig tried to persuade Duke Albrecht of Prussia and King Sigismund of Poland to intercede on their behalf, they may well have regretted their earlier pride.[96] Furthermore, in the autumn of 1536, they would have realised that noble birth and blood connections counted for little in a changing Scandinavia where the social and political trends favoured Protestantism.

[93] See M. Schwarz Lausten, *Religion og Politik. Studier i Christian IIIs forhold til det tyske rige i tiden 1544–1559*, Copenhagen 1977, 193–4 and 341–2.

[94] O. Garstein, *Rome and the Counter-Reformation in Scandinavia*, I, Oslo 1963, 12–21.

[95] K. Johannesson, *The Renaissance of the Goths in Sixteenth-Century Sweden. Johannes and Olaus Magnus as Politicians and Historians*, Berkeley 1982, 32.

[96] *Ibid.*, 67.

CHAPTER 5

The consolidation of Lutheranism in Denmark and Norway

Thorkild Lyby and Ole Peter Grell

When the Reformation king, Christian III, died in 1559, an era had come to an end. By then most of the evangelical/Lutheran theologians who had worked for the Reformation in Denmark had either died or were to pass away within the next couple of years.[1]

Christian III was succeeded by his son, Frederik II (1559–88), who differed substantially from his father. Christian had been a godly and politically cautious monarch, whose reign had been determined to a large extent by the economic restraints imposed by the civil war (1534–6) which had preceded his accession to the throne in 1536.[2] Frederik II proved both politically and militarily far more adventurous. He may not have differed from his father in religious outlook, but in personal commitment he did, and he was less directly involved in the affairs of the new Lutheran church in Denmark and Norway than his father had been. Frederik's reign was characterised by the growing influence of the nobility, which was the only estate represented on the Council (*Rigsrådet*) after the Reformation. In spite of having been hailed as his father's successor in Denmark in 1542, and in Norway in 1548, Frederik II had to accept a coronation charter in August 1559 which confirmed and augmented the power of the nobility.

Frederik had already demonstrated his political and military ambitions when he, together with his uncle, Duke Adolph of Gottorp, conquered the Ditmarshes in the summer of 1559. This campaign served as a dress rehearsal for the realisation of his dream to re-establish the Union of the Scandinavian Kingdoms under his personal rule, which was all part of a greater scheme to gain total control over the Baltic region. Consequently, Frederik attacked Sweden in 1563 and initiated the Seven Years War. Apart from financially exhausting both kingdoms,

---

[1] Frants Vormordsen died in 1551; Peder Laurentsen in 1552; Jørgen Jensen Sadolin in 1559; Peder Palladius in 1560 and finally Hans Tausen in 1561, see *DBL*.
[2] For Christian III, see chapter 2.

the war proved inconclusive. Retrospectively, however, it can be seen to be the start of more than a century of inter-Scandinavian rivalry and war, which eventually served to remove Denmark from her position as the dominant power in the north and to replace her with Sweden.[3]

The end of the Seven Years War with Sweden and a general European economic boom which led to a growing demand for Danish agricultural products, boosted the economy and made the second half of Frederik II's reign a prosperous and felicitous period for the country. It resulted in a cultural and educational renaissance in Denmark, more often than not guided and promoted by a small circle of influential noble administrators. Particularly influential were the Lord High Stewart, Peder Oxe, whose financial acumen was instrumental in the economic revival which took place from 1570 onwards, and the chancellor, Niels Kaas. Both keenly supported the major cultural and educational initiatives during the second half of Frederik II's reign. After Oxe's death in 1575, this policy was continued by Kaas and others, during most of the regency leading up to the rule of Christian IV.[4] Included in this circle was the naval commander, Herluf Trolle, whose proverbial emphasis on the national duties of the nobility as a natural corollary to their privileges offers insight into the motives of these men. Their policies, combined with Frederik II's support, secured the start of a golden age of learning in Denmark, which produced a number of famous scholars, of whom the most internationally famous was the astronomer, Tycho Brahe, while figures of purely national importance such as the minister and historian, Anders Sørensen Vedel, should not be overlooked.[5]

Theologically, the period which started with the accession of Frederik II and lasted until the beginning of the seventeenth century, may be termed Melanchthonian or Philippist. By the time Frederik II was enthroned the most necessary regulations for a Protestant national church were in place. The ecclesiastical structure is probably best described as Erastian or a state church. Legally and institutionally, as well as economically, the new Protestant church in Denmark and Norway was inseparable from the state. The break with Rome and the Reformation had been introduced by the king and Council, and institutionally the new Lutheran church was an arm of the state.

[3] H. Gamrath and E. Ladewig Petersen, *Gyldendals Danmarkshistorie*, II, part II, Copenhagen 1980, 359 and 443-78.
[4] For Peder Oxe and Niels Kaas, see *DBL*, 3rd edition.
[5] For Herluf Trolle, Tycho Brahe and Anders Sørensen Vedel, see *DBL*. For the cultural renaissance in general, see O. P. Grell. 'Caspar Bartholin and the Education of the Pious Physician', in O. P. Grell and C. Cunningham (eds.), *Medicine and the Reformation*, London 1993, 78-100.

This state of affairs does not appear to have worried the ecclesiastical leaders of the day. They saw the church as constituted by the preaching of the gospel and the administration of the sacraments and not by the sanctity of ecclesiastical office. Accordingly, they found the close relationship with the crown unproblematic. The king was in full control of the ecclesiastical administration. He expected the clergy, as loyal servants of the crown, to provide the necessary religious legitimation of his rule. However, if royal supremacy meant influence, it also meant liability for the crown. The responsibility for keeping up the ecclesiastical apparatus and for providing parishes with pastors rested with the king. It was his responsibility to secure the undisturbed practice of all ecclesiastical functions. This was what the churchmen wanted, and evidently they considered it a matter of course to be loyal to a godly government which made it possible for them to work in peace in 'the Lord's vineyard'.

DENMARK

This view would have been further enhanced by the Philippist Lutheranism which was the dominant theology of the age in Denmark. It meant that the king was considered *custos utriusque tabulae legis*. He was, in other words, responsible not only for the regulation of society, but also for the spiritual welfare of his subjects, i.e. for their religion. According to the Lutheran clergy, a good king should model himself on Old Testament kings, like David, Solomon, Hezekiah and Josiah.[6] For them responsibility and power went hand in hand.

Furthermore, it has to be remembered that the concept of law did not occupy exactly the same position in the theology of Melanchthon and his pupils, as in Luther's. In practice the Philippists did not distinguish as sharply between law and gospel as Luther, and consequently they did not retain the separation of the two regiments either. They considered Christianity as much a matter of beliefs and morals as of faith and evangelical liberty, and consequently their teaching came to serve as a conservative element and a stabiliser in society. Through the practical identification of Christian virtues with civil loyalty, the teaching in the churches could become a consolidator of the existing social order and an upholder of social discipline, as imposed and enforced by the government.

With hindsight it may seem surprising that it was never stated at the Reformation which confession should be normative in Denmark. It has,

---

[6] M. Schwarz Lausten, *Christian 3. og Kirken*, Copenhagen 1987, 120.

however, to be borne in mind that the first generation of reformers neither imagined nor wanted a split of the occidental church into a number of competing Christian churches. Instead, they wanted to cleanse the Christian church of all its medieval aberrations and restore it to its original purity. They considered this an unambiguous goal and they saw no need to explain what sort of Christianity they had in mind.

In spite of this lack of clarity, there can be no doubt that the reformers considered the Augsburg Confession normative for Denmark. It was the implicit presupposition of the church Ordinance of 1537/9.[7] Later in 1538 the Augsburg Confession was mentioned as the basis of the alliance between Christian III and the Schmalkaldic League.[8] Likewise, Christian III repeatedly stated in his letters, that he would tolerate no doctrine which was at variance with it.[9] However, the Augsburg Confession was not directly referred to in any Danish law until the Strangers' Articles of 1569, and not until 1665 was its normative character established in the Danish constitution.

Because the Reformation resulted in a break-up of the church, it made the establishment of some form of authoritative formula imperative. The doctrinal quarrels which followed within the Lutheran camp accentuated this need further. As early as 1561, the German evangelical princes made an abortive attempt to reach a common policy at a conference in Naumburg. Frederik II, who had been invited, stayed away from this meeting. The king's decision to have a Danish confession drawn up at the same time as an account of the ecclesiastical system in the country – in other words, a new Church Ordinance – may well have been a consequence of this invitation.[10]

These two documents were ready for publication in 1561. Both of them were written in a clear and lucid style with exact definitions. If we compare the second part of the proposals with the Church Ordinance of 1537/9, they constitute a major improvement as far as clarity, balance and beauty of style is concerned. The proposed confession refers specifically to the Augsburg Confession and has a strong anti-Catholic tenor. It is Lutheran in doctrine, but a considerable Melanchthonian tendency is recognisable on several important points. The author's name is not known, but it may well have been Niels Hemmingsen.

[7] M. Schwarz Lausten (ed.), *Kirkeordinansen 1537/39*, Copenhagen 1989, 136 and 230.

[8] L. Laursen (ed.), *Danmark-Norges Traktater*, I, Copenhagen 1907, 279.

[9] C. F. Wegener (ed.), *Aarsberetninger fra det Kongelige Geheimearchiv*, I, (Copenhagen 1852–5), 271, 280, 282, 283, 284, 286, 288, 293.

[10] B. Kornerup (ed.), *Confessio et Ordinatio ecclesiarum Danicarum anno MDLXI*, Copenhagen 1953, XX–XXII.

Considering the strength and clarity of this document, it is surprising that it was never authorised, but was shelved and forgotten until it was published in the 1950s. The reason for this is probably to be found in the personal attitude of Frederik II, who was conservative in religious matters and anxious not to introduce any changes to the Reformation established by his father. This was already evident in 1560, when he assured Queen Elizabeth of England that he would, in the spirit of his father, oppose all errors and protect the true religion.[11] Worries about generating unwanted religious debate within the kingdom, even when clarification and strengthening of orthodoxy was the intended objective, probably convinced Frederik II that the risks of introducing a new church order were greater than the possible benefits.

It is symptomatic of Frederik II's reign that a deep fear of religious unrest characterised his church policy. Doubts concerning the accepted religious truths were not tolerated. The differences which existed between Luther and Melanchthon were ignored, and a simple reference to the Augsburg Confession was considered sufficient.

Initially, the most serious threats against this policy of uniformity seemed to come from abroad. Consequently, the government took steps to guard the kingdom against the entry of heretical influences. As early as 1537/9 the Church Ordinance had introduced a general censorship, prohibiting the printing and importation of books in Danish, Latin and German which had not received the prior approval of the university and the superintendents/bishops.[12] As theological strife in Lutheran Germany flared up, there was good reason to renew this precaution. Thus during 1562 the government realised that unapproved books were imported from Germany, which might represent a danger for both the true religion and the purity of the Danish language. Consequently, a new general censorship of books, administered by the university, was created to protect both language and religion. The printing of approved Danish books was monopolised by printers in Copenhagen. Evidently the censorship proved difficult to enforce and in 1576 the import ban was reiterated, emphasising the need for strict observance.[13]

Immigration was also perceived to represent a threat to uniformity. Already in 1553 the fear of Anabaptists and 'Sacramentarians' (Calvinists) had induced Christian III to issue injunctions forbidding foreigners to settle in Denmark and Norway, unless they could give satisfactory

---

[11] *Calendar of State papers, Foreign, Elizabeth I*, III, London 1865, no. 181.
[12] *Kirkeordinansen*, 136 and 231.
[13] H. F. Rørdam (ed.), *Danske Kirkelove*, I–III, Copenhagen 1883–9, II, 59–61 and 264–6.

accounts of their beliefs. The arrival in Copenhagen of nearly 200 refugee members of the Dutch Reformed church in London, under the leadership of Johannes a Lasco, made the problem still more poignant. In 1555 the prohibition was renewed with threats of capital punishment for both the heretics and those who sheltered them.[14]

A steady stream of religious exiles from the Netherlands had begun to arrive in Denmark in the wake of the sanguinary Counter Reformation begun by the duke of Alva in 1567. It was rumoured that Anabaptist and Sacramentarian services were held among them, and in June 1569 the king ordered the professors of the university to investigate the matter. A consequence of this investigation appears to have been the drawing up of a confession of twenty-five articles. It was authorised only a few months after the professors had begun their investigation and was posted on the doors of major churches and guildhalls. All foreigners were ordered to subscribe to the articles or leave the country within three days.[15]

As mentioned above, these so-called Strangers' Articles constitute the first officially binding Danish confession. They were presented as a supplement to the three creeds of the early church and the Augsburg Confession, which by implication became officially binding for Denmark and Norway. Like the draft confession of 1561, they are strongly anti-Catholic, and best characterised as moderately Melanchthonian. Their author was undoubtedly the country's leading theologian, Niels Hemmingsen.

During the following years the Strangers' Articles were used regularly by the government. It proved impossible to seal off a country as dependent on commerce as Denmark, and consequently the question of foreigners and their beliefs came up several times during the following years. Generally it was in relation to the major trading towns of Copenhagen, Malmø and Elsinore, which traditionally, owing to their strategic position on the Sound, had considerable immigrant populations. Later in the century the problem of heterodoxy was not restricted to Dutch settlers, but included Englishmen and Scots as well, who had a strong presence in Elsinore in particular.

In the long term it also proved impossible for the government to prevent all differences of religious opinion from surfacing internally.

---

[14] *Danske Kirkelove*, I, 362–3 and 485–8. For the arrival in Copenhagen of the Marian refugees led by Johannes a Lasco, see M. Schwarz Lausten, *Biskop Peder Palladius og Kirken 1537–1560*, Copenhagen 1987, 206–24.
[15] E. Pontoppidan, *Annales Ecclesiæ Danicæ Diplomatici*, III, Copenhagen 1747, 416–21 (Latin); *Danske Kirkelove*, II, 126–34 (Danish).

However strong the notion of uniformity, and however strict the orders given to the clergy not to dispute publicly on dangerous subjects, the theological differences could not remain concealed. Eventually, such differences led to the suspension of Niels Hemmingsen, the most famous Danish theologian of the early modern period from his chair in theology.

Niels Hemmingsen (1513–1600), who had inherited the position as the country's leading theologian after Peder Palladius' death in 1560, had studied in Wittenberg under Philip Melanchthon.[16] He became professor of Greek in Copenhagen around 1543, and in 1553 he was appointed professor of divinity. For more than twenty years he was the most prominent figure within the university, which he served as vice-chancellor (*Rektor*) on several occasions. Hemmingsen was immensely productive as a theological author, publishing a series of works aimed not only at the university, but also at the people and the church. While he was celebrated as the general teacher of Denmark (*praeceptor universalis Daniae*), the impact of his works was not limited to his own country. Most of his books were written in Latin, which made them accessible to foreign scholars, and soon they were to be found in libraries all over northern and western Europe. As mentioned above, Hemmingsen was for years entrusted by the government with drawing up normative documents, when needed.

By the mid-1570s, however, it was no longer possible to keep Denmark insulated from the doctrinal strife in Germany. The most serious episode was the controversy over crypto-Calvinism, where the so-called gnesio-Lutherans accused Melanchthon and his disciples of Calvinist tendencies in their doctrine of the eucharist.[17] Undoubtedly there was some justification for this accusation in the case of Hemmingsen. For example, in his *Demonstratio* of 1571 he bitterly opposed the tenet of ubiquity, which was an integral part of the teaching of Melanchthon's opponents.[18] In 1574 he published his great *Syntagma*, which was a general exposition of the Christian doctrine, and which can be considered his major work. Here his teaching on the eucharist is certainly Calvinistic.[19]

This caused Frederik II to intervene. Hemmingsen was summoned to the castle in Copenhagen and reprimanded; a few days later the clergy

---

[16] For Niels Hemmingsen, see *DBL*.

[17] For a recent introduction to these issues, see R. Po-Chia Hsia, *Social Discipline in the Reformation: Central Europe 1550–1750*, London 1989, 28–32.

[18] N. Hemmingsen, *Demonstratio indubitatæ veritatis de Domino Jesu vero Deo et vero homine unico Christo, Mediatore atque Redemtore nostro unico*, Copenhagen 1571.

[19] N. Hemmingsen, *Syntagma institutionum christianarum perspicuis assertionibus ex doctrina prophetica et apostolica congestis, plerisque propositis et disputatis in Acad. Hafniensi*, Copenhagen 1574.

were ordered to stick to the Augsburg Confession, and to avoid new and subtle disputations on the sacraments or other tenets. However, the question of Hemmingsen's orthodoxy quickly acquired international significance. In Germany passions ran high, and the strife was exacerbated by the fact that the Religious Peace of Augsburg in 1555 only legalised Lutheranism within the German Empire which was in accordance with the Augsburg Confession. Accordingly, Crypto-Calvinism could be considered a political crime, and princely protection or toleration of it could have political repercussions.

In 1574 the elector, August of Saxony, who was married to Frederik II's sister, became aware that the theologians in Wittenberg consisted predominantly of crypto-Calvinists. He took action against them while they tried to defend themselves by pointing to the famous Danish theologian, Niels Hemmingsen, who shared their views. The elector reacted by sending Frederik II a copy of Hemmingsen's *Syntagma*, advising him to restrain this gross Sacramentarian and Calvinist. Neither did he forget to remind his brother-in-law that Calvinism was considered politically subversive.

Frederik II realised that action was urgently needed. In 1575 he called a meeting of the professors of the university, the clergy in Copenhagen, and three prominent noblemen, who represented the crown. Under pain of death the theologians and clergy were ordered to stick to the Augsburg Confession, while Hemmingsen was ordered to retract his heterodox statements in *Syntagma*. Hemmingsen, however, tried to defend his position, and although there were differences of opinion, a compromise seemed possible.

But in 1576 new letters arrived from Saxony, which made the king request Hemmingsen to recant immediately. A series of dramatic and painful meetings followed, where Hemmingsen tried to avoid the humiliation. Eventually he was forced to yield and to ask the king to be forgiven. A public recantation was prepared, but it had to be re-drafted several times before it proved acceptable to Frederik II.

Finally, the matter seemed settled. However, the elector of Saxony was not yet satisfied, and more complaints arrived from him and his wife. Frederik II retorted angrily, but when in 1578 a fresh edition of *Syntagma* was published in Geneva, it mattered little that Hemmingsen had not been involved, and protests were received from the king's mother-in-law, Duchess Anna of Mecklenburg. They were supplemented by further complaints from the elector and in June 1579 Hemmingsen was suspended. This amounted to a *de facto* dismissal since Hemmingsen was never re-instated in his professorship. Hemmingsen's fall was clearly politically motivated, and it was a severe blow to the university that it should be deprived of its most famous teacher on such grounds. The experience was, of course, also extremely painful for Hemmingsen himself, but it could have been worse. Since his suspension had been primarily dictated by foreign policy, Hemmingsen's reputation was untarnished. He took up residence in Roskilde, where he held a canonry. Here he could continue his studies in peace, though he could no longer teach. Despite being removed from his professorship, he was still held in high esteem by colleagues at home and abroad. He even participated in the drawing up of the substantial Marriage Act of 1582 – by which divorce and re-marriage was made possible in Denmark.[20] On this occasion he drew upon the Genevan Church Ordinances of Calvin. In 1590 when James VI of Scotland visited the country, he travelled down to Roskilde in order to discuss theological matters with Hemmingsen.[21]

As the doctrinal strife had direct political implications, the German Lutheran princes could not leave their theologians to fight it out between themselves. Consequently, they put pressure on them to obtain some sort of agreement, and in 1577 the Formula of Concord was drawn up. Undoubtedly the gnesio-Lutherans achieved most; yet the Formula proved a viable method of settling the controversies. In 1580, fifty years of the Augsburg Confession were celebrated by a publication of all the recognised creeds of the Lutheran churches including the Formula of Concord. This collection, the *Book of Concord*, became the basis of Lutheran orthodoxy, which was to dominate the cultural life of Lutheran Germany and Scandinavia during most of the seventeenth century.

Considering Frederik II's strong reaction against crypto-Calvinism, it might have been expected that he would have welcomed the Formula of Concord. However, that was not the case. A number of factors, such as his conservatism in religious matters, political considerations and, of course, the risk of generating a theological schism, may have caused him to take a dim view of the Formula. From the outset the king refused to be involved. He rejected the request of the elector to let Danish theologians participate in the preparatory work, and all subsequent attempts from Germany to make him change his mind proved futile.

By then, however, Frederik II was also under pressure from other rulers. In May 1577 the Formula was accepted by the German Lutheran princes. Five months later, Queen Elizabeth of England sent a letter to

[20] *Danske Kirkelove*, II, 339–53.
[21] H. F. Rørdam, *Kjøbenhavns Universitets Historie fra 1537–1621*, II, Copenhagen 1872, 433.

Frederik, protesting against the anathematising of other Protestants who were close to the Lutherans, although they did not agree with them on every doctrinal point. That attitude, she pointed out, would only lead to a strengthening of the pope.[22] Frederik forwarded this letter to the elector, who was still busily engaged in winning him over to his side. Frederik's mind, however, was made up. He was not prepared to abandon the middle course he had chosen, nor would he give up friendly relations with commercially important nations such as England. Consequently, he rejected the Formula.[23]

Similarly he kept up friendly relations with the Huguenot king, Henry of Navarre, who later became king of France under the name of Henry IV. He sympathised with Henry's efforts to create a comprehensive Protestant alliance against the Counter Reformation, and in 1586 he sent an expeditionary force to assist Henry in the religious wars in France.[24]

Furthermore, when the *Book of Concord* was published, Frederik II did not disguise his dislike of gnesio-Lutheranism. Under pain of death it was prohibited to possess or import this work into Denmark, and when his sister sent him two magnificent copies, he personally saw to it that they were burnt 'on a good hearth fire'. Thus, through this mini *auto-da-fé*, Frederik II made sure that the religious order created by his father was preserved.[25]

NORWAY

In Norway the consolidation of Lutheranism followed a different route from that in Denmark. There had been little if any popular support for the evangelical cause, and the Reformation was primarily an act of government. The Norwegian clergy remained solidly Catholic throughout the Reformation period while most of the bishops had been thoroughly compromised during the civil war from 1534 to 1536. Accordingly, the government was faced with the difficult task of converting a predominantly Catholic church, which had been purged of its leaders, and a conservative Catholic population to Lutheranism.

Prudence dictated a slow and cautious approach under such circumstances in order to keep clashes with ancient rites and teachings to a minimum, without losing sight of the ultimate objective. Government

---

[22] Pontoppidan, *Annales*, III, 472–4.
[23] H. F. Rørdam, 'Kirkelige Forhold og Personligheder i Kong Frederik II's Tid', in *Kirkehistoriske Samlinger*, Series 2, 4 (1867–8), 253–75.
[24] Pontoppidan, *Annales*, III, 502–3.
[25] *Danske Kirkelove*, II, 322–3 and *Kjøbenhavns Universitet*, II, 209–10.

officials were expressly instructed to act cautiously, while the government's policy was determined by the wish to avoid all controversy in religious matters. It is characteristic that the first Lutheran superintendent/bishop of Bergen, Geble Pederssøn, who was appointed in 1537, had originally been elected by the chapter as their Catholic bishop in 1535. Pederssøn seems to have been a Christian humanist with very little knowledge of Lutheranism, who was happy to ease the transition from one ecclesiastical system to another. An even more striking example is Hans Reff, who had served the see of Oslo as its Catholic bishop from 1525 until his resignation in 1537. As it proved impossible to find another suitable candidate, he was appointed superintendent of the combined dioceses of Oslo and Hamar in 1541.[26]

The archbishopric of Trondheim remained vacant for no less than nine years. It was not filled until Torbjørn Olavssøn Bratt was appointed superintendent in 1546. This delay was probably dictated by political considerations. The government may well have concluded that a transition from Catholicism to Lutheranism would be smoother in Norway without an incumbent of the old archbishopric, who might be tempted to provide the leadership which traditionally had been associated with Trondheim. The example of its last Catholic archbishop, Olav Engelbriktsson, who died in exile in 1538, would have served as a warning to the government. A new incumbent might so easily be encouraged to emulate his troublesome predecessor. Torbjørn Olavssøn, however, proved to be not only a well-educated Lutheran, but also a loyal servant to the crown, well suited for the cumbrous work of reforming his diocese.

It is noteworthy that apart from Hans Reff, the first generation of Lutheran superintendents/bishops in Norway were all Norwegians, as opposed to later in the century when practically all the bishops were Danes. At this later stage the government in Copenhagen may have felt confident enough to pursue a more determined Lutheran course, but found it difficult to find enough Norwegian theologians who were either sufficiently familiar with Lutheran thought or considered to be confessionally reliable enough to implement such a policy.

However, the fact that they were Danish does not appear to have caused the bishops any problems. Several of them proved successful in promoting evangelical Christianity, often under difficult circumstances. Frants Berg, who was bishop of Oslo and Hamar from 1548 to 1580, and who had supported the evangelical cause in Denmark before the official

---

[26] For Hans Reff, see chapter 4.

introduction of the Reformation, did much to improve the financial situation and standard of education among the clergy. Hans Gaas, who succeeded Torbjørn Olavssøn in Trondheim in 1549, tried to remedy the lack of a Church Ordinance for Norway by adapting an old Norwegian church law in 1559, as a temporary expedient. Jens Skjelderup, who succeeded Geble Pederssøn as bishop of Bergen in 1557, worked hard to improve the training and education of the clergy while trying to rid the country of the remnants of Catholicism. In 1570 he clashed with the town council of Bergen over the removal of images of saints.[27]

Most influential of them all was Skjelderup's son-in-law, Jørgen Erickssøn, who became bishop of the much neglected diocese of Stavanger in 1571. Through his diocesan synods and his visitations, he managed to promote evangelical teachings and the significance of his work can be seen from the fact that he was labelled 'the Norwegian Luther'.[28] Through his sermons, which were published in 1592, Erickssøn became immensely influential in the whole of Norway. Another son-in-law, Jens Nielssøn, who had been headmaster of the Latin school in Oslo, initially served as an assistant for his father-in-law, Frants Berg, succeeding him in 1580. Nielssøn's visitation books show him to be a dedicated and effective supervisor of his diocese, while his sermons reveal the strong theological influence of Niels Hemmingsen.[29]

On the whole, the attitude among the post-Reformation Norwegian clergy resembled that of their Danish colleagues. Ideologically they found it unproblematic to undertake the change from a late medieval type of Catholicism, which more often than not was influenced by Christian humanism, to a 'liberal' Philippist variety of Lutheranism most poignantly represented by the kingdom's leading theologian, Niels Hemmingsen. As in Denmark, Calvinism or crypto-Calvinism also found adherents in Norway. Thus in 1571 Torleif Gregoriussen, who, at the expense of the chapter in Bergen, had studied at the University of St Andrews, was disciplined for Calvinistic teaching on the eucharist.

The Latin school in Oslo became a centre for a circle of Norwegian humanist scholars, not least through the efforts of its headmaster, Jens Nielssøn, while similar attempts to improve education and learning were

27 For Frants Berg, Hans Gaas, Torbjøn Olavssøn, Jens Skjelderup and Geble Pederssøn, see *NBL*. See also S. Imsen, *Superintendenten. En studie i kirkepolitik, kirkeadministrasjon og statsutvikling mellom reformasjonen og eneveldet*, Oslo 1982; and Lausten, *Peder Palladius*, 380–5.
28 For Jørgen Erickssøn, see *NBL* and chapter 7.
29 For Jens Nielssøn, see *NBL*.

undertaken in Bergen by Geble Pedersson. His foster-son, the historian, Absalon Pedersson, became the leader of a similar humanist circle to that in Oslo, the only difference being that the Bergen group came to represent a more nationally conscious tradition.

However, the necessary books and documents for the new Lutheran services and catechising remained scarce. Danish books were used to some extent, and in 1541 Peder Palladius had published an exposition of his catechism dedicated to Norwegian pastors.[30] The lack of any normative document for the new Lutheran church in Norway until the beginning of the seventeenth century clearly presented the bishops and their clergy with serious problems. Consequently, the government authorised the Norwegian bishops to draw up a Church Ordinance for the country. Their proposal, which differed from the Danish Church Ordinance, being specifically geared to Norwegian needs, was ready in 1604. It did not, however, appeal to the government in Copenhagen, which eventually, in 1607, decided to introduce a revised version of the Danish Church Ordinance. If, from a national point of view, this outcome was less than satisfactory to the Norwegians, they had, at least, finally received a much needed Church Ordinance. Its introduction can be seen as a sign that the Reformation had finally succeeded in Norway. From then on the religious developments in the country were to follow events in Denmark closely, while the interchange of personnel and ideas became so extensive that only minor variations can be seen.

THE REIGN OF CHRISTIAN IV

In 1596 Christian IV (1588–1648) had come of age and took control of the government from the regency. The young king's impressive energy and ability made him the centre of all government activity. Often he would be personally involved in political decisions down to the last administrative details. His direct involvement is strongly in evidence in the commercial policies undertaken during his reign, in his personal interest in the expansion of the navy – he even contributed to the design of several new ships – and his direct involvement in town planning. Christian IV's autocratic rule is probably best illustrated by the increasingly infrequent meetings of the Council (*Rigsrådet*), with whom he was obliged to rule (*Monarchia mixta*), not to mention the disappearance of the annual meeting of parliament (*Herredag*) after 1596. Likewise, his personal

---

[30] P. Palladius, *Brevis Expositio Catechismi*, Copenhagen 1541.

attempts to glorify the crown found an expression in his extensive building programme of castles and other buildings in the capital, Copenhagen.[31]

Christian IV continued the aggressive foreign policy which had characterised the first half of his father's reign. Like his father, he advocated a strongly anti-Swedish policy in order to dominate the Baltic region. His more conservative councillors were only able to hold the king back until 1611 when the so-called War of Kalmar (1611–13) with Sweden began. Victory in this confrontation, which saw a war indemnity of one million thalers imposed on Sweden, which was to be paid personally to Christian IV, must have encouraged him to continue to pursue an aggressive foreign policy. In 1625 he entered the Thirty Years War in support of the German Protestants for a mixture of religious, political and dynastic reasons. This proved a fateful decision which had disastrous consequences. The Danish army was defeated in 1626 and Jutland was occupied and devastated by Wallenstein's troops. Three years later, in May 1629, Christian IV signed a peace treaty with the emperor in Lübeck. The king escaped defeat lightly, having to pay no war reparations nor make any concessions on territory; by 1629, financially devastated by the campaign, the emperor was just as much in need of peace as Christian IV.

However, the defeat had been costly for king and kingdom – in financial terms the final bill was somewhere between six and eight million thalers, not to mention the cost of rebuilding a devastated Jutland. In political terms the defeat served to discredit Christian IV as a Protestant leader of international importance. Furthermore, coinciding as it did with Sweden's subsequent and successful intervention in the Thirty Years War under Gustavus Adolphus, the defeat came to constitute the end of any realistic hope of Denmark being able to dominate the Baltic region. Instead, Sweden became the dominant power in the north and punished Christian IV for his anti-Swedish diplomacy by occupying Jutland in 1643. Two years later Christian IV was forced to conclude the peace of Brömsebro which forced him to make heavy territorial concessions to Sweden: Denmark lost two important islands in the Baltic while Norway relinquished the provinces of Härjedalen and Jämtland. This proved only the first in a series of concessions to an increasingly dominant Sweden which from now on became the main power in Scandinavia.[32]

Coinciding and closely connected with the centralising tendencies of

[31] *Gyldendals Danmarkshistorie*, II, part II, 480–4.
[32] See G. Parker, *The Thirty Years War*, London 1984, 71–81.

the autocratic government of Christian IV, a change of church policy took place. The years from around 1600 to 1614 were marked by an increasingly bitter confrontation between the Melanchthonianism which had characterised the Danish church during the second half of the sixteenth century and the Lutheran orthodoxy which was to dominate the country for most of the seventeenth century. By 1614 the orthodox had gained a complete victory.

This development can be seen in parallel with, or even as part of, the political development. From the late Middle Ages a process of particularisation had taken place within western Christendom. The idea of the universal empire had never been successful in practice, and gradually the national or territorial states had asserted themselves as the basic political unity. At the Reformation, the occidental church had also been particularised, while secular power had taken over the political control of ecclesiastical life. In other words, western Christendom had been incorporated into the autonomous state.

However, the concept of society had never been secularised. It was still considered a divine construction and kings were still seen as reigning by divine right and on behalf of God. Consequently, enemies of kings were perceived to be enemies of God and true religion. Since religious antagonisms were intertwined with political conflicts, they only corroborated the sense of fighting godly wars against satanic adversaries.

The latter half of the sixteenth century and the first half of the seventeenth saw the resurgence of Catholicism following the disasters of the Reformation; and the Counter Reformation became increasingly politically influential. Heightened religious fervour guaranteed that religiously motivated wars became the dominant feature of the age. A general anxiety prevailed, generated more often than not by the perceived politico-religious threat from territorial states belonging to a hostile confession, which saw domestic policies being introduced in most European countries against religious heterodoxy and political deviance. Accordingly uniformity became the main preoccupation for most of the period's leading national churchmen and rulers. Doctrinal variations which had hitherto been tolerated were considered politically dangerous. In the case of Denmark and Norway, this meant the introduction of a strict orthodoxy at the expense of the less rigorous Melanchthonianism which had characterised Lutheranism in these countries since the 1560s.

The dominant figure of Danish orthodoxy was Hans Poulsen Resen. Born in 1561 in a remote part of Jutland, he was educated at the universities of Copenhagen, Rostock and Wittenberg where he graduated. Later he travelled to Italy, where he studied at Padua and visited Rome, Sicily and Malta. On his journey home he stayed briefly in the Calvinist stronghold of Geneva. On his return to Copenhagen in 1591, he was appointed professor of dialectics. Three years later he was elected dean of the faculty of arts. By 1597 his career had progressed further; he became doctor of divinity and was appointed to one of the two chairs in theology.

Little if anything is known about Resen's theological leanings in his early years. Some evidence, however, would indicate that until his appointment to the theological faculty, Resen remained anchored in the Philippist tradition with its associated crypto-Calvinist tendencies which had dominated the Lutheran church in Denmark for decades. By the turn of the century Resen had changed his position and had become an advocate of Lutheran uniformity. Personal experiences and studies of the Bible, Augustine, German mysticism and Luther may well have brought about this change. By 1605 Resen had changed into a staunch champion of a Lutheran orthodoxy which was bitterly opposed to Calvinism. The effects of this theological re-orientation proved detrimental to a number of his colleagues who continued to hold crypto-Calvinist views, since Resen was soon to lead the government's drive for uniformity within church and state.

The new translation of the Bible into Danish which appeared in 1607, was the first fruit of Hans Poulsen Resen's attempt to impose his brand of Lutheranism on the whole nation. From the start of the Reformation, the vernacular Bible had been an essential part of the new Lutheran church and two translations had already been completed before Resen's edition, the so-called Christian III's Bible (1550) and Frederik II's Bible (1589). Both these Bibles were magnificent and costly books which would be an ornament to any church. They were, however, very expensive to buy and therefore beyond the reach of the average Christian. Furthermore, they were not flawless and were open to scholarly criticism since they had not been translated from the original Hebrew and Greek texts, but were mainly re-translations of Luther's German translations.

In 1603 Christian IV ordered the university to take responsibility for an edition of a new Danish Bible where all faults had been corrected. As the professors were well aware that suspicion of heterodoxy might emerge from quite harmless corrections, they, at first, tried to excuse themselves. Eventually, in 1604, Resen undertook the task and within three years he had completed the huge work. Compared with the previous editions, Resen's Bible was a modest book. It was clearly intended for ordinary people. Textually, however, it was a pioneering work. Originally, Resen had only intended to produce a revision of the two previous Danish Bibles. Eventually, he ended up comparing them with the original Hebrew and Greek texts and wherever he found discrepancies, he followed the originals. He adhered to this principle even in cases where the discrepancies originated from his esteemed Luther. In effect, Resen produced the first translation of the Bible into Danish, from the original Hebrew and Greek texts, even if he was greatly assisted by the work of Luther and his Danish predecessors.

Due to his skills in the ancient languages, Resen was able to remain faithful to the original text. Unfortunately, his scholarly concerns did not always result in the clearest translation. Furthermore, Resen was not a great writer in the vernacular and his Bible often proves cumbersome reading. Nevertheless, his work remained an important tool for later Danish translations of the Bible well into the twentieth century.

Resen's newly found orthodoxy was prominently displayed in 1607, when he tackled the question of exorcism. The Lutheran church had taken over the ritual exorcism preceding baptism from Catholicism. Luther had been in doubt whether or not to retain it, but had eventually opted in favour. Melanchthon had considered it to be of no significance. During the doctrinal strifes within Lutheranism it had become evident that Luther's theology was marked by a distrust of the intellect and a passionate irrationalism with an inclination to paradoxes, while Melanchthon emphasised the concept of the church as *ecclesia doxtrix* – a doctrinal community – and consequently opted for intellectual clarity and rationality. Thus, exorcism became a bone of contention between the factions. The Melanchthonians wanted to abolish it, because they considered it to be a manifestation of superstition. The gnesio-Lutherans wanted to keep it, because they considered it to be a consequence of the doctrine of original sin. What had been a matter of indifference grew into a shibboleth.

Exorcism had been preserved in the Church Ordinance 1537/9 and in the service book of 1556, but gradually under the influence of Niels Hemmingsen many clergymen became dissatisfied with it, and some of Hemmingsen's pupils wanted it abolished. In 1567 the minister of Stege, Iver Bertelsen, stopped using the exorcism on his own initiative. He was dismissed from office, in spite of a very competent defence of his views, and later others were to follow him.

At the beginning of the seventeenth century, however, the Melanchthonian interpretation had begun to influence the royal family in

Denmark. In 1606 Christian IV ordered the professors of divinity and the bishops to submit their views on abolishing exorcism. Only a month later, when the answers of the theologians were not yet available, the king ordered Bishop Winstrup of Lund to omit the exorcism at the baptism of his daughter.[33]

Meanwhile the orthodox position was being strongly promoted by the two professors of theology, Jørgen Dybvad[34] and Hans Poulsen Resen, who both wanted to retain exorcism. Resen, who voiced his opinion in a thorough response, argued that exorcism was a time-honoured ecclesiastical tradition, which had nothing to do with superstition, but served to comfort many of those baptised for the rest of their lives.

The bishops had their doubts, but dared not advise abolition, faced, as they were, with the adamant Resen. This all happened while the Norwegian Church Ordinance was being prepared. In the draft version exorcism was left out. However, Resen objected, and his personal power and influence were already so great that he managed to have it reinstated. In 1607 Bishop Winstrup found it necessary to impress on his pastors that exorcism was not to be omitted. The first open confrontation between orthodoxy and Philippism in Denmark ended in victory for orthodoxy. Consequently, exorcism was preserved in the Danish liturgy until 1783. The Philippist view, however, survived within the royal family where princes and princesses continued to be baptised without exorcism.

During the following years a series of different religious controversies and cases emerged which served to strengthen Resen's personal position as well as to consolidate orthodoxy. First came the deposition in 1607 of Resen's cantankerous colleague within the theological faculty, Jørgen Dybvad. Officially, Dybvad lost his job because he had overstepped his powers and neglected his office through his sharp criticism of the government's policy. Theological questions were not mentioned, but Dybvad was known to have crypto-Calvinist leanings. Furthermore, his downfall considerably strengthened Resen's position within the faculty. It might not be too rash to suggest that Resen was involved in the affair which fitted neatly into his plans for supremacy within the church.

However, Resen was openly involved in the next clash. In December 1608 he accused another professorial colleague, the equally quarrelsome Iver Stub, of violating university regulations, of Calvinist heterodoxy, and of an infringement of Resen's privilege on Bible printing. The last point was occasioned by the fact that Stub, in a treatise on the Book of

[33] For Winstrup, see *DBL*.   [34] For Dybvad, see *DBL*.

Job, had printed parts of Resen's translation paralleled by another by himself. The controversy was long and bitter and was finally resolved by Stub being deprived of his professorship in 1609. Stub subsequently left Denmark and died abroad two years later.

The antagonism between the two sides was now openly acknowledged and in 1613 Resen was virulently attacked by the Norwegian minister, Oluf Kock, who held a living in Copenhagen. Kock was undoubtedly a crypto-Calvinist and his coarse and aggressive attacks guaranteed that he could not be ignored, especially since in 1614 he personally lodged a complaint with the king, accusing Resen of heterodoxy.

Kock's assertive behaviour meant that his case developed along two lines. Firstly, after an investigation into the matter, Kock was suspended from office for insubordination against his bishop who, in vain, had tried to call him to order. Secondly, Kock's charges of heterodoxy against Resen necessitated the creation of a special court with ecclesiastical, as well as lay, members. It was presided over by the king, who intervened in the discussions in favour of Resen. After Kock had presented his accusations, Resen responded in detail. The court found that Kock's charges were totally unsubstantiated and that Resen was absolutely sound in doctrine. Consequently, Kock was banished from the kingdom. This was a sentence which was considered a mitigation of the capital punishment Kock might well have received.

Resen, however, was tackling other potential antagonists during 1614. He confronted his colleague in the divinity faculty, the Norwegian Cort Aslaksen, who inclined towards the crypto-Calvinist position. Aslaksen may in fact have been the instigator of Kock's action against Resen. However, finding himself under attack from his powerful colleague, Aslaksen gave in immediately and from then on toed the orthodox line adopted by Resen.[35]

Another offshoot of the Kock controversy was the case against Niels Mikkelsen Aalborg who was deposed as dean of Helsingborg. In 1616 Resen's relentless drive for uniformity saw his brother-in-law, the bishop of Funen, Hans Knudsen Vejle, deposed for crypto-Calvinism. The effects could be felt as late as 1620 when Dr Christopher Dybvad, a son of the above-mentioned Jørgen, lost his academic position in the university for both political and theological heterodoxy.

In effect, Resen's victory over Kock and Aslaksen in 1614 ended the struggle. Then, for the first time, the government clearly and officially

---

[35] For Aslaksen, see O. Garstein, *Cort Aslakssøn*, Oslo 1953.

accepted Lutheran orthodoxy at the expense of crypto-Calvinism. In 1615 Resen was elevated to the bishopric of Zealand, the highest office of the Danish church. Two years later he was able to celebrate the victory of orthodoxy and the centenary of the Reformation simultaneously, by publishing a history of the Reformation entitled *Lutherus triumphans*.[36]

The contest between Philippism and gnesio-Lutheranism was to a large extent characterised by the fear of Calvinism, combined with a deep worry about resurgent, Counter-Reformation Catholicism.

Obviously, Catholic traditions and rites remained part of popular beliefs and customs. Jens Skjelderup's troubles concerning the abolition of images have already been mentioned, and Christian IV was obliged to drink to St Olav during his travels in Norway. Catholic customs in Denmark survived the Reformation for at least a couple of generations.[37]

Rome had not entirely given up Scandinavia, either. In 1561 Pope Pius IV staged an invitation to the Danish and Swedish kings to participate in the third session of the Council of Trent. Frederik II, however, turned it down emphatically, even before the papal envoy had reached Denmark.[38] During the latter half of the sixteenth century the Jesuits played an increasingly important part in promoting the Counter Reformation. One of their strengths was education, where they developed a skill which won them European fame. There are indications that the Jesuits were active in Copenhagen as early as 1560 but, of course, at that time their possibilities were limited. With a view to the Scandinavian countries, they did, however, found colleges in nearby Catholic cities like Braunsberg and Vilna, and in the more distant Olmütz. Soon a fair number of gifted young Scandinavians were crossing the Baltic in order to get the best possible education.

At first nobody seems to have objected to this practice, and even sons of orthodox Danish churchmen, such as the hymn writer, Hans Christensen Sthen, were sent to Jesuit colleges.[39] However, as time passed it gradually dawned on the authorities that Jesuit education, disregarding its quality, could influence students to embrace Catholicism. A substantial proportion of the students converted and later returned home to continue their studies at the University of Copenhagen or to take up employment as ministers and schoolmasters in Norway and Denmark.

---

[36] See B. Kornerup, *Biskop Hans Poulsen Resen*, 2 vols., Copenhagen 1928 and 1968.
[37] See O. P. Grell, 'Scandinavia' in R. W. Scribner, R. Porter and M. Teich (eds.), *The Reformation in National Context*, Cambridge 1994 and chapter 7.
[38] *Confessio et Ordinatio*, XIX–XX, and O. Garstein, *Rome and the Counter-Reformation in Scandinavia*, I, Oslo 1963, 23–35.
[39] For Hans Christensen Sthen, see *DBL*.

Initially they were treated rather leniently by the authorities. Somehow the bitter controversy over crypto-Calvinism appears to have softened the attitude to Catholicism. It was, for instance, part of the accusations against Professor Jørgen Dybvad that he had treated the pope and Catholicism far too virulently in his writings. Gradually, however, apprehension grew. In 1604 Resen demanded that a student from one of the Jesuit colleges who wanted to study at the University of Copenhagen, should have his opinions on controversial points thoroughly examined and afterwards receive the eucharist according to the Lutheran tradition. From then on scholars from Jesuit colleges had to go through this procedure before they could be matriculated. Later that year the University of Copenhagen received an open letter which must have stunned the professors. After a moderate ecumenical introduction, the letter ended in a eulogy of Catholicism and a denunciation of Luther's teaching as the work of the devil. Its author was probably the Norwegian Jesuit, Laurentius Nicolai Norvegus, who had already been actively promoting the Counter Reformation in Sweden.[40] If Laurentius Nicolai had expected a reply, he must have been disappointed, since the professors chose to ignore his letter.

Meanwhile, the headmaster of the Latin school in Malmø, Jens Aagesen Raaby (Johannes Haggæus) had openly confessed his sympathy for Catholicism at an ecclesiastical meeting. This was too much for the authorities and Aagesen was dismissed. Later in October the government issued a prohibition against the employment of students, who had been educated at Jesuit colleges, as ministers and teachers in Denmark.[41] It had an immediate effect. The majority of Danish students stopped attending these colleges. At the same time, a major educational reform was introduced in Denmark which served to make domestic schooling more attractive.

Two years later the Catholic church made its most determined attempt to win back Denmark. It was spearheaded by the above-mentioned Laurentius Nicolai who had become a Jesuit in 1565 and who had worked as an agent for the Counter Reformation in Sweden in the 1570s. Laurentius Nicolai had published an extensive apology for Catholicism in 1604, entitled *Confessio Christiana*. His work ended with an urgent appeal to the Danes, especially to the king and the nobility, for a return to Catholicism. In 1606 he appeared in Copenhagen with copies of his work which he forwarded to Christian IV, the chancellor and Hans Poulsen

[40] See chapter 6 and Grell, *'Scandinavia', in Reformation in National Context'*.
[41] *Danske Kirkelove*, III, 16–17.

Resen. Laurentius Nicolai had hoped for an interview with the king, but was not granted one. Instead he was reprimanded by the senate of the university for his reckless behaviour and told that Christian IV had banished him from his countries with only one day's notice.[42]

Laurentius Nicolai's attempt may have been naive, but it served to draw the government's attention towards the dangers posed by the Counter Reformation in general and the Jesuits in particular. In 1613 decrees were issued which forbade Catholics to settle and hold office in Denmark and Norway, while people who were convicted of holding Catholic beliefs were to be disinherited.[43] That year Christian IV was present at a parliament in Norway where an interrogation by Bishop Niels Klaussøn Senning resulted in the banishment of six Norwegian crypto-Catholics, four of whom were clergymen.

Further Catholic missionary efforts were undertaken between 1622 and 1623. The *Congregatio de propaganda fide* had been established in Rome, and from the beginning there were plans for a mission to the north. In July two Dominicans arrived in Copenhagen. They visited the towns around the Sound and made thorough studies about the feasibility of the planned mission, but apparently obtained no substantial results.

Around New Year 1623 a new Jesuit mission was launched, but not without some friction with the Dominicans. The missionaries stayed with a foreign Catholic merchant in Malmø, but as their prospects of success proved disappointing, most of them soon returned. They were fortunate, because shortly afterwards their activities were discovered by the authorities. The only remaining Jesuit was banished with three days' notice. Their host was arrested and accused of a whole series of crimes. Finally he was sentenced to death on the grounds of theft and forgery and hanged. The case ended as a normal criminal case, but it can hardly have benefited the accused that he was a Catholic.

The Catholic missionary interest in Denmark was not rewarded with much success. Instead it resulted in reinforcing official hostility towards Rome. Furthermore Christian IV's involvement on the Protestant side in the Thirty Years War meant that a Catholic mission stood no chance of a positive or even tolerant reception by the authorities.

From 1614 Lutheran orthodoxy became the dominant and only officially acceptable doctrine in Denmark and Norway. The period leading up to the introduction of absolutism in 1660 is probably best described as one of Lutheran consolidation. Government control of the

---

[42] See V. Helk, *Laurentius Nicolai Norvegus S.J.*, Copenhagen 1966.
[43] *Danske Kirkelove*, III, 38–9.

clergy's discharge of their duties was strengthened and the standard of education of ministers improved. In 1621 the university received new statutes and the curriculum was modernised. Two years' study at a university was made conditional for the employment of future ministers or teachers at the Latin schools. Likewise, from 1625 all professors at the university had to accept the Augsburg Confession. A formal university exam for students of divinity was introduced in 1629, which became conditional for employment within the church.

In accordance with his programme for the unity of state and church, Christian IV had chosen as his motto: *regna firmat pietas* – piety strengthens the kingdoms. This was to be taken literally. Piety was thought to make the kingdoms prosper, while lack of it, in belief as well as deeds, would prove detrimental to the kingdoms. The losses of the Thirty Years War brought this principle to the test. Clearly, if piety would strengthen the kingdoms, and lack of piety weaken them, then the misfortunes of the war had to be taken as a sign that the nation was found wanting. Consequently the political and ecclesiastical establishment had to cooperate in order to improve matters. Even before entering the war, the government appears to have been worried about the godliness of the nation. In 1623 prohibitions were issued against swearing and the neglect of holidays, prescribing penalties. It was expressly stated that such failings were the cause of the wrath of God, clear signs of which were at hand, and that the prohibition was necessary in order to try to avoid further punishment.[44]

However, such worries did not stop Christian IV from entering the Thirty Years War. When he suffered defeat in 1626, new and serious measures had to be taken. Days of public penance, including special services, were prescribed every Friday for the towns, while the rural parishes were allowed to concentrate their activities to one Wednesday a month. Furthermore, on several occasions the government found it necessary to enjoin the population to observe three consecutive days of penance.

This policy reached a peak in the comprehensive penitential ordinance of 27 March 1629. The ordinance in effect introduced a regular church discipline. It stated that although the light of the gospel did not shine as brightly in other countries (i.e. Calvinist) as in Denmark, people were in fact more pious. Many people in Denmark and Norway lived in the erroneous opinion that outward signs of piety, such as church

[44] *Ibid.*, III, 98–102.

attendance, the taking of the sacraments, singing of psalms and praying were adequate, even if their lives did not conform to the word of God. Consequently, a body of elders was to be appointed in every parish. These leading parishioners were to serve as assistants to the ministers. They were to assemble with the ministers at least four times a year in order to discuss parish matters and the behaviour of their parishioners. Where impiety was detected, they were to take action according to Matthew 18.15ff., first through private admonition, next by official reproof by the minister in the presence of witnesses, then by exclusion from the sacraments, and finally by excommunication and exclusion from the Christian community. If the culprit did not repent and do penance within a year, he or she was to be banished. Likewise, it was enjoined that ministers should avoid drinking, and that they and their families should dress modestly and avoid extravagance in clothing.[45]

The regulations of the penitential ordinance were incorporated in the comprehensive law of 1643 (*Store Reces*), and later reiterated in the Danish law of King Christian V (1683). Unfortunately, we do not know how the ordinance worked in practice. It remains, however, a fascinating document because it reveals an important streak in Lutheran orthodoxy which is often overlooked. Traditionally orthodoxy has been seen as characterised by exactly the signs which the penitential ordinance stigmatised as insufficient – the outward observance of ecclesiastical customs and lack of personal commitment.

There is, of course, some basis for this interpretation. Some of the most notorious examples of Christian IV's ecclesiastical laws, the decrees of 1645, prescribe that in order to prevent members of the congregation from sleeping during sermons, wardens should be appointed to wake up sleepers, prodding them with long sticks.[46] This order can be seen as a consequence of the Lutheran tenet that the word of God is the only means of salvation, to which man can offer no assistance, even if it was largely a caricature and showed a total disregard for personal commitment. The numerous examples of extended, learned sermons, with detailed polemics against Catholics or spiritualists, of whom the congregations would have had little or no knowledge, only serve to corroborate this impression. It is on such evidence that orthodoxy has been generally assumed to have equalled barren formalism. The ordinance of 1629, however, demonstrates that this is a simplification. There was a

---

[45] *Ibid.*, III, 140–69.   [46] *Ibid.*, III, 317–18, 322.

movement towards penitential piety within Lutheran orthodoxy ('reforming orthodoxy'), which pointed towards a later period's Pietism.

A totally different theology to that of Lutheran orthodoxy was that promoted by the nobleman, Holger Rosenkrantz, who had been one of the most celebrated members of the Danish Council, but ended his days out of favour and suspected of dangerous heterodoxy. Rosenkrantz, who belonged to one of the oldest and most influential aristocratic families in Denmark, had spent most of the 1590s studying abroad. His letters from this period show him as a typical gnesio-Lutheran who had little sympathy or tolerance for other views. However, around 1600 he experienced a religious crisis which caused him to abandon his orthodoxy. He found that contemporary theology was marked by intransigent controversies about sterile doctrine which could not possibly lead to true piety. Instead, he was convinced that theology ought to focus on Biblical exegesis and encourage the believer to lead a pious life. Initially these views did not bring him into open conflict with the orthodox theological establishment. On the contrary, he became a close friend of the kingdom's leading orthodox theologian, Hans Poulsen Resen, whom he supported during his drive for uniformity in 1614. Rosenkrantz became a member of the Council in 1617, and during the following years he played a prominent part in Danish politics, especially within the domain of foreign policy. Not surprisingly, he appears to have wielded considerable influence over the penitential ordinance mentioned above. Rosenkrantz remained preoccupied with his theological studies throughout. He wrote a number of books, which, however, he refrained from publishing. He was undoubtedly one of the most respected intellectuals of his generation and enjoyed a considerable reputation abroad.

During the 1620s he became increasingly tormented by religious scruples. He considered his involvement in politics a burden, and he felt personally responsible for the disasters of Jutland during the Danish intermezzo in the Thirty Years War. Time and again he requested the king to relieve him of his membership of the Council, until he finally withdrew on his own initiative in 1627. For a short while Rosenkrantz even left the country. Christian IV, however, never forgave him for what he considered a betrayal of his duties.

Following his resignation, Rosenkrantz began to publish his works, and in 1636 he found himself in serious trouble with the kingdom's leading theologians. By then he had developed his own, deeply original theology which deviated not only from orthodoxy, but also from the teachings of Luther and Calvin.[47] Rosenkrantz advocated a 'doctrine of double justification', according to which man is justified first by faith and then by works. The latter had to be the consequence of faith and are accepted by God as truly good works because of being the effects of grace. The inspiration for this profoundly original theology may well be the writings of Erasmus of Rotterdam, even if Rosenkrantz was also influenced by contemporary German, pre-Pietist Lutherans, such as Johannes Arndt.

Christian IV intervened and demanded a revocation of such ungodly opinions and the faculty of divinity described them as dangerous. Rosenkrantz defended his views, but the faculty submitted a thorough refutation which condemned them as 'Socinian'. Most likely Rosenkrantz was only saved from a heresy trial by his social position and the influence of his son-in-law, who had become chancellor and head of the university. In 1642 he died peacefully, but isolated and abandoned by many former friends.

Although Rosenkrantz represented a heterodox position, his theological influence was considerable, especially before his troubles began in 1636. His views demonstrated that the age was not solely characterised by formalism. There was a deeply rooted yearning for the personal religious experience which could offer guidance for the lives of believers and provide comfort during the tribulations of the age. The 'pre-Pietism' of Rosenkrantz and his followers points towards a later period's Pietism, which was not inspired by Rosenkrantz's theology, but which shared important concerns and ambitions with it.

Among Rosenkrantz's antagonists was his former friend and pupil, Jesper Rasmussen Brochmand, who had become Resen's successor as the kingdom's leading theologian. He seems to have drafted the refutation of Rosenkrantz's theology issued by the faculty of theology in Copenhagen. Brochmand, who had studied in Copenhagen and the Netherlands, had, in spite of Rosenkrantz's teaching, developed into a typical orthodox churchman. He had been appointed professor of pedagogy at the University of Copenhagen in 1610, later advancing to the vacant chair in Greek. During the controversies of 1614, he firmly supported Resen and he quickly came to be seen as Resen's spiritual heir. When Resen became bishop in 1615, Brochmand received his doctorate in theology and became professor of divinity, and when Resen died in 1638, Brochmand succeeded him as bishop of Zealand.

---

[47] J. Glebe Møller, *Doctrina Secundum Pietatem. Holger Rosenkrantz den Lærdes Teologi*, Copenhagen 1966.

That Brochmand should end up confronting his former mentor may be due to the fact that only in 1636, when Rosenkrantz published his opinions for the first time, did he fully appreciate the implications of Rosenkrantz's theological opinions. Brochmand's bitterness towards Rosenkrantz can also be explained to some extent by the changes his own theology had undergone while he was teaching at the university. Thus in 1633 Brochmand published a huge book, *Universa Systema Theologiæ*, which became a classic in the orthodox literature. An abridged version was published in 1649 which became the standard manual for the Danish clergy during the next century. It is an Aristotelian work which reiterated the theology of the Formula of Concord. The Bible was the centre of Brochmand's theology and he forcefully advocated the tenet of verbal inspiration.

Given his scholarly inclinations, Brochmand's considerable ability and popularity as a writer of devotional literature is somewhat surprising. In 1635 he published a collection of sermons, *Huspostil*, which remained popular with pious Danish households for more than two centuries. In this work Brochmand was not influenced by mainstream Lutheran orthodoxy, but by the pastoral theology of the German pre-Pietist, Johannes Arndt. Both Arndt and Rosenkrantz inspired a number of Danish theologians of whom the most important was Jens Dinesen Jersin, since 1625 archdeacon in Copenhagen, who gained considerable following as a revivalist preacher and author. Jersin's appointment as bishop of Ribe in 1629 shows that some flexibility still existed within the Danish Lutheran church in spite of Resen's policy of uniformity.[48]

The ecclesiastical situation in Norway did not differ significantly from that of Denmark in these years. The majority of the clergy in both countries were educated at the University of Copenhagen. Consequently, Norwegian bishops, several of whom continued to be Danes, shared a common outlook with their Danish colleagues. The bishop of Bergen, Anders Foss, was a learned historian, while the bishop of Oslo, Niels Glostrup, had identical plans to those of Resen, wanting to introduce an evangelical confirmation. Another bishop of Bergen, Niels Paaske, who was a personal friend of Holger Rosenkrantz, maintained a positive attitude to Calvinists in spite of his orthodox Lutheranism. His successor in the see, Ludvig Munthe, actively argued against the existence of witchcraft.

Similarly, a strict control of beliefs and manners was maintained in

---

[48] For Jesper Rasmussen Brochmand, see *DBL*; for Jens Dinesen Jersin, see S. M. Gjellerup, *Biskop Jens Dinesen Jersin*, Copenhagen 1868–70.

Norway. Thus, in 1622, Bishop Anders Arrebo was deposed for having behaved in an unseemly manner at a party. As in Denmark, a more pious atmosphere is generally identifiable and the devotional works of Brochmand and Jersin proved popular. Niels Svendsen Chronick who was a divinity teacher at the Latin school in Oslo from 1640 to 1652, exerted a similar influence in Norway to that of his father-in-law, Jersin, in Denmark. Like Arndt, he was concerned with the mystical unification with Christ. However, because of his involvement with conventicles and derogatory attacks on the clergy, an action was brought against him. Only the protection of the influential courtier, Hannibal Sehested, who was governor of Norway from 1643 to 1651, saved Chronick. However, when Sehested was removed, Chronick was forced to leave Oslo. Later Chronick was imprisoned in Copenhagen. In 1658 he was liberated by the Swedes and subsequently settled in the Netherlands.

ABSOLUTISM

Christian IV died in 1648. His favourite son and designated successor, Prince Christian, had died the previous year from excessive drinking. Instead he was succeeded by his second son, Frederik III (1648–70), who had already acted as governor of the German archbishopric of Bremen and Verden. Frederik III was a considerably more introvert character than his father. He was probably one of the best educated monarchs ever to succeed to the Danish throne, and throughout his life he promoted scholarship and learning, while concentrating on his own scholarly interests. He continued his father's church policy with its emphasis on uniformity. The church remained subservient to the crown, but played a decisive part in the introduction of absolutism in 1660 through its leader, the bishop of Zealand.

The ongoing struggle for power with Sweden was significant in bringing about this major political change. Shortly after his accession to the throne, the Swedish king, Charles X, had become involved in a war with Poland. The Danish government and Frederik III perceived this to be an opportune moment to try to regain the provinces which had been lost to Sweden in the 1640s, and subsequently declared war in 1657. Charles immediately turned his weapons against Denmark which was unprepared for the onslaught of the full military might of Sweden. Furthermore, the extreme cold of the winter of 1657/8 made the Danish straits freeze, thereby making it possible for Charles to march his army across to Zealand. Consequently, the Danish government was forced to accept peace in Roskilde in 1658, on the worst possible conditions. The eastern provinces of Scania, Halland and Blekinge had to be ceded, while Norway lost a further two provinces, which effectively cut the country in half.

Initially Charles seems to have been satisfied with his achievements at the Peace of Roskilde, but later that year he changed his mind and attacked Denmark and Norway in order to subject them fully. He laid siege to Copenhagen and launched a decisive assault on the city in February 1659. Frederik III personally led the defence of his capital and managed to beat off the Swedish attack with Dutch support and stubborn resistance from the capital's citizens. The defeat of Charles and the interference of the Dutch Republic on Denmark's side guaranteed that Sweden was forced to sue for peace. The peace treaty of May 1660 meant that Denmark and Norway regained some of the territories lost three years earlier. The sea-faring powers, England and the Dutch Republic, made sure that the coasts of the Sound in future would remain split between Denmark and Sweden.

Thus Swedish hegemony over the whole of Scandinavia was narrowly avoided, but the costs had been colossal. The financial situation of the government in Copenhagen was disastrous. A parliament was called in order to deal with the crisis. It met in Copenhagen in September 1660 with the brief of introducing a new system of taxation in order to restore the kingdom's finances. The nobility, however, refused to pay any of the new taxes, referring to its traditional privilege of exemption. Considering the unimpressive role most noblemen had played in the recent wars, this proved an insensitive and dangerous road for them to take. The popular hostility towards them, already considerable, now reached new heights, especially in Copenhagen. The nobility was bypassed in the negotiations between the mayor of Copenhagen, Hans Nansen, and the bishop of Zealand, Hans Svane, on one side, and the court on the other. A bill was introduced to make the crown hereditary, thus removing the nobility's privilege of negotiating a coronation charter with the king. The nobility yielded, not least because of the personal danger they were exposed to in Copenhagen, but a final settlement proved impossible. Consequently, Bishop Hans Svane suggested that parliament left it to the king to lay down the details of the new political system. This was approved and allegiance was sworn to Frederik III as hereditary monarch, while his coronation charter was declared null and void.[49]

---

[49] See C.-J. Bryld, *Hans Svane og gejstligheden på stændermødet 1660*, Odense 1974.

However, the courtiers who framed the new system realised that the moment had come for the introduction of absolutism through the statutes which were to be drawn up for the new hereditary monarchy. This law was introduced the following year, and the absolutist system was solidly anchored in the new constitution known as the King's Law (*Kongeloven*) in 1665. Thus the leaders of the Lutheran church in Denmark were instrumental in the peaceful political revolution of 1660. The foundations had been laid for an even closer and more harmonious co-operation between king and clergy than had been the case during the reign of Christian IV. The law introducing absolute and hereditary monarchy was signed by the clergy, and Hans Svane was rewarded through the appointment as titular archbishop. Special privileges for the clergy, as an estate, were issued which, however, proved of little significance. The King's Law stated that the king was the supreme head of the church. He was, however, confessionally bound by the Augsburg Confession, and soon his authority over the clergy was interpreted as the highest in external ecclesiastical matters only, and not in internal doctrinal matters (*jus circa sacra*) not (*in sacris*).

Thus the union of state and church became fully formalised in the 1660s. From then on, however, the secular authorities gradually lost interest in the unity of the political and ecclesiastical establishments, for which they had worked so hard since the Reformation. This development was conditioned to a considerable extent by the growing mercantilism in the late seventeenth century. This predominantly economic theory served to make religious considerations subservient to the economic interests of the state. Under such circumstances, the policy of religious uniformity proved difficult for the government to sustain. Consequently, during the second half of the seventeenth century, several attempts were made to mitigate the policy of religious uniformity in Denmark and Norway. The governor of Norway, Hannibal Sehested, introduced a limited tolerance in three places in Norway, and in 1685 an edict of tolerance for adherents of the Reformed church was issued, in spite of bitter opposition from the bishops. This signalled the collapse of the policy of Lutheran uniformity in Denmark and Norway which had been the objective of government church policy since the introduction of the Reformation in 1536.

CHAPTER 6

The institutionalisation of Lutheranism in Sweden and Finland

Ingun Montgomery

Officially, Sweden was slow in committing herself fully to Protestantism. Traditionally, and with some justification, the parliament (*Riksdag*) of Västerås in 1527 has been seen as the birth of evangelical Sweden. This view is based on parliament's decision that 'the word of God should be purely preached all over the kingdom'. However, very little changed within the church in the aftermath of Västerås and none of the Catholic bishops was removed from office. It was not until 1544, during the Succession Parliament which met in Västerås, that it was unambiguously decided to promote Protestantism. It was during this meeting that the king and the representatives of the estates promised never to deviate from 'the teaching which has become accepted' and to take action against 'those who argue against such Christian teachings or try to suppress them'.[1] At this occasion the clergy debated the ecclesiastical ceremonies and agreed to remove some ancient rites which made no sense in an evangelical Lutheran church. The adoration of saints was to be stopped, as was the use of holy water and incense; furthermore, requiem masses and a number of Catholic holidays were no longer to be celebrated.[2]

In Sweden the recently established royal house of Vasa proved of tremendous significance for the introduction and development of the Reformation. The church policies initiated by Gustav Vasa came to determine developments in the reigns of his three sons who succeeded him.[3]

---

[1] S. Kjöllerström, 'Laurentius Petris Kyrkoordning 1571–1971'. *Den Svenska Kyrkoordningen 1571*, Lund 1971, 209.

[2] The same demand, 'that the many holidays, which have no ground in scripture are to be abolished', had been raised in 1540 in 'Regementsform i Västergötland', see A. A. Stiernman, *Alla Riksdagars och Mötens Besluth...*, I, Stockholm 1728, 162. The reason for this demand was that the holidays were seen to obstruct honest work and encourage drunkenness and murder. Consequently 'Our Church Order must ordain which holidays shall be celebrated and which not.'

[3] See chapter 3.

ERIK XIV – KING OF AN EVANGELICAL KINGDOM

Following the death of Gustav Vasa, the development towards a confessionally uniform, hereditary kingdom accelerated. When Erik XIV succeeded his father in 1560 it was in accordance with the order of succession which had been introduced at the parliament of Örebro in 1540 and confirmed at the Succession parliament of Västerås in 1544. This arrangement was consolidated in the will of Gustav Vasa from 1560. Here he established that his eldest son, Erik, in accordance with the succession agreement, should succeed him, and he added:

We command him also, above everything else, to love and defend the honour of God and his holy and sacred word. To let it (as We, with the help of the Almighty, have introduced and promoted it) be spread and preached uncorrupted and without superstition or inventions of Man.

He also took the opportunity to admonish his younger sons, Johan and Karl, to have faith in God and not to be enticed away from His pure teaching, 'but remain steadfast until the end'.

At Erik XIV's accession in 1560 the ceremonies and rules for a change of government were yet to be developed. That Sweden and Finland then became a hereditary kingdom, where the eldest son succeeded his father while his younger brothers were endowed with duchies, had been determined in the Act of Succession and confirmed in the will of Gustav Vasa. However, it still remained to be decided what, if any, demands were to be made on the succeeding ruler. The oath Erik swore at his coronation did not correspond with the common law of the realm and was phrased in very general terms. The king only promised to fear and love God, to preserve the pure word of God and the Christian faith, to suppress all false teachings and heresy, to protect the church and its ministers, and to love all his subjects.[4]

Erik XIV's church policy was decidedly anti-Catholic without any clear doctrinal definitions. Thus the new king avoided espousing anything which amounted to a distinctive confessional position. He was tolerant of the different views expressed by the Swedish clergy, and demonstrated a similar flexibility towards his subjects' religious preferences. In a charter of 1561 he invited Protestant exiles to settle in Sweden. The only condition these immigrants had to fulfil was that they

---

[4] E. Hildebrand and S. Tunberg, 'Gustav Vasas söner', *Sveriges historia till våra dagar*, V, Stockholm 1923, 12.

should adhere to the true and Christian teachings in accordance with the Bible, and live in peace as loyal subjects. The charter resulted in a growing immigration into Sweden of Huguenots and Dutch Calvinists. Inspired by the king's former tutor, Dionysius Beurreus, a more Calvinist theology, especially concerning the eucharist, took root in the country. These Calvinistic tendencies were censured by Archbishop Laurentius Petri, who denied the possible substitution of wine with other liquids such as cherry juice, as argued by Beurreus. This peculiar debate was occasioned by a shortage of wine in Sweden caused by the Danish naval blockade during the Seven Years War (1563–70). Laurentius Petri tried to suppress such ideas. He was influenced by a southern German Lutheranism, as well as by Philippism, and he wanted to preserve as many ecclesiastical forms and traditions as possible while strongly promoting evangelical doctrine. Personally, Erik XIV was attracted to the teachings of Melanchthon and was inclined to employ followers of Melanchthon within the church, as well as the central administrations.[5] His flexible and tolerant attitude benefited both gnesio-Lutherans and the more Calvinistic, humanist wing of the church.

It was during his reign that a debate began among church leaders about the definition of true evangelical faith. Consequently, in August 1563 Erik XIV was forced to moderate his positive attitude to foreign Protestants. He issued an order which forbade Calvinist immigrants to proselytise among Swedes and spread 'wrong teachings'. They were, however, granted freedom of conscience and were allowed to take part in services. We find the same attitude in the order Erik XIV issued in connection with the April 1565 synod which met in Stockholm. Here the Calvinist teaching on the eucharist was condemned, but its adherents were permitted 'to continue in such errors', as long as they did not cause scandal, because the king would not 'master anyone's conscience'. Erik XIV's religious position is undoubtedly best characterised as Melanchthonian-humanist and anti-sacramental Lutheranism.[6] Among other things, he attempted to suppress ceremonies which could contribute to the survival of Catholic traditions. He had reservations about the elevation of the communion wine and bread and the use of exorcism in connection with baptism and wanted such rites abolished. In this, however, he was opposed by the archbishop, Laurentius Petri.

---

[5] S. Kjöllerström, *Striden kring kalvinismen i Sverige under Erik XIV. En kyrkohistorisk studie*, Lund 1935, 17ff. See also O. P. Grell, 'Huguenot and Walloon Contributions to Sweden's Emergence as a European Power, 1560–1648', *Proceedings of the Huguenot Society*, 25 (4), (1992), 371–84.
[6] H. Holmquist, *Svenska Kyrkans Historia*, III, Uppsala 1933, 402f.

ARCHBISHOP LAURENTIUS PETRI AND THE DEVELOPMENT
OF AN EVANGELICAL CHURCH ORDER

The greater religious tolerance permitted by Erik XIV resulted in increased activity within the church. Laurentius Petri's position as the most prominent of the leaders of the Swedish church was confirmed when the archbishop preached the sermon at Erik XIV's coronation in 1561. Laurentius Petri emphasised that even if lay authority is ordained by God, this means not only that it has certain rights with regard to the church, but also certain obligations. Lay authority has the ultimate responsibility for the church, but the church is not passively subjected; it has its own responsibility and obligations. According to the archbishop, the crown's power is restricted to the 'secular and transient' domain. This was the principle on which the archbishop based his view of the relationship between state and church and which can be found in all his ecclesiastical activities.

It was during the reign of Erik XIV that the long drawn out work on an evangelical Church Order was finally finished. Laurentius Petri had a draft ready shortly after the coronation. The so-called Church Order of 1561 was modelled on some German church orders, the first part on the Württemberg Order, and the second on the Mecklenburg Order. The chapter on the eucharist in this edition was influenced by Melanchthon's *Augustana Variata*. It does not distinguish between Luther and Melanchthon. The episcopal organisation which was suggested differed from the practice in Denmark and England. Petri advocated a richer liturgy than that used in any of the other Reformation churches. As in similar church orders from the Reformation period, Petri's draft also included a comprehensive plan for schooling. The strong belief in the education of the people which characterised the Reformation is emphasised. However, this Church Order was not accepted by the parliament which met in 1562. It only became law nearly a decade later, in 1571, in the reign of Erik XIV's brother and successor, Johan III, and then in a revised version.

The 1560s was an eventful period for the Swedish church. Apart from his work on the Church Order, Laurentius Petri translated several of the books of the Old Testament from Hebrew. At the parliament of 1561 it was finally forbidden to celebrate communion without participants. The following year the debate about the eucharist surfaced for the first time. In 1566 Laurentius Petri published a small pamphlet entitled: *About Ecclesiastical Laws and Ceremonies*. It is characterised by its author's humanistically inspired *via media* theology, which seeks to retain the old ceremonies, but simultaneously argues that they do not contribute anything to salvation.

It was also during these years that the so-called 'Gävle school' developed. It was a liturgically moderate, but doctrinally orthodox, Lutheran movement, whose leading figure, around this time, was the superintendent in Gävle, Martinus Olai Gestricius. This movement, which bore the stamp of Lutheran orthodoxy and was deeply hostile to Calvinism, was later to play an important part in the decisions of the Uppsala Assembly of 1593. This period also witnessed an improvement in the financial situation of the Swedish church as can be seen from the restoration and decoration of local churches. Likewise, the possibilities for providing the congregations with proper evangelical education improved through the publication of sermons, prayer books and collections of psalms. In addition to the collection of sermons by Laurentius Petri (*The History of the Suffering and Death of Christ*), *The Swedish Psalmbook* was published in 1567, which contained contributions from the archbishop, as well as from his successor and namesake, Laurentius Petri Gothus.

JOHAN III. CHRISTIAN HUMANISM AND COUNTER REFORMATION

In 1569 Erik XIV was succeeded by his brother, Johan, who initially pursued the same general evangelical church policy which Gustav Vasa had laid down in his will. In his coronation oath, Johan III promised to 'uphold the true religion, the pure word of God and Christian faith while suppressing and obliterating all false teachings and heresy'. However, Johan gradually moved towards a Christian humanist position. For him faith and religion meant an emotional experience. Johan III was undoubtedly a highly intelligent monarch, but he appears to have been liable to considerable emotional changes. He tried to adapt the ideals of renaissance absolutism to the government of his realm. He wanted not only to control all appointments to ecclesiastical positions and the property of the church, but also the doctrine and liturgy of the church.

The type of Catholicism which appealed to Johan III was pre-Tridentine and did not generate much sympathy within the *Curia* which was dominated by Counter Reformation Catholicism. Johan III, however, also had reasonable political and economic motives, such as the possibility of receiving the considerable Sforza inheritance, to try to improve the contacts to Rome. If he received this inheritance, Sweden's economic problems would be solved immediately. It is in this context that the opposition towards the *Nova Ordinantia*, which he had drawn up in 1575 as a supplement to the Church Order of 1571, has to be seen. In reality it was only an addition to the Church Order, and in many ways it only realised the intentions which Laurentius Petri had already argued for in his writings. Among other things it sought to provide the foundation for a better system of primary and secondary education. This was nothing new since the Church Order of 1571 had already included provisions for schooling. Accordingly, the *Nova Ordinantia* was initially accepted by the bishops without much hesitation. Even Bishop Nicolaus in Strängnäs appears to have accepted it, if only under duress, as later claimed.

Not even Johan III's brother, Duke Karl, was totally disinclined to accept these changes from the outset, in spite of doing his utmost to try to preserve the religious customs which had been in use during his father's reign. The new ceremonies were only to be used in the cathedral of Strängnäs within his duchy, with the strict proviso that care should be taken that no popery re-emerged. However, in the parish churches in the countryside no changes were permitted. It is noteworthy that the duke offered no theological explanation for his cautiousness. It may well have been his recollection of the opposition his father, Gustav Vasa, had encountered when he tried to purge some of the many surviving Catholic rites, which made Karl err on the side of caution. In the meantime, however, the negative consequences of the tendency in Europe to decide doctrinal questions by political means, had gradually become evident. An example of this was the Augsburg Interim of May 1548. Later in December that year the Wittenberg theologians tried to introduce a compromise, the Leipzig Interim, which allowed the re-introduction of the mass in Latin, images, traditional holy days, the teaching of the seven sacraments, and the ecclesiastical hierarchy's jurisdiction. This was justified with the argument that questions of rites were *adiaphora* (matters of indifference). It was thought that this provided an arrangement which would allow the reformatory teachings to continue more or less unchanged. However, as it turned out, there were no *adiaphora* in questions of doctrine.

What served to arouse the confrontation in Sweden was the new liturgy which was introduced in 1576.[7] It was intended to be an improvement on the order of service written by Olaus Petri. Its supporters

---

[7] S. Serenius, *Liturgia svecanae ecclesiae catholicae et orthodoxae conformis. En liturgihistorisk undersökning med särskild hänsyn til struktur och förlagor*, Åbo 1966.

wanted no theological, but only aesthetical improvements. They had evidently learnt nothing from the above-mentioned conflicts in Germany.[8]

Johan III had been influenced by the irenical theology, promoted by Georg Cassander (1513–66) in particular, who looked back to the early church in order to find the true faith which, according to him, would unite Christendom once more.[9] Like the reformers, Johan wanted to emphasise the importance of scripture as the foundation of true faith. However, he also underlined the significance of the church Fathers and tradition.

In 1577 Johan III summoned all the bishops to a meeting in Stockholm where he presented them with a new liturgy, which became known as the Red Book, because of its red binding. It was accepted and signed by the bishops, but after the meeting they expressed serious reservations, especially the bishops of Linköping and Strängnäs, Martinus Olai Gestricius and Nicolaus Olai Helsingius. Nicolaus of Strängnäs claimed that he had only accepted the liturgy for the kingdom and not the duchy, which in effect excluded his own diocese. Duke Karl adopted the same attitude to the liturgy as he had to the *Nova Ordinantia*. In spite of disapproving of the liturgy and having no intention of introducing it in his duchy, he showed hardly any interest in how the Red Book was received in the rest of the realm.[10]

The opposition soon accused the king of trying to introduce Catholicism through the back door. It was pertinent to make such accusations since Johan III was married to a Catholic Polish princess, Catherine Jagellonica, who was allowed her own Catholic chapel and court priests. Furthermore, the young Prince Sigismund was brought up in the Catholic faith. Initially it does not appear to have caused any worries in Sweden that the country was to receive a Catholic ruler in the near future. However, it has to be borne in mind that the type of Catholicism which appealed to Johan III was the moderate, pre-Tridentine variety. The king wanted communion in both forms (*sub utraque*), mass in the vernacular, and clerical marriage permitted. Some years earlier such demands would have been met with sympathy at the *Curia*.[11] The queen's Catholic court priest seems to have distributed communion in

---

[8] Compare with Leipzig Interim, see A. Adam, *Lehrbuch der Dogmengeschichte*, II, Gütersloh 1968, 364f.
[9] G. Ivarsson, *Johan III och klosterväsendet*, Lund 1970, 62f.
[10] O. Söderqvist, 'Studier rörande förhållandet mellan Johan III och hertig Karl (1576–1582)', *Historisk Tidsskrift*, 1 (1903), 223ff.
[11] Ivarrsson, *Johan III*, 53ff.

both forms.[12] But with the growing dominance of the Counter Reformation such demands were no longer acceptable to Rome.

The orthodox Lutherans who opposed the new liturgical forms prescribed in the liturgy were in many cases removed from office by Johan. A number of these deposed clergymen sought refuge in Karl's duchy. At first Karl had not seen Johan's reforms as attempts to re-introduce Catholicism. Thus, when in 1578 his father-in-law, Ludwig VI of the Palatinate, had inquired abut Johan's orthodoxy, Karl had vouched for his brother.[13]

It was during these attempts to introduce changes in religion over and above the Church Order of 1571 that the religion of the ruler acquired constitutional importance. Duke Karl strongly emphasised his fidelity to the will of Gustav Vasa.[14] In a letter of 1575 to the bishop of Strängnäs, the leading ecclesiastical figure within his duchy, Karl had instructed the bishop to suppress all false teaching and the pope's lies and resolutely defend the teaching which had been preached during the reign of Gustav Vasa.

However, the traditional way of defining correct doctrine through general references to 'the time of old King Gustav and Archbishop Laurentius' was no longer sufficient. In a period of growing confessionalisation, a more precise definition of what constituted correct doctrine was urgently needed, not only in Germany, but also in Sweden, which had tried to remain outside the doctrinal confrontation. As mentioned above, Duke Karl had felt obliged to vouch for his brother's orthodoxy when queried by his father-in-law. In the marriage contract between Duke Karl and his fiancée, Maria, the couple bound themselves to the Augsburg Confession and promised to bring up their children in accordance with it.[15]

Doctrinal definitions had been slow in making an impact in Sweden. Not until 1558 was the first book concerned with evangelical doctrine published. It was a work by Bishop Erik Falck of Skara, based on Melanchthon's *Loci Communes*, published under the title *Margaritha theologica*. The bishop supported the same liberal views on ceremonies as those expressed by Laurentius Petri.[16] *Confessio Augustana* was translated into Swedish for the first time in 1581 by Petrus Johannis Gothus and

[12] O. Garstein, *Rome and the Counter-Reformation in Scandinavia*, I, Oslo 1963, 72ff.
[13] O. Holmdahl, 'Karl IX:s fömenta kalvinism', *Kyrkohistorisk Årsskrift*, 20 (1919), 249.
[14] K. Strömberg-Back, *Lagen, Rätten, Läran. Politisk och kyrklig ideedebatt i Sverige under Johan III's tid*, Lund 1963, 273ff.
[15] O. Holmdahl, 'Karl IX:s förmenta kalvinism', 250.
[16] Holmquist, *Svenska Kyrkan*, III, 358.

published in Rostock. Subsequently, this confession grew in importance within the Swedish church.

Johan III's ecclesiastical innovations, the *Nova Ordinantia* and the liturgy should also be seen as attempts to demonstrate the king's Catholic credentials in order that Sweden might profit, economically and politically, from preferential treatment by the Catholic powers on the continent. This foreign policy dimension of his church policy, however, found little support internally among the clergy, and the laity. It is noteworthy that negotiating with representatives of the *Curia*, Johan III claimed that the liturgy was only part of the religious changes he intended to introduce, while for domestic purposes he underlined his loyalty to the evangelical inheritance from Gustav Vasa. Whether or not Johan III converted to Catholicism is doubtful, even if he attended mass celebrated by the court priests of his Catholic queen, and had his son, Sigismund, the future king of Sweden, brought up as a Catholic. However, the political opposition to Johan III quickly exploited the growing aversion against what was perceived, at least, as the king's crypto-Catholic policies.

When disassociating himself from the church policies of King Johan, Duke Karl, the youngest of the three brothers, also referred to the religious inheritance from Gustav Vasa. It was to the evangelical teaching, as expressed in the reign of his father, that he pointed the people and clergy of his duchy in 1575. Thus it is no coincidence that it is during the mid-1570s that the paragraph on religion in Gustav Vasa's will becomes important. More than anyone else it is Duke Karl who gives this paragraph prominence in order to justify his opposition to his brother's church policy.[17]

A SOLUTION TO THE DOCTRINAL QUESTION IS FOUND

When Johan III died in November 1592 he was, in accordance with an earlier agreement between king and Council, succeeded by his son, Sigismund. Sigismund, who had been king of Poland since 1587, was a staunch Catholic. Evidently, the succession principle had taken precedence over the significance of the new ruler's religious allegiance in the negotiations which had taken place between Johan III and the Swedish Council. However, all the formalities had been dealt with and the

[17] I. Montgomery, *Värjostånd och lärostånd. Religion och politik i meningsutbytet mellan kungamakt och prästerskap i Sverige 1593–1608*, Uppsala 1972, 114f.

succession was agreed. In spite of this, Duke Karl succeeded in pushing the religious question to the front of the political agenda. In this the duke was able to collaborate with the majority of the clergy. Both he and the clergy wanted to defend the Swedish Reformation against the threats of Counter Reformation Catholicism. The clergy, however, were concerned solely with the preservation of Protestant teaching, while the duke, via his defence of Protestantism, wanted to expand his political influence. Consequently, the collaboration between the two sides became strained when the threat from Catholicism began to recede. Already during the Uppsala Assembly in 1593 a certain antagonism between the clergy and the duke is in evidence. The clergy's view that the duke should only call the assembly while they should be left to make the decisions about religion did not correspond with the duke's concept of his responsibility for his subjects' religion.

Since the new king belonged to an alien faith, he was incapable of performing the task of *custos ecclesiae*, defender of the church. This left an ecclesiastical vacuum which could be filled only by the duke who, in his capacity as the leading member of the royal family belonging to the evangelical faith, could take it upon himself to defend the Protestant church. It was in this capacity that he was able to summon the clergy to a synod in Uppsala, but not a parliament. The decisions by the assembly in Uppsala on 20 March 1593 were of paramount importance for the Lutheran church in Sweden. It was decided that because it 'has been acknowledged that nothing is more damaging to a country or a kingdom than disputes and disagreement, and nothing more beneficial and profitable, or binds the hearts closer together than concord and harmony, and especially in religion', it was of the greatest importance to reach agreement on doctrine and ceremonies in the kingdom. The idea of unity in religion as a precondition for harmony in the whole country gained ground in the wake of the Uppsala Assembly.

Gustav Vasa's will had confirmed that Sweden had become a hereditary monarchy based on primogeniture. In that connection it had been argued that an organised succession was an important condition for peace and order in the country. In constitutional law the idea of the hereditary monarchy as the most functional form of government had won increasing support in the first half of the sixteenth century, not least because of the constantly growing administrative tasks of government, which ill suited a noble republic, the only available government alternative. Naturally the struggle between the prince, who sought to expand his powers, and the nobility, who refused to renounce its established privileges, was concerned primarily with the control of government. In this connection unity of religion was of the utmost importance. Uniformity was considered a precondition for a harmonious and well-ordered society. To tolerate more than one faith within a country was considered absurd since there could only be one true religion. This explains why the paragraph about religion in Gustav Vasa's will is given similar weight and prominence to the principle of primogeniture.

However, during the confrontations of the 1580s between King Johan and Duke Karl over the liturgy it became evident that the duke did not share the religious position of those who were opposed to the liturgy for purely theological reasons.[18] That he eventually collaborated with them is best explained by his ambition to maintain his duchy's independence of the king. For him the religious independence of his duchy constituted part of its political independence. It is, however, also possible that Karl had yet to understand the full religious implications inherent in Johan III's church policy. There is evidence to support such a view. During the synod in Stockholm in 1577, when the clergy discussed whether or not they should accept the new liturgy, Bishop Nicolaus of Strängnäs wrote to the duke asking him for his opinion of 'the new mass book which has recently been drawn up'. Karl responded by explaining his personal attitude while referring to what had been decided concerning religion in the duchy. But surprisingly enough he leaves it to the bishop's discretion to decide what to do 'in such a highly important affair, but to reach a decision which he could defend temporally and eternally'.[19] Even in that part of the letter where he stated his personal religious views, the duke avoided an open and reasoned condemnation of the liturgy. Instead he only referred to the fact that unanimous agreement on the Church Order of 1571 had been reached in 1572 at the synod of Uppsala.

We recognise no other church order or order of service than that which for some time has been in use thanks to God, and which was sealed and agreed by the clergy, bishops as well as others, in Uppsala in the year 72, which you, as well as some of those who are now present with you in Stockholm, signed and sealed.

Furthermore, concerning the duchy, he referred in his letter to 'what had recently been decided by the clergy concerning religion in our duchy'.[20] This was as far as Duke Karl was prepared to commit himself in 1577, and it cannot have clarified matters significantly for Bishop Nicolaus. If we

[18] Strömberg-Back, *Lagen, Rätten, Läran*, 290ff.
[19] *Svenska Riksdagsakter jämte andra handlingar som höra till statsförfattningens historia*, edited by E. Hildebrand *et al.*, I:I; 1–4, Stockholm 1887–1938, II, 554f.
[20] *Ibid.*, 1002f. The clergy's oath of loyalty is dated Nyköping 25 September 1576.

are to take the letter on face value then the duke appears to have been of the opinion that the Church Order of 1571, together with the oath of loyalty of September 1576 from the duchy's clergy, fully expressed his theological position. In their oath of loyalty the clergy had promised to uphold 'God's holy, clear and pure word' and not to permit 'any other teaching or ceremonies' to be introduced in the duchy 'than those used in the time of his Highness, blessed King Gustav, which have been in Christian usage since then and until the present'.

Traditionally the opposition to the liturgical innovations of King Johan has been seen to have been generated by Duke Karl on one hand and a group of orthodox Lutheran theologians, educated at the University of Rostock, on the other.[21] In Rostock the leading theologian was David Chytraeus who taught at the university from 1551 to 1600 and who was internationally famous for his orthodoxy. Like the rest of the theological faculty in Rostock, Chytraeus had accepted the Formula of Concord, as well as the doctrine of *ubiquity* (Christ's presence in the communion). In questions of doctrine Chytraeus was close to Martin Chemnitz, whose works were very popular in Rostock.[22] A fair number of the many Swedish ministers who had been educated in Rostock eventually sought refuge in Karl's duchy during the confrontations surrounding the liturgy. They developed an aggressive and often unshakingly hostile stance towards the liturgy.

A decade later, in 1586, the duke stated that the Church Order of 1571 ought to be sufficient and the only norm for both teaching and ceremonies.[23] Until then, however, Karl had avoided identifying his position fully with that of the Church Order and only referred to 'the pure word of God' as the guide to be used together with the practice from the reign of his father. Here he differed from the 'anti-liturgists', who considered the Church Order and the letter of ratification of 1572, which rejected all later additions to the Church Order, as their sole doctrinal foundation.

Yet, during his discussions with Johan in January 1587, Karl seems to have considered the possibility of postponing the question of ceremonies to a later synod. His negotiator, Karl Sture, stated:

---

[21] H. Cnattingius, *Uppsala möte 1593. Konturer av en kyrkokris*, Uppsala 1943, 44.

[22] H. Cnattinguis, 'Nicolaus Bothniensis' teser om skriften 1584 . . . ', *Kyrkohistorisk Årsskrift*, 37 (1938), 161ff and 192ff.

[23] Stiernman, *Alla Riksdagars och Mötens Besluth*. See the articles of Örebro of 27 May 1586: 'Furthermore concerning ceremonies during church services, no changes shall be made within the duchy, except in cases where they will return to those which have long been in use after the Reformation', 360ff.

neither can his princely Grace force his subjects to accept what they are not prepared to undertake and believe, and legally no lay authority can decide in such spiritual matters, but they have presented them to the most learned, in order that they can look into them and pass judgement.[24]

Following the death of Johan III towards the end of 1592 Duke Karl immediately tackled the two most important issues upon his arrival in Stockholm. One was the need for a synod of the church in order to resolve the religious dispute caused by the liturgy; the other was the summoning of parliament. The idea of a synod was, however, hardly new. As early as 1580 the Council had proposed that the controversy surrounding the liturgy be solved at a general synod.[25] During the parliament of Vadstena in 1587 it had furthermore been decided that it was for the clergy, not lay authority, to decide the ceremonies of the church.[26] When King Johan and Duke Karl were reconciled in 1590, they had agreed that a synod should be summoned in order to reach a decision about ceremonies.[27] The idea of a general synod had, in other words, been aired repeatedly and appears to have been widely supported.

THE UPPSALA ASSEMBLY: SYNOD OR PARLIAMENT?

Only two days after the death of King Johan, Karl approached the Council with an inquiry as to whether or not a synod should be summoned to make a decision about doctrine and ceremonies.[28] The deceased king had contemplated a similar meeting shortly before his death. That a synod was called at this time was, in other words, not unexpected. The clergy took the lead offered, and on 3 January they requested a general synod, 'in order that a constant and godly unity can be established once more'.[29] In a letter to the Council, Duke Karl drafted the directives for the planned synod.[30] Here he stated that it was the synod's task to provide the foundations for unity in religion 'and that biblical and apostolical scripture alone should provide the guidelines'.

The participants assembled in Uppsala on the appointed day, 26 February 1593. The first couple of days were spent on preparations. The assembly was formally opened on 1 March by a speech given by the chancellor, Nils Gyllenstierna. He expressed himself with great care and

[24] *Svenska Riksdagsakter*, II, 723.
[25] *Ibid.*, II, 576. [26] *Ibid.*, II, 723f. [27] *Ibid.*, II, 1040.
[28] *Ibid.*, III, 2. [29] *Ibid.*, III, 3f. [30] *Ibid.*, III, 84.

stressed that the meeting took place at the request of the clergy. The duke and the Council had accepted it, partly because King Johan – shortly before his death – had 'accepted and promised' that such a meeting would take place, and partly because 'our country should not suffer a similar fate to France, Holland and the Netherlands, where great cities have been destroyed because of religious conflicts: because where there is no agreement in doctrine and faith, there can never be any unity in society, except conflict and ruin'. Already in his opening address Gyllenstierna underlined that 'what was to be decided according to the pure word of God, should be drafted in a Christian manner and signed by everybody'. He also pointed out that the Council intended to adhere to the Augsburg Confession and the corresponding confession written by Archbishop Laurentius Petri. However, Gyllenstierna emphasised that the assembly should be a free synod. Accordingly, it was to be chaired by a person of its own choice.[31]

The assembly started its proper work on 3 March by trying to establish the official doctrine of the Swedish church. The dominating perspective was to let scripture be normative for all religious questions. Then the assembly accepted the three creeds of the early church and began a systematic treatment of the individual paragraphs of the *Confessio Augustana*. On 6 March the assembly began debating and criticising the liturgy. Two days later it was decided to return to the Church Order of 1571 and the manual written by Olaus Petri.

The prime task of the Uppsala Assembly was to establish religious unity. Through that would follow political agreement and peace in the country. The substance of this unity had yet to be decided. But it was obvious that Catholicism had no supporters among the participants in Uppsala. It was acknowledged that some of the ceremonies retained in the Church Order of 1571, especially concerning baptism and communion, had been abolished in most of the other evangelical churches, because they tended to lead to superstition and misuse. However, the assembly found it unnecessary to take such steps in Sweden, where it was assumed that such misuse could be halted through education and admonition.

It was around the traditional evangelical doctrine of the 'pure and saving word of God' which the Swedish clergy rallied in Uppsala. The Uppsala Resolution stated that apart from scripture, the three creeds of the early church and *Confessio Augustana* were binding, as was:

[31] *Ibid.*, III, 38ff.

the religion which was practised in this kingdom, in both teaching and ceremonies, during the reign of the late, departed King Gustav, God rest his soul,
and during the life of the late archbishop, Laurentius Petri (Nericiani), and
stated in the printed Church Order published in 1572, which has been consented
to and agreed.

The theological discussions in Uppsala show that the Swedish clergy
had begun to be influenced by gnesio-Lutheranism, even if no direct
references are made to either the Formula of Concord nor the *Book of
Concord*. According to paragraph ten in the Formula of Concord, ceremonies should be considered as in *statu confessionis* (as part of doctrine). It
is exactly this gnesio-Lutheran perspective which now, for the first time,
acquires importance in the theological debate in Sweden.

The main aspects of the Uppsala Resolution were the following.
Firstly, Sweden now approved *Confessio Augustana* as a symbolic book.
The clergy united around *Confessio Augustana* which made it possible for
them to reject some of the duke's suggestions for reforming the ceremonies of the church. Secondly, through the Resolution the unity of the
Swedish church had been demonstrated and the religious stability of the
country re-established. A compromise had been reached over the most
contentious ceremonies, especially elevation and exorcism in connection
with baptism. They were only to be abolished if it proved impossible to
prevent the superstition and misuse attached to them. Thirdly, during
the negotiations of the assembly the *Nova Ordinantia*, as well as the liturgy,
had been branded Catholic. This was a new development. Never before
had such labels been used about Johan III's ceremonial innovations,
either by their protagonists or antagonists.

The Uppsala Assembly has achieved great importance in Swedish
history for several reasons. Through the Resolution, religious uniformity
was formally established. This official unity is confirmed by the considerable number of ecclesiastical, as well as lay, leaders who signed it, not
only in Uppsala, but later when it was circulated in the kingdom. Those
who signed were obliged to see that the Resolution was adhered to,
which carried with it considerable political obligations. Considering that
Duke Karl was given the ultimate responsibility for putting the Resolution into effect, he was indirectly given additional political power,
which gave him more room for manoeuvre in his struggle with his
Catholic nephew and the crown prince, Sigismund, for control over
Sweden.

Undoubtedly the Uppsala Resolution, issued 20 March 1593, finally
established the confessional and doctrinal foundation for the Protestant

church in Sweden. Apart from its theological and religious importance, the decisions taken in Uppsala had far-reaching political consequences for early modern Sweden. The Swedish estates took a revolutionary political decision in 1593, recognised as such by a number of contemporary European governments, by questioning the order of succession and rejecting the ceremonies which, only fifteen years earlier, they had accepted. The full consequences of what was decided in Uppsala may not have been immediately visible, but shortly afterwards during the negotiations with the country's chosen king, Sigismund, they became evident.

The Resolution was issued on behalf of the duke, the Council, the bishops and the common clergy, but the signatories consisted of a much wider group, including a considerable number of the nobility, gentry and burghers. That the resolution was circulated so widely and attracted such a considerable number of signatures (more than 2,000 lay and ecclesiastical members of the estates signed, most of whom took no part in the debate in Uppsala), has made it very difficult to place this event constitutionally and legally. Scholars have generally tried to chose either the label 'synod' or 'parliament' for the Uppsala Assembly, but neither has proved satisfactory.

Above all, the similarities to the emergence and sealing of the *Confessio Augustana* spring to mind. The Augsburg Confession had not been a response to purely ecclesiastical needs either. It had been drafted on the initiative of Duke Johan, elector of Saxony, who wanted to justify the evangelical changes which had taken place in the rites and organisation of the church of Saxony. Thus it was on his order that Melanchthon began drafting the confession. The Schmalkaldic Articles, the doctrinal statement drawn up by Luther, were drafted in similar circumstances, on the order of Duke Johan Friedrich, in anticipation of the council of the church which was planned to meet in Mantua in 1537. Accordingly, these confessions were not drawn up and signed by synods, but by the lay authorities. The Formula of Concord came into existence through a similar procedure, and among the princes who signed it was Duke Karl's father-in-law, Duke Ludwig VI, elector Palatine.[32]

The importance of the Uppsala Assembly lies precisely in its twofold character as simultaneously an ecclesiastical and political event.[33] It should be seen on a par with the above-mentioned German confessions,

---

[32] See *Die Bekenntnisschriften der evangelisch-lutherischen Kirche*, Göttingen 1956, 3rd edn., 762 (Duke Ludwig VI's name heads the list of princely signatories).

[33] H. Cnattingius, *Den centrala kyrkostyrelse i Sverige 1611–1636*, Uppsala 1939, 41.

which attempted to create doctrinal uniformity in a potentially dangerous political situation. The Council's attempt to avoid a parliament by
calling a synod proved impossible to accomplish. The decisions taken in
Uppsala had unavoidable political consequences, which were further
emphasised by the decision to circulate the Resolution in order to
maximise the number of signatories. That was why it was, and could be
seen as, a confederation directed against the king-in-waiting.[34]

In spite of being entitled to succeed his father in accordance with the
order of succession, King Sigismund, who had been the ruler of Poland
since 1587, was forced to negotiate with the estates about terms for his
coronation. He was forced to accept the Augsburg Confession and the
Uppsala Resolution before he could be crowned. Duke Karl founded his
political opposition to his nephew on the decisions made in Uppsala.
Accordingly, he demanded that King Sigismund should provide religious guarantees for his Protestant subjects before his coronation.
Sigismund refused, emphasising that an heir to the throne did not need
to fulfil any obligations in order to be crowned; it was simply his right.
Karl did not yield, however, and finally, together with the estates, he
forced Sigismund to provide the required religious guarantees. These,
however, were given by the young Catholic king with a *reservatio mentalis*
(silent reservation, meaning that the concessions had been forced upon
him).

Later, at the coronation of Duke Karl as King Karl IX, on 15 March
1607 the estates once more tried to secure religious guarantees before the
coronation. This time they failed, but Karl found it necessary to provide
the guarantees shortly after his coronation. Karl's son and successor, the
great Protestant 'icon', Gustavus Adolphus, however, was obliged to
provide detailed religious guarantees, promising to adhere to the Augsburg Confession and the Uppsala Resolution.[35] Thus the decisions of the
Uppsala Assembly had become generally acknowledged as the basis for
correct doctrine in Sweden.

DUKE KARL: DEFENDER OF TRUE DOCTRINE

Since lay authority and subjects were no longer of the same religion,
doctrine became an issue of paramount importance in their interrelationship and acquired an increased political significance. According

---

[34] Montgomery, *Värjostånd och lärostånd*, 98f.
[35] I. Montgomery, *Gustav Adolf och religionen', in Gustav II Adolf – 350 år efter Lützen*, Uddevalla 1982, 64.

to Lutheran constitutional theory, it was one of the most important tasks of lay authority to guard the law and, with it, true religion. The oath of allegiance which Duke Karl swore to Sigismund at the latter's coronation, was not without reservations. It referred to the religious guarantees given by the king, stating that for as long as his duchy was allowed to remain with the pure and unadulterated Augsburg Confession and the will of Gustav Vasa, Karl considered himself bound by his oath. If, however, that was not the case, the duke felt obliged to break his oath in order to defend the Protestant church, in his capacity of *Praecipuum membrum ecclesiae* (leading member of the church). However, the estates were not willing to follow him into open opposition to the king; they found that Sigismund's coronation charter offered adequate protection. Furthermore, the accusations of Calvinism which began to be directed against the duke can only be interpreted as a deliberate attempt to circumscribe his efforts to utilise the religious issue to strengthen his opposition to the king. These accusations might have proved dangerous to the duke had they won general credence. They would have made it impossible for him to portray himself as a 'defender of the true religion'. Thus it was significant that the cathedral chapter of Uppsala was forced to retract such accusations and beg him to continue as regent in 1595.

It was during the parliament of Söderköping in 1595 that the antagonism between the duke and the king became manifest. Sigismund had tried his utmost to prevent a parliament from being summoned. The question of religion was, in other words, the only way of legitimating the calling of such an assembly in the face of royal opposition. In Söderköping Duke Karl, once more, demanded that the disputed ceremonies, such as exorcism, should be abolished.[36] This time, however, he wanted it done through a reform of the church manuals. He underlined the significance of unity in doctrine and ceremonies. He repeated these arguments a couple of months later when he demanded a revision of the manual, and a new and improved edition of the catechism, including a stronger denunciation of 'the papal errors'. By now he appears to have come to the conclusion that a revision of the church manuals was a necessary precondition for a reform of the ceremonies. King Sigismund intervened and accused the duke of trying to introduce Calvinism in Sweden through his proposed reforms of the ritual.

In the wake of the parliament of Arboga in 1597, the Council was dissolved because its members could not agree on an answer to the

---

[36] *Svenska Riksdagsakter*, III, 535.

religious question. Accordingly they were unable to solve the continuing political crisis. But in spite of his wish to protect Protestantism, a goal Duke Karl shared with the majority of the clergy, his relationship with this estate was far from harmonious. The duke clashed with Skepperus, the minister in Stockholm, about the right of lay authority to interfere in ecclesiastical matters. The duke's claim to hold the right and duty to intervene worried the clergy who considered it to be an abuse of power.

Meanwhile, the confrontation between the duke and King Sigismund came to a head the following year. During the summer of 1598, Duke Karl informed Sigismund that he could no longer serve him, because the king had not fulfilled his coronation charter. Later, in the autumn, when Sigismund had secretly left Sweden, against all his promises, the religious question acquired renewed importance. It became generally accepted that unity in religion was a necessary precondition for peace and stability in the country.

By taking upon himself the role of defender of the evangelical faith and guarantor of the will of Gustav Vasa, Duke Karl was able to legitimise and carry through an opposition for which it would otherwise have been impossible to generate support. He was able to use the idea of religious unity to considerable effect as a precondition for political stability and peace in the country. In this connection he was able to find support in the Lutheran theory of state, where lay authority was assigned responsibility for the law, including religion. Since the Swedish people were of a different religion from their ruler, their allegiance was no longer straightforward. Accordingly, the religious question became highly politicised and served to make Sigismund's and Karl's co-rule a period of constant conflict and division.

GOVERNMENT AND SUBJECTS UNITED IN THE SAME FAITH

Finally after a prolonged period of strife the estates formally renounced their allegiance to Sigismund during a parliament which met in Stockholm in July 1599. They emphasised that this was not a revolutionary act since they retained their loyalty to the Vasas, but they underlined that in future Sweden could only be governed by a Protestant. They pointed out that it was possible for Sigismund's son, Vladislav, to become king of Sweden, if he was sent to Sweden and brought up in the Protestant faith; until then Duke Karl was to serve the country as regent.

Finally government and subjects were of the same religion. During the reign of Sigismund, the Uppsala Resolution had provided the platform for the political opposition to him. Duke Karl had justified his summoning of parliaments on this basis. At these gatherings Karl had claimed that the evangelical faith based on the holy Bible was a necessary condition for the welfare of the country. Against this view, the estates pointed towards the importance of doctrine. Their strong emphasis on doctrine was a product of the growing influence of gnesio-Lutheranism, which considered scripture to be insufficient to decide what true teaching was. According to these orthodox Lutherans, scripture needed interpretation and its content had to be expressed in doctrinal form. This, of course, was a task which could only be performed by the clergy.

Even after Sigismund had left Sweden, religion continued to play a prominent part in Swedish politics. The nature of the debate changed, however, and it became concerned with who should control the spiritual domain, the king or the clergy, lay or ecclesiastical authority. Thus, during the parliament of Linköping in 1600 the estates demanded that Karl govern the country in accordance with the Uppsala Resolution. On this occasion the clergy also wanted to secure the church's freedom to fill vacant ecclesiastical posts and decide all doctrinal matters without lay interference. Here the clergy came into conflict with the duke's concept of the territorial church. He considered himself to be *Custos utriusque tabulæ* and as a consequence he presented them with his personal draft for a new church order and manual. The duke wanted to take holy scripture as the basis for his planned revision. He presented a report entitled: '*On the Lord's Eucharist, Baptism and Other Things*' for the clergy's consideration. Firstly, Karl dealt with the eucharist, emphasising its importance and meaning, but playing down its ritual dimension. He expressed scepticism about *manducatio indignorum* (participation of the unworthy in communion), while he no longer wanted to retain exorcism in connection with baptism.

In their answer, the clergy rejected the changes suggested by the duke. According to them, his proposals included 'some dangerous opinions inspired by Calvinists and Sacramentarians'; furthermore, if they were to be accepted it would mean a clear departure from the Uppsala Resolution. The clergy pointed out that by abolishing exorcism, there was a danger of invalidating the significance of original sin, which would also be contrary to article nine in the Augsburg Confession. This latter argument constitutes the first use of *Confessio Augustana* as a guide to correct doctrine in the theological debate in Sweden.

The accusations of Calvinism angered Karl who pointed out that he based himself solely on the word of God: 'because such decisions should only rest on the word of God without any human considerations'.

Accordingly, the duke would give neither Luther nor Calvin precedence over Moses and the prophets:[37] in other words *Sola Scriptura!* In their response, the clergy agreed that the word of God ought to be the sole guide for the teaching and ceremonies of the church. But they emphasised, at the same time, that the word of God is open to misinterpretation and 'that even the greatest heretics claim to be in accordance with the word of God, as did the devil in his disputation with Christ'. Among the examples of such heretics, the clergy mentioned Zwingli, Karlstadt and Calvin, while they pointed to Luther as an example of correct interpretation of the scripture.

In several cases, what the clergy described as false Calvinist doctrine in their controversy with Karl turns out to have been no more than traditional practice within the Swedish church, originating from the time of Olaus and Laurentius Petri. The clergy emphasised ubiquitarianism, the real presence of Christ in the eucharist. They condemned Karl's view of the eucharist as taking part in Christ in a eucharistic way, which they interpreted as Calvinist, in spite of it having originally been promoted by Laurentius Petri with reference to Paul. What was perceived by the clergy as a conflict between crypto-Calvinism and orthodox Lutheranism was in reality a clash between an older Philippist, humanist theology and the new, gnesio-Lutheran theology.

The clergy refused to accept Karl's draft for a revised manual. They were of the opinion that the task of revising the church manuals was their prerogative. It was only for the regent to make sure that the revision was done, not to determine how. In vain the clergy made a serious attempt during the parliament of 1600 to limit the duke's responsibility for religion. Duke Karl's response to the clergy's demand to be sole arbiters of doctrine is interesting. He suggested that a committee should be formed by the estates which should revise the manual and Church Order. Thus he emphasised the responsibility and superior position of the estates *vis-à-vis* the clergy in doctrinal matters. Parliament assented to the creation of such a committee. However, parliament was not able to solve the succession question which was so closely connected to the religious debate. Karl refused to be bound by the Uppsala Resolution, confessionally as well as constitutionally, and accordingly his coronation was postponed. The duke's goal remained religious unity under royal supremacy.

The religious debate had been initiated by the estates at the parliament in Linköping. They had attempted to determine the religion of

---

[37] Montgomery, *Värjostånd och lärostånd*, 295.

their regent. This was a radical novelty which was doomed to failure. Subjects had no right to decide the religion of their ruler. In early modern Protestant Europe it was the ruler who would determine the country's religion, according to the decision of the Diet of Augsburg in 1555, *cuius regio, eius religio*.[38]

The question of whether the clergy or the regent was to be in charge of religion emerged once more during the parliament of 1602 in Stockholm. It found clear expression in the demands of the estates that Karl should be crowned and provide a coronation charter which would offer the clergy guarantees against Calvinist heterodoxy. Duke Karl refused to accept such limitations on his church policy. His position may well have been dictated by foreign policy concerns, rather than by personal conviction. The clergy continued to want sole responsibility for the interpretation of the word of God. It was on this doctrinal basis that they expected lay authority to provide the church with the necessary support and direction. However, such a division of responsibility was not yet feasible.

Eventually during the parliament of Norrköping in 1604 a new succession was put in place. But even at this parliament conflicts arose between Duke Karl and the clergy about the right to determine doctrine. Significantly, in the succession agreement which secured the throne for Karl's line of the Vasa family, no reference was made to the Uppsala Resolution. Thus it no longer provided the guide to orthodoxy within the Swedish church, and Duke Karl could proceed to reform the teaching and ceremonies of the church solely according to the word of God.

Karl was finally crowned on 15 March 1607. During the previous parliament Karl had obtained agreement that his coronation would not be conditional on a coronation charter. He had informed the nobility that he was only implementing his father's church policy, since he 'was promoting the clear, pure and saving word of God without any superstition, human invention or additions'. He added that even if the word of God had been purely preached for seventy years, many papal customs and ceremonies remained in the country. Consequently, 'a reformation with the concession and agreement of His Royal Majesty and the estates of the realm was needed'.

It was, in other words, the idea of the continuous Reformation which determined the church policy of Karl. For him the Reformation was an ongoing concern for which he, as ruler, had responsibility. The Swedish

38 M. Heckel, *Staat und Kirche nach den Lehren der evangelischen Juristen Deutschlands in der ersten Hälfte des 17. Jahrhunderts* (Jus ecclesiasticum, VI), Munich 1968, 227ff.

clergy, however, who adhered to the Formula of Concord (1577), no longer considered ecclesiastical ceremonies to be *adiaphora*, but rather an important part of the true faith. Accordingly, the clergy remained hostile to Karl's attempts to reform the order and rites of the Swedish church.

The leader of the ecclesiastical opposition to Karl was Olaus Martini. He was a son of Martinus Olai of Gävle, who had become Bishop of Linköping and who had been prominent among those who had opposed the liturgy of Johan III.[39] Olaus had received his MA in 1583 from the University of Rostock which was then strongly influenced by the ideas of Peter Ramus. On his return to Sweden the following year, he had become a schoolmaster in Nyköping in Karl's duchy, where he was promoted to minister ten years later. He had been the leading antagonist of Johan III's liturgy within the diocese of Strängnäs, and he had been elected one of the secretaries to the Uppsala Assembly. In 1599, together with the chapter of Uppsala, Olaus Martini had drafted a new manual which Duke Karl had rejected and which did not agree with the duke's own suggestions for a revision of the Church Order and manual, which he presented to the clergy at the subsequent parliament in Linköping. Parliament had then suggested that the duke and clergy should collaborate on a new draft. During the summer of 1600, Olaus Martini was elected archbishop. His election was eventually accepted by Karl after some prevarication. The theological confrontation between the two leaders of church and state, however, continued unabated. They both published a series of religious tracts until the archbishop died in the spring of 1609, followed only two years later by Karl IX.

In spite of the opposition of the clergy, Karl had published his manual in the autumn of 1602.[40] According to its title, it was to be used at court, thus precluding the estates from any formal right of interference.[41] Archbishop Olaus Martini wrote a hostile response, arguing that the book was unnecessary, harmful and, furthermore, Calvinistic, since the teaching on ubiquity and the real presence of Christ was missing.[42] With regard to the ceremonies, the archbishop argued that they were not arbitrary, as claimed by Karl and the humanists, but were in *loco confessionis*. Consequently they constituted part of confession and

---

[39] C. Annerstedt, *Olaus Martini. Minnesteckning*, Uppsala 1904 (Svenska Akademiens handl. ifrån år 1886; XVIII).

[40] H. Block, *Karl IX som teolog och religiös personlighet*, Uppsala 1918; for Karl's manual, see 247–88.

[41] *Kristelig Ordning och Sätt huruledes hållas skall uti den Högborne Furstes och Herres, Herr Carls med Guds nåde Sveriges Rikes Regerande Arvfurstes, Hertig till Södermanland, Närke och Värmland etc. Hovförsamling med Gudstjänsten*, Stockholm 1602 (no author).

[42] O. Martini, *Kristeligt betänkande* ... , Uppsala Universitetsbiblitek MS T. 79.

doctrine and could only be determined by the clergy. It was, in other words, a question of who should administer the teaching of the church: regent or clergy. In 1604 Karl published his *Bevisbok* (Book of Proof), where he, using quotations from the church Fathers, Luther and Melanchthon, tried to reject ubiquitarianism. The archbishop immediately responded, publishing a tract in which he agreed with Karl's general approach of interpreting scripture through the writings of the church Fathers, but emphasised his misunderstandings and Calvinist interpretations. Karl followed this up by issuing a public letter to the nation in December 1604 where he rejected the archbishop's accusations, eventually providing a more detailed response in a tract which he published two years later.

An anonymous catechism was published in November 1604, of which Karl later acknowledged authorship. It was intended to educate the people and was written in an evangelical and direct style. It drew predominantly on Luther's Small Catechism, but it also includes passages from the Reformed Heidelberg and Emden Catechisms. Yet it does not appear to have intended to introduce reformed ideas. Naturally, the archbishop produced a hostile response to the catechism. In January 1607 Karl published a pamphlet on the eucharist, which further demonstrates his general evangelical position that the Bible should be normative in all matters of faith. The theological debate continued through 1608 with King Karl IX accusing the clergy of being inclined towards crypto-Catholicism, since they refused to suppress many of the old holy days. Finally, the clergy was ordered by the king to produce a revision of the Church Order for his approval. By 1609, however, the king's active involvement in ecclesiastical affairs came to an end after he suffered a stroke from which he never fully recovered.

GUSTAVUS ADOLPHUS AND THE RELIGIOUS INHERITANCE FROM GUSTAV VASA

The accession of Gustavus Adolphus in 1611 signals the end of the Reformation era in Sweden.[43] However, it was during his reign that Sweden entered the Thirty Years War, and together with the evangelical German territorial states, fought for the survival of Protestantism. The young king's succession to the throne was far from unproblematic. The estates had shown their support by disregarding the paragraph in the

[43] See N. Ahnlund, *Gustav Adolf the Great*, Princeton 1940 and M. Roberts, *Gustavus Adolphus*, 2nd edition, London 1992.

succession agreement which stated that the regent had to be twenty-four years old in order to be crowned. In spite of Gustavus Adolphus being only seventeen years old, he was considered to be of age and his guardians, the queen dowager and Duke Johan, had already renounced their guardianship. The promises which Gustavus Adolphus was forced to make when taking over the government after his father anticipated the coronation charter he had to issue at his coronation in 1617. He had to give religious guarantees which included restrictive provisions against heterodox immigrants. Later, when he tried to exclude these stipulations from his coronation charter, the estates requested him to include them.

The significance attached to the religious guarantees by the estates is remarkable. Admittedly, in 1593, King Sigismund had been forced by Duke Karl and the estates to provide such guarantees in order to be crowned. But then Sigismund had been in the unusual situation of belonging not only to a different religion, but one which was hostile to that of the majority of the population. Karl IX, however, had managed, with the acceptance of the estates, to wait until after his coronation to offer any guarantees. He had then given these as a confirmation of his Lutheran faith, not as a condition for his coronation. Gustavus Adolphus was not in a position to impose such conditions on the estates, not least because of his extreme youth. However, with regard to his future foreign policy, he must have been relieved to have avoided a public condemnation of Calvinists and Reformed.

THE CORONATION OF 1617 AND ITS RELIGIOUS AND POLITICAL SIGNIFICANCE

Gustavus Adolphus was crowned in the cathedral of Uppsala on 12 October 1617.[44] The coronation ceremony can be seen as a significant step on the way to breaking the isolation of Sweden and laying claim to a position among the important powers of Europe. At the beginning of the year the peace treaty of Stolbova had been signed with Russia. It was significant to the extent that it was the first Swedish peace treaty to be based on military victory. Furthermore, the recently re-opened University of Uppsala was able to celebrate the awarding of its first degrees in July, thereby laying claim to a place within the world of learning. The following month a parliament met in Stockholm in order to prepare the

[44] I. Montgomery, 'Gustav Adolf von Schweden – Der Held aus Mitternacht' in K. Scholder and D. Kleinmann, *Protestantische Profile*, Berlin 1983.

coronation. On this occasion Gustavus Adolphus took the opportunity to promise to guard the evangelical inheritance from Gustav Vasa and defend the pure teaching. The young prince described himself as God's instrument, elected to carry out God's will for the country.

The solemn coronation with its traditional ceremonies fulfilled not only a religious design, but also a political one. Sweden, by rallying round a strongly evangelical king, emphasised that Sigismund's claim to the Swedish throne was considered null and void. The new Swedish national consciousness was prominent in the coronation, especially in the chivalrous tournaments in which the king took part, and in the poetry and songs performed at the occasion. This new national consciousness was characterised by an old-fashioned Lutheran certainty: Sweden was compared with Israel of the Old Testament and, accordingly, seen as a nation chosen by God. The Lutheran faith confirmed and gave meaning to the political and intellectual gains of recent years.

It is in this context that the conferring of the doctoral degrees in theology, which ended the coronation, has to be seen.[45] This event underlined that it was no longer necessary for learned Swedes to travel abroad to receive this distinguished degree. The ceremony, however, was a predominantly political affair. The king issued the invitations and selected those who were to be awarded the degree, while the chancellor, Axel Oxenstierna, acted as promoter. Those who became doctors of divinity, the archbishop Petrus Kenicius, the bishop of Strängnäs and later archbishop, Paulinus Gothus, and the two court preachers, Johannes Rudbeckius and Johannes Bothvidi, had all been personally selected by Gustavus Adophus. It has been debated why these four were elected. They were undoubtedly important people, but so were a number of other candidates who were not considered. Significantly, two of those rewarded had been faithful royal servants since the reign of Karl IX. Both Kenicius and Paulinus had played a major part in the Uppsala Assembly where Swedish Reformation doctrine had finally been established. Gustavus Adolphus may well have followed one of Karl's maxims: 'Love your father's loyal servants: reward them properly'. Both Rudbeckius and Bothvidi must have been obvious candidates, being the king's court preachers and his personal chaplains. They had furthermore executed a number of important tasks for the government to the satisfaction of the king.

The King stated his purpose in the invitations to the degree ceremony.

[45] S. Göransson, 'Teologin i 1600-talets Uppsala', in S. Lundström, *Gustav II Adolf och Uppsala Universitet*, Uppsala 1982, 37.

First, he referred to the traditional saying that reward and punishment are aids in governing the state. He intended to encourage virtue by rewarding the deserving:

Since the King has decided to reward some of his subjects, who through the honours they receive from him become examples of virtue, as well as of the King's grace, he was of the opinion that the spiritual estate should not be forgotten, because of the elevation and necessity of the clergy's office, as well as the King's great love of the faith itself, and even of the clergy, whom God has personally entrusted to his care and protection.

Second, those who had been chosen are mentioned and it is stated that they: 'through their loyalty to God and religion, to King and country, through their talents, learning and diligence, understanding of Holy Scripture, through lectures, disputations and sermons' are 'particularly deserving to be rewarded by the King with a distinguished honour'. Apart from the speech given by the promoter, a prepared question had traditionally to be addressed by the doctoral candidates in this period. It was: 'Can several faiths which are false and erring be tolerated together with the true orthodox religion by the Christian government in a well-organised state?' Paulinus answered on behalf of the candidates, but unfortunately his answer has not been preserved. Whether or not religious toleration was feasible and acceptable had become an important political issue in the wake of the Peace of Stolbova that year, when a number of adherents of the Russian Orthodox church had become Swedish subjects. It is significant that the question was a practical and not a theoretical one, focussed, as it was, on how lay authority should deal with the problem.

The question of toleration achieved prominence in Sweden during these years when the country became a major European power and came under the influence of European culture and politics.[46] That Gustavus Adolphus remained concerned with toleration can be seen from the funeral sermon Bothvidi preached at the king's death in 1632. Bothvidi related that Gustavus Adolphus had asked 'if not several faiths could be accommodated in the kingdom'. However, he had been given the answer that it would only lead to so much conflict and disagreement that it would cause the destruction of the kingdom, as well as the true faith. Consequently the king had abandoned the idea. The reason why Bothvidi included this incident in his sermon was, of course, to demonstrate how sensible the king had been in taking the clergy's advice and

---

[46] For the interest in the Orthodox church, see T. Kälvemask, 'Petrus Petrejus' och Johannes Botvidis skildringar av den ryska kyrkan', *Kyrkohistorisk Årsskrift* (1969), 85–96.

avoiding such a hazardous undertaking. Rather than Bothvidi's orthodox view that unity in religion was a necessary precondition for peace and prosperity in the country, it is the fact that Gustavus Adolphus raised the question at all which is significant.

Bothvidi's orthodoxy was unquestionable. The day after having received his doctorate, he presided over a disputation which disproved the validity of the Calvinist teaching on predestination. These theses were dedicated to the king and were undoubtedly intended to show his subjects that the previous dissociation from the reformed faith was still valid.

THE REFORMATION CENTENARY OF 1621

The centenary of the Reformation which Gustavus Adolphus allowed to be celebrated in 1621 represents the climax of the accentuation of Gustav Vasa's significance for Sweden. It was decided to celebrate the centenary on 21 January, 21 February and 21 March. Sweden had missed out on the celebrations which took place in most evangelical countries in 1617. Instead, the choice fell on 21 January 1621 which was the centenary of Gustav Vasa's election as leader (*hövitsman*) by the peasant population of Dalarna. It was undoubtedly an important event in bringing about the country's independence, while for Gustavus Adolphus and Archbishop Kenicius, who encouraged him to commemorate the centenary, the introduction of the Reformation was a logical consequence of Gustav Vasa's seizure of power.[47]

The king personally drafted a detailed order on 3 December 1620 which stated that 'a jubilee or solemn and glorious day of prayer' should be celebrated the following year in order to commemorate the centenary of the Reformation of Sweden. He explained that Gustav Vasa had been chosen by God as

an instrument and tool, through whom the papal idolatry has been suppressed and ousted, and who in its place has introduced the pure and saving word of God preached to our congregations and hearts. For a century God has upheld among us his holy word and correct teaching.

These three days of commemoration were to be celebrated like the traditional rogation days and, as was his habit, Gustavus Adolphus personally chose the texts to be preached. Three were chosen for each day, all from the Old Testament. It was common practice to choose texts

---

[47] See O. P. Grell, 'Scandinavia', in R. W. Scribner, R. Porter and M. Teich (eds.), *The Reformation in National Context*, Cambridge 1994, 111–12.

from that part of the Bible during this period, because it was easy for the congregations to identify with many of the Old Testament figures. Bishop Laurentius Paulinus Gothus had the sermons printed which were to be given on the commemorative days in the cathedral of Strängnäs. They are particularly interesting because of their national patriotism which the bishop linked with the Reformation. At the beginning of the book is the royal order of 3 December, followed by a list of the texts chosen for the different days, including the psalms to be sung. Then follows a dedication to Gustavus Adolphus which compares him with Emperor Constantine. Finally come the elaborate sermons which utilise the texts from the Old Testament to rationalise events in Swedish history. The theme is very strictly developed, drawing a parallel between Biblical history and Swedish history – as God had controlled the history of Israel so he controls that of Sweden. Accordingly, Gustav Vasa and his successors were portrayed as staunch defenders of the faith on a par with the heroes of the Old Testament.

Through these sermons, Gustavus Adolphus received confirmation from the church of the Vasas' importance for Sweden in political, as well as religious, terms. Apart from Paulinus Gothus, Kenicius and Bothvidi took the opportunity to publish their sermons. Bothvidi, who preached his sermons in the Great Church in Stockholm, reflects the same intimate relationship between religion and politics in the title he chose for the publication of his sermons: *Three celebratory sermons about the reformation which took place in Sweden a century ago, in government, as well as religion through ... King Göstaff Ericsson [Gustav Vasa] ...*

By the early seventeenth century, Sweden had become one of the strongest champions of Lutheranism in Europe, as can be seen by Gustavus Adolphus's decision to enter the Thirty Years War in order to assist his evangelical co-religionists in Germany. Sweden had finally become a recognised and valued member of evangelical Europe, notwithstanding her earlier hesitation and lack of clear religious direction.

FINLAND

Simultaneously with the installation of 'Finland's reformer', Mikael Agricola, as bishop of Åbo in 1554, the country was divided into two bishoprics, and Paavali Juusten was given the new diocese of Viborg. Juusten had studied in Wittenberg between 1543 and 1546. Upon his return he became the first headmaster at the Latin school in Åbo, where he played an important part in training the new evangelical ministers. The evangelical faith which, according to contemporary perception, represented a definite guarantee for the unity of the state, was to be promoted through education. Furthermore, Juusten sought to consolidate the Reformation through synods and synodal acts, along the same lines as those of Archbishop Laurentius Petri in Sweden. In 1563 Juusten was promoted to the more important see of Åbo where he remained until his death in 1575. He was rewarded for the political support he had offered King Erik XIV against the latter's brother, Duke Johan, who ruled Finland. This happened at the time of Erik XIV's imprisonment of Duke Johan, when most of the Finnish clergy remained loyal to the duke. Later, when Duke Johan had managed to dethrone his brother, Juusten was allowed to retain the bishopric of Åbo. However, as a form of punishment and test of his loyalty to his new king, Johan III, he was forced to take part in a diplomatic mission to Russia which lasted from 1569 to 1572. By the time Juusten returned to Finland he was a broken man and he died a few years later.

Juusten spent considerable energy and time in organising his diocese through numerous visitations. Likewise, he worked hard at improving the educational standards among his clergy. Thus in 1573 he organised the first post-Reformation synod in Finland. He also issued regulations from which it can be seen that his concept of the eucharist was identical to that of Laurentius Petri.[48] He wanted to keep the rites of baptism unchanged and he rejected the possibility of exchanging wine with other liquids, such as water, in the communion. He also considered penance a sacrament. Juusten was concerned with the same issues which had come to the fore in the clash over Calvinism in Sweden under Erik XIV. The Finnish bishop was undoubtedly influenced by the Wittenberg Church Order, as well as Laurentius Petri's Church Order. In spite of his unpopularity with the government of Johan III, Juusten took part in the consecration of Archbishop Laurentius Petri Gothus in 1575.

In addition, the bishop of Åbo was a diligent author of educational and ritual books. He wrote the first book of sermons to be published in Finnish,[49] and he translated and adapted Luther's catechism. In 1575 he published a new and changed edition of Mikael Agricola's *Manual* in

---

[48] W. Schmidt, *Finlands kyrka genom tiderna*, Stockholm 1940, 123 (*Sedicim capita rerum synodicarum*). See also S. Heininen, 'Biskopsutnämningarna i Finland 1554–1642', in I. Brohed (ed.), *Reformationens konsolidering i de nordiska länderna 1540–1610*, Oslo 1990, 240–50.

[49] Schmidt, *Finlands kyrka*, 124 (*Explicationes evangeliorum dominicalium et praecipuarum totius anni* (no copy is extant)).

Finnish. Among his historical works, his *Bishops' Chronicle* is undoubtedly the most important.[50]

However, Johan III made sure that his church policy also affected the see of Åbo. The medieval chapter had been dissolved by Gustav Vasa in 1555. A new chapter had been instated by the king before 1571, and one of Johan's loyal servants, Henricus Canuti from the diocese of Strängnäs, had been made dean. Canuti energetically promoted the king's liturgical reforms within the see, but he found that his work was opposed by the leading minister in Åbo, Henricus Jacobi, who had been passed over for the office of dean.

The episcopacy of Åbo was left without an incumbent for eight years following the death of Juusten. During this period, the diocese was in the hands of superintendents who had no right of ordination. Henricus Canuti was made superintendent in 1579, but when Johan III failed to secure apostolic succession for the Swedish/Finnish bishops, he decided to fill the episcopacy once more in 1583. The king appointed the Finn, Ericus Erici Sorolainen, as bishop of Åbo and placed the see of Viborg under his administration.

From the outset the Jesuits had taken a lively interest in Johan III's pro-Catholic church policy, and they had tried to promote the Counter Reformation in Sweden and Finland through diplomatic initiatives and missionary efforts. In particular, the king's plans for a restitution of the monasteries had raised their expectations. Their recatholisation efforts were spearheaded by the Norwegian Jesuit, Laurentius Nicolai (Kloster-lasse) and the former secretary-general of the Jesuit order, Antonio Possevino. The theological college which the king allowed Laurentius Nicolai to open in the former Franciscan monastery in Stockholm became the centre for their attempt to engineer the country's return to the Catholic fold.[51]

The most important Finnish Jesuit was Johannes Jussoila from Raumo, who returned to Rome with Antonio Possevino and was ordained. Later he became court priest to King Sigismund, only to be imprisoned in Sweden where he appears to have died in 1604. Around twenty Finnish students attended the Jesuit college in Braunsberg towards the end of the sixteenth and beginning of the seventeenth centuries. Those Finns who chose a Jesuit school did so for both political and religious motives. There was a feeling in Finland that the personal

[50] *Ibid.*, 125 (*Catalogus et ordinaria successio episcoporum*).
[51] See V. Helk, *Laurentius Nicolai Norvegius*, Copenhagen 1966 and O. Garstein, *Rome and the Counter-reformation in Scandinavia*, I–IV, Oslo 1963 and 1980 and Leiden 1991.

union between Sweden/Finland and Poland provided protection against Russian expansionism, and Sigismund accordingly retained a substantial following in the country. One of the most illustrious Finnish pupils of the Jesuit college in Braunsberg was Johannes Messenius, who studied there from 1595 to 1602, and who wrote the extensive history, *Scondia illustrata* and a smaller history of Finland, *Finlands krönika*.[52] In 1616 Messenius was removed from the University of Uppsala and imprisoned in the castle of Kajaneborg, where he died in 1636.[53]

Even if the Jesuits had substantial support in Finland, they were faced with considerable local hostility. Thus the pupils at the Latin school in Viborg refused to attend when a Jesuit, Gregorius Clementis, was made headmaster in 1584.[54]

Finland was represented at the Uppsala Assembly by just over ten clerics. The small number was indicative not only of the strength of Catholicism in the country, but also of the tension between Duke Karl and Klas Fleming who, since 1591, had been the governor of Finland and Estonia and controlled the eastern part of the realm. Fleming deliberately made use of Catholicism to indicate his independence of Duke Karl. However, he appears to have been genuinely interested in theology and he wrote a small tract on the eucharist, *En kort Undervijsning*. Undoubtedly, Fleming could rely on the support of the majority of the population in his political and religious confrontation with Duke Karl.

Following the death of Juusten in 1575 and of Härkäpää in 1578, the bishoprics of Åbo and Viborg remained vacant for years because of the general religious and political instability in the country. Johan III's liturgy was quietly introduced and accepted in Finland which, after all, had been his duchy. Furthermore Johan made attempts to re-establish the monastery of Nådendal and he intended to make the Latin school in Åbo a centre for humanist education. All these initiatives were greatly encouraged by the *Curia*.

Finally in 1583 a new bishop of Åbo, Ericus Erici Sorolainen, was appointed. He remained in charge of the see until his death in 1625, while also administering the diocese of Viborg, which remained vacant for nearly forty years, until 1618. The historical reputation of Sorolainen has been mixed. He has been portrayed in a number of ways, ranging from a humanist scholar who disliked politics to an inane and spineless

[52] H. Schück, *Messenius. Några blad ur Vasatidens kulturhistoria*, Stockholm 1920, 20f.
[53] *Ibid.*, 239ff.
[54] J. Nourteva, 'Finlands studerande vid jesuiternas kollegier', in Brohed (ed.), *Reformationens konsolidering i de nordiska länderna*, 155.

opportunist. However, to provide leadership for the Finnish church in a period characterised by considerable fluctuations in both politics and religion cannot have been a simple task. Sorolainen had received his education in Germany, where he had studied under David Chytraeus in Rostock and where he had encountered the Philippist-inspired Rostock orthodoxy. His interest in the writings of the church Fathers was probably also generated by his experiences in Rostock. Shortly after his return he was made court preacher by Johan III. In 1578 the king made him headmaster of the important Latin school in Gävle, as successor to Petrus Olai Gestricius, who had been forced out because of his opposition to the liturgy, and five years later he was given the bishopric of Åbo. He promised to introduce the *Nova Ordinantia* and the liturgy, to celebrate mass in Latin on the important holidays, to use chasubles and pay attention to church singing and to interest his clergy in the writings of the church Fathers. Sorolainen worked tirelessly with his clergy to introduce the liturgy in his diocese. Among the liturgy's most forceful advocates in Finland was the dean, Jacob Geet.

Sorolainen was also actively involved in Johan III's attempt to enter into a dialogue with the Greek Orthodox church. He translated the liturgy and a type of catechism into Greek as a basis for discussions which, however, never took place. When Klas Fleming tried to convince Sigismund to introduce purely Catholic ceremonies in Finland, Sorolainen, however, desisted. His relationship with Duke Karl, later King Karl IX, remained tense throughout his life. When Duke Karl arrived in Finland in 1602 he imprisoned Sorolainen together with twenty Finnish ministers and brought them back to Uppsala to be prosecuted by the chapter. The chapter of Uppsala acquitted Sorolainen. Undoubtedly his opposition to Fleming's papism now stood him in good stead. He was pardoned and re-instated in his office.

Sorolainen made a significant contribution to the ecclesiastical literature in Finland. In 1614 he translated the new Swedish manual into Finnish. Four years later he published a catechism intended for students and ministers. A smaller catechism was published posthumously. It is characterised by Sorolainen's liberal use of the works of Luther, Agricola and Juusten. In spite of his use of these authors, his model was probably the catechisms of J. Tettelbach, D. Chytraeus and S. Musaeus. Thus Sorolainen's catechisms are closer in their theology to gnesio-Lutheranism than Reformation Lutheranism. Sorolainen's most important works were his books of sermons. The first was published in 1621 and the second four years later. It was the first work of its kind to be published in Finnish.

It draws on German sources. Sorolainen was also involved in the translation of the Bible into Finnish and was elected a member of the committee which oversaw the translation of the Bible.

In 1583 the first hymn book in Finnish appeared, edited by the headmaster of the Latin school in Åbo, Jacobus Petri Finno (Suomalainen). Later, between 1611 and 1614, it was expanded by the minister, Henrik Hemming, who published a collection of more than 200 hymns under the title, *En liten finskspråkig psalmbok*. Around the same time another hymn book, *Andeliga Psalmer och Wijsor*, was published by Sigfrid Aron Forsius. He was the first Finnish-Swedish hymn writer and was an exponent of a neo-platonic natural philosophy with a strong astrological element.

It is possible to detect a religious and political consistency in Sorolainen's actions. Even if he was positively inclined towards the liturgy from the outset, he never sought to force it upon the clergy and laity of his diocese. Theologically, he was probably closer to such humanistically inclined Lutherans as the archbishops Laurentius Petri Gothus and Andreas Björnram, who both supported the liturgy. Sorolainen considered ecclesiastical ceremonies to be *adiaphora* which could be shaped according to the demand of the times. Furthermore, he remained loyal to King Johan III, who had ruled Finland as a duke. In accordance with his view, there was nothing in the liturgy which was contrary to Lutheran teachings. However, at the Uppsala Assembly, Sorolainen was forced to change his position publicly and apologise for his earlier support of the liturgy. He admitted that he had realised that the liturgy was an expression of false teaching, and neither he nor his clergy would defend it.[55]

Only thirteen ministers from Finland took part in the Uppsala Assembly of 1593. All members of the chapter in Åbo were present, apart from the dean who was ill. The Finnish clergy were united with their Swedish colleagues in their wish to abolish the liturgy. The Finnish clergy's changed position could not fail to attract attention since they had hitherto been united behind the liturgy. The stadtholder of Finland, Klas Fleming, scorned them for changing their view with such ease and accused them of passively bowing to the directives of lay authorities.

Not surprisingly, it was the bishop of Åbo, Sorolainen, who took the lead among the Finnish representatives. He appears to have been prominent among those who engineered the meetings' condemnation of Calvinism. Sorolainen's view seems to have swayed the Finnish clergy,

[55] *Svenska Rigsdagsakter*, III, 52ff.

who all signed the Uppsala Resolution, while hardly any members of the Finnish nobility and local authorities followed suit. Undoubtedly they were encouraged not to by Klas Fleming's hostile attitude to the Resolution.

A synod of the Finnish clergy was held in Åbo in the summer of 1593.[56] Here they took the opportunity to explain their actions in Uppsala, pointing out that, in their opinion the Resolution expressed the true apostolic doctrine. Accordingly, they had agreed and confirmed it with their signatures and seals. For the Finnish church, as well as the Swedish, the Uppsala Resolution served to bind it firmly to the Lutheran faith. Here, as in Sweden, it signalled the end of the theological strife of the Reformation era.

When Gustavus Adolphus succeeded to the throne the situation was considerably more difficult in Finland than in other parts of the realm, because of the prolonged war with Russia and Poland. Politically the peace with Russia at Stolbova in 1617 proved of lasting importance for Finland. The border was now moved further east, and the western part of Karelia and part of Ingermannland became part of the realm. It was as a direct consequence of this that the diocese of Viborg was re-established and Olaus Elimaeus appointed bishop in 1618. He received special instructions to try to teach and convert those people of the Russian Orthodox faith who had now become Swedish/Finnish subjects. Over the next decade Elimaeus, until his death in 1627, managed to revert the serious decay which had imperilled the Protestant church in that part of Finland during the preceeding decades. Gustavus Adolphus took a personal interest in the missionary efforts of the Finnish clergy, especially among the Lapps. By then, however, the Lutheran church in Sweden/Finland needed only to extend its influence to these marginal, indigenous people living at the barren edges of the kingdom in order to complete successfully the Reformation which had begun a century earlier.

[56] E. Anthoni, *Till avvecklingen av konflikten mellan hertig Carl och Finland*, Helsinki 1935, 41f.

CHAPTER 7

Faith, superstition and witchcraft in Reformation Scandinavia

Jens Chr. V. Johansen

In a book of sermons, published in 1592, the Lutheran bishop of Sta-vanger, Jørgen Erickssøn, pointed out the unambiguous connection between superstition and witchcraft. He blamed the papists for trying to teach the peasantry that they could subdue storms through the burning of consecrated herbs and suppress the forces released by the devil with incense. This was nothing but 'sheer idolatry and witchcraft' which Man had been forbidden to use.[1]

The view of Jørgen Erikssøn coincided with that of the fathers of the Reformation, Luther and Calvin. For both reformers, the fight against superstition and its instigators on one hand, and the persecution of witches on the other, represented identical concerns: the need to expose the false play of the devil.[2] Superstition was contrasted with the true religion.[3] During the sixteenth and seventeenth centuries when this concept was used in Denmark against remnants of Catholic ideas and more generally about every deviation from official doctrine,[4] it was directly inspired by Luther's view of the mass, purgatory, the sacraments, fasts, worship of saints, baptism of bells and wax candles, worship of relics, indulgences and pilgrimages.[5] Luther considered such rites to be superstitious, because believers did not put their faith in God alone.

Theologically the early Danish reformers were rooted in Christian

---

[1] J. Erickssøn *Jonæ Prophetis skiøne Historia vdi 24 Predicken begreben*, Copenhagen 1592, sig., SIII.
[2] J. Delumeau, 'Les réformateurs et la superstition', *Actes du Colloque d'Amiral de Coligny et son temps (Paris, 14–28 octobre 1972)*, Paris 1974, 462.
[3] *Ibid.*, 451.
[4] A. Wittendorff, 'Fire stolper holder et skidehus'. Tidens forestillingsverden', in S. Ellehøj (ed.), *Christian IVs verden*, Copenhagen 1988, 214. Some scholars appear to have missed this double aspect and consider superstition to be solely concerned with witchcraft and magic, see J. M. Kittelson, 'Visitations and Popular Religious Culture: Further Reports from Strasbourg', in K. C. Sessions and P. N. Bebb (eds.), *Pietas et Societas. New Trends in Reformation Social History. Essays in Memory of Harold J. Grimm*, Kirksville, MO, 1985, 89: 'the presence of what modern scholars define as magic *or* superstition ... the casting of signs, spells, or hexes, and *the like*' (my emphasis).
[5] Delumeau, 'Les réformateurs', 454f.

179

humanism rather than Lutheranism. This can be seen from several of their writings from the early 1530s. Their official views were expressed in the so-called Copenhagen Confession of 1530, while their differences can be seen from a comparison of their individual works.

The Catholic prelates and the evangelical preachers had been asked to present their views at the parliament which met in Copenhagen in July 1530. Eventually, no official religious debate took place during parliament and no solution was found to the growing religious conflict between Catholics and evangelicals. Other more urgent issues came to dominate the agenda of the parliament.[6] However, people were informed about the forty-three articles of the Copenhagen Confession through sermons preached over each article by the evangelical preachers assembled in Copenhagen. Printed versions by Jørgen Jensen Sadolin and Peder Laurentsen were quickly published, as were the twenty-seven-point answer and complaint by the prelates.[7]

The Malmø reformer, Frants Vormordsen, adopted the most rigorous position concerning the worship of saints. He rejected it as offending the honour of God and the atonement of Christ. For Vormordsen it was the historical, perfect and unique atonement of Christ which mattered above everything else. Consequently he had to fight the saints and their role as expiators, which detracted from the uniqueness of Christ's atonement, even more forcefully than Luther,[8] Another Malmø reformer, Peder Laurentsen, and the later Lutheran bishop of Ribe, Hans Tausen, showed greater flexibility with regard to the worship of saints. Tausen in particular was prepared to be indulgent towards the weaker members of the church. Thus, Laurentsen asked why we should worship saints, when Christ was our expiator and defender before his heavenly father.[9] Tausen, who was one of the few Danish evangelical preachers who had studied under Luther in Wittenberg, understood the religious feeling behind the invocation of saints – that Man in his sinfulness and disgrace did not dare 'to ask too much of God'. Furthermore, he considered it a gradual process to teach the weak to approach God directly.[10]

---

[6] N. K. Andersen, *Confessio Hafniensis. Den københavnske bekendelse af 1530*, Copenhagen 1954, 52–64. See also O. P. Grell, 'The City of Malmø and the Danish Reformation', *Archiv für Reformationsgeschichte*, 79 (1988), 323–5.

[7] See chapter 2 and Andersen, *Confessio*, 56.

[8] Andersen, *Confessio*, 315. See Frants Vormordsen's two pamphlets, *Een korth oc lydhen forklaring oc forskell . . .* , Malmø 1531, 4f. and *En oc Tiue de allerskøniste oc hugsualestigste Artickle . . .* , Malmø 1534, art. 7–10.

[9] Andersen, *Confessio*, 316. See P. Laurentsen, *En stacket vnderuisning*, Malmø 1533, 21ff.

[10] Andersen, *Confessio*, 316–17.

In the Copenhagen Confession, however, it was the much more uncompromising position of Vormordsen which carried the day; article thirty-two rejected saints as intercessors and expiators. This article, like *Confessio Augustana*, was definite in its rejection of the Catholic teaching on saints.

The Danish reformers were much more categorical than Luther in their rejection of the teaching on purgatory too. While Luther considered purgatory to represent a purification of souls, the Danish preachers did not vacillate.[11] Vormordsen used the same arguments as Zwingli, pointing out that the concept of purgatory challenged the belief in the full atonement of Christ.[12] Accordingly, the rejection of purgatory led to the rejection of vigils.[13]

Iconoclasm played a part in the popular evangelical movement. Thus, in November 1529 the preacher Claus Mortensen and his supporters destroyed all images in St Peter's church in Malmø. A year later a prominent mayor of Copenhagen, assisted primarily by members of the guilds,[14] led a similar iconoclasm in the church of Our Lady. Officially, in the Copenhagen Confession, however, the evangelical preachers did not demand the removal of all images. They only warned of the danger of idolatry which the images presented. This view corresponded closely with that of Peder Laurentsen: Christians were at liberty to decide whether or not they wanted images in their churches. Images were neither evil nor good. However, if someone was of the opinion that they should be honoured and worshipped, and that they possessed spiritual power, and that one could receive assistance and comfort from them or for their sake, then they had to be removed, because 'insane and simple folk' would abuse them for idolatry.[15]

Frants Vormordsen took a more stringent approach – all images made and honoured by Man should be removed and destroyed by the authorities.[16] Hans Tausen, on the other hand, appears to have leant towards

---

[11] *Ibid.*, 327ff.
[12] Vormordsen, *Een korth oc lydhen forklaring*, 20f.
[13] See P. Laurentsen, *Aarsagen oc en ret Forklaring paa den nye Reformats ... vdi den kristelige Stad Malmø*, Malmø 1530, 40v–41v. This pamphlet is known under the title: *Malmøbogen*, and is the only evangelical publication to treat the question of vigils.
[14] H. Lundbak, *Såfremt som vi skulle være deres lydige borgere. Rådene i København og Malmø 1516–1536 og deres politiske virksomhed i det feudale samfund*, Odense 1985, 97ff.
[15] Andersen, *Confessio*, 419ff. See Laurentsen, *Aasagen oc en ret Forklaring*, 53v ff. and O. Chrysostomus, *Lamentatio Ecclesiæ*, Malmø 1529, 27.
[16] Vormordsen, *Een korth oc lydhen forklaring*, 21f.

the more flexible position of Peder Laurentsen, when he stated that only crucifixes and edifying images should be hung in churches.[17]

The debate about images continued during the following decades, but the leading Protestant theologians were unable to reach an agreement. In his *Visitation Book*, the first Lutheran Bishop of Zealand, Peder Palladius, wrote that images were allowed in churches. He emphasised, however, that if they were worshipped, they had to be removed and burned.[18] His brother, Niels Palladius, who succeeded Vormordsen as bishop of Lund in 1551, however, fought vigorously against the use of images. In his work *Commonefactio de vera Dei et de vitandis Idolis*,[19] he stated that no images, which he consistently referred to as idols, could be tolerated in churches. The peasantry was still rooted in profound darkness and ignorance about the true worship of God. They worshipped the old images, honoured them with wax candles, sacrifices, suits of clothes and genuflections. They invoked the Virgin Mary, many still carried rosaries, and they continued to go on pilgrimages to the traditional sacred places. Not only did Niels Palladius reject the old pictures and statues of saints, he rejected all images in the churches. Most contemptible were attempts to picture God himself and here Niels Palladius referred to the prohibition of images laid down in the Mosaic law.[20]

Following the introduction of the Lutheran Reformation in Denmark-Norway in 1536, the government never intended to remove all Catholic parish priests. In the main, most Catholic priests continued their work and cure more or less undisturbed. It was for this reason that the leaders of the new Lutheran church considered the fight against Catholic relics one of their most important tasks. Bishop Peder Palladius carried out a visitation of all the parishes in his diocese between 1538 and 1543. This experience caused him to write his so-called *Visitation Book*, intended for contemporary and future bishops as a guide to provide assistance in their work of instructing ministers and congregations. Here Palladius

---

[17] 'Have no images of idolatry to kneel in front of. But have crucifixes and other such images and pictures which remind us of the kindness of God.' Hans Tausen, 'Sendebrev til alle Provster og Sognepræster i Ribe Stift', in H. F. Rørdam (ed.), *Smaaskrifter af Hans Tavsen*, Copenhagen 1879, 258.

[18] 'Paintings and images can be fixed to the walls, in order that they can serve as a mirror for good, simple folk, when they are told who these images portray. But the images which are greatly frequented, and where wax models of children and crutches are hung, should be removed and burned.' In L. Jacobsen (ed.), *Peder Palladius' Danske Skrifter*, V, Copenhagen 1925, 36.

[19] Published in Wittenberg 1557. A German translation was published in Heidelberg in 1563.

[20] M. Schwarz Lausten, *Biskop Niels Palladius. Et bidrag til den danske kirkes historie 1550–1560*, Copenhagen 1968, 50f.

described indulgences and pilgrimages as the work of the devil.[21] He was no less severe in his treatment of the worship of saints, requiem masses and purgatory.[22] The Catholic traditions, however, could not be swept aside quickly and some years later, in 1554, Palladius renewed his attacks in another work entitled: *A Useful Book about St Peter's Ship.*[23]

The worship of saints and relics was undoubtedly among the most difficult traditions to eradicate in the new Lutheran church. Concerning relics, Palladius was vitriolic in his sarcasm, pointing out that the Virgin Mary could not but have been constantly milking herself if she was to have produced all the milk ascribed to her.[24] He had already, in his *Visitation Book*, attacked the abuse which took place in connection with pilgrimages.[25]

The close co-operation between church and state in Denmark guaranteed that Palladius' complaints were given serious attention. Often the local authorities were ordered to take action against the continued use of Catholic rituals. In 1532 the royal administrator, Hans Barnekow, was ordered personally to inspect the church in Holmstrup. Much idolatry, many sacrifices of geese and lambs, and the worship of images, were apparently taking place in the church, and Barnekow was ordered to remove 'all the idolatry from the church'.[26] Four years later the administrator was ordered to stop the use of idolatry in the church in Bidstrup. Previously, he had been ordered to demolish the church. Having refrained from taking action he was now ordered to demolish it once more and to level it and the churchyard with the ground.[27] Similarly, in 1553, Knud Gyldenstjerne, was ordered to demolish the

---

[21] *Palladius' Danske Skrifter*, V, 31 and 130.

[22] 'The other altars, apart from the straight high altar, belong to the deluded teachings about the invocation of saints and the torment of purgatory, which the pope and monks introduced. They are nothing but similar to the cow-sheds and market-stalls which our Lord Jesus personally destroyed when he cleared the Temple in Jerusalem of shopkeepers', *ibid.*, 36 and 39.

[23] Palladius wrote the following about purgatory: 'such trash was brought on board the ship by the devil through ghosts and false revelations in order that he could establish idolatry and the worth of Man's own deeds', in *Palladius' Danske Skrifter*, III, Copenhagen 1916–18, 88.

[24] *Ibid.*, 87 and 89.

[25] 'This our pilgrimage, which they wrongly even call holy walk, is running to the dead Iacob of Compostella, to Karop, and Vilsnap, and the seven dead churches in Rome, to the dead blood in Bystrup near Roschild; to the dead Søren in Holmstrup, to the dead blood in Kipping on Falster; there and elsewhere the devil has produced his portents and blurred our eyes, and we rush there, as I can see the multitude does'. In *Palladius' Danske Skrifter*, V, 131.

[26] *RA* (Royal Archive in Copenhagen) Letterbooks of the Chancellery, Tegnelser no. 4, f. 142. For all subsequent references to the Letterbooks of the Chancellery, see also the printed edition, *Kancelliets Brevbøger 1551–1648*, Copenhagen 1885–1991.

[27] *Ibid.*, no. 5.

chapel in Skjerrum, which he had recently acquired, because he allowed idolatry and other objectionable practices to take place.[28]

It proved difficult to overcome Catholic traditions among the Danish-Norwegian peasantry. Shortly after the Reformation, Christian III had advocated a cautious approach in Norway, occasioned by evidence that the population in the western part of the country was hostile towards the new religion. The people refrained from presenting their children for baptism and did not ask the ministers to attend the mortally ill, they refused to pay tithes, the churches decayed, and they stayed away when the bishop carried out his visitations. Consequently, the government decided to placate the population and encouraged the ministers to continue to celebrate mass in accordance with Catholic tradition.[29] Furthermore, the murder of a number of ministers must have encouraged the government to take a cautious approach.[30] Around 1570 it was finally decided to take action against the surviving Catholic traditions. This happened after the bishop of Bergen, Jens Skjelderup had discovered that some women still worshipped the remaining statues of saints in the cathedral.[31]

In Blekinge in Scania most of the people still used their rosaries, lit candles and knelt in front of images of Mary, while images of saints were decorated and worshipped in a number of parishes. By 1590 similar images of saints still existed in at least four parish churches in Funen, where they constituted part of the remaining side altars.[32] As late as 1606 Christian IV learned that there was an image in the church in Krogstrup in the district of Horns, named St Dionysius, which the peasants honoured according to the old popish religion and dressed and decorated at certain times. The royal administrator was ordered to remove it from the church.[33]

A more cautious approach was initially taken in Sweden. At the synod of Örebro in 1529 it was decided to keep the old rituals as long as they were not contrary to the word of God. However, fifteen years later, during the parliament (*Riksdag*) of Västerås the king, Gustav Vasa, raised

[28]   *Ibid.*, no. 4, f. 286.
[29]   O. Koldsrud, 'Folket og reformasjonen i Noreg', in *Heidersskrift til Gustav Indrebø på femtiårsdagen 17. november 1939*, Bergen 1939, 24f.
[30]   *Ibid.*, 27.
[31]   H. Rieber-Mohn, 'Reformasjonen – brudd eller overgang', in I. Semmingsen *et al.* (eds.) *Norges Kulturhistorie*, II, Oslo 1979, 324; and T. Troels-Lund, *Dagligt Liv i Norden i det sekstende Århundrede*, 6th edition, Copenhagen 1969, VI, 71.
[32]   Troels-Lund, *Dagligt Liv*, VI, 71.
[33]   *RA*, Letterbooks, Sjællandske Tegnelser no. 20, f. 113.

these issues himself. He argued that the simple people were deceived to believe that consecrated water and salt and Latin masses were more powerful than the holy gospel and true Christian faith and knowledge of Jesus Christ.[34] Consequently, the worship of saints, requiem masses, pilgrimages and other popish traditions were forbidden by parliament. Shortly afterwards, Archbishop Laurentius Andreae had the great crucifix at the holy spring in Svinnegarn, which had been a considerable attraction for pilgrims, removed.[35] However, these changes were far from popular with the population at large. When the minister in Ovensjö interfered with the 'cross-crawling' on Good Friday, tumult broke out in the congregation. A minister in Piteå was threatened with an axe when he refrained from rubbing oil on a child during baptism.[36] The articles of Vadstena from 1552 warned against the practice of sick and unbaptised children being carried forward in the church while the gospel was read. Evidently, magic protection was sought through the words of the gospel.[37]

Throughout the sixteenth century, as we have seen above, Swedish society was troubled by confessional problems, and it was not until the Uppsala Assembly in 1593 that the Swedish Reformation moved decisively in a Lutheran direction.[38] It was during the succeeding decades that the Lutheran faith gained adherents in the villages. It was assisted by the destruction of images of saints and the prohibition of old customs. The population remained hostile, but expressed their hostility solely through silent disapproval.[39] Simultaneously, the Swedish house examinations (*husförhör*) became regularised. In 1596 the minute book of the cathedral chapter in Uppsala stated that the common people knew so little of the gospel that they ought not to receive communion. Accordingly, it was suggested that the local ministers should visit all villages once a year and catechise the inhabitants in the Christian faith.[40] This practice achieved the greatest importance for the propagation of the Lutheran faith in Sweden.

In Denmark and Norway the government continued its fight against superstition. In 1622 Christian IV had to renew his prohibition against pilgrimages in Norway, for example to the church of St Thomas in

[34] H. Pleijel, *Hustavlans värld. Kyrkligt folkliv i äldre tiders Sverige*, Stockholm 1970, 164f.
[35] H. Holmquist, *Från reformationen til romantiken, Handbok i svensk kyrkohistoria*, II, Stockholm 1953, 30.
[36] Pleijel, *Hustavlans värld*, 166.
[37] *Ibid.*, 169.
[38] See chapters 3 and 6; see also Pleijel, *Hustavlans värld*, 17.
[39] Pleijel, *Hustavlans värld*, 18.
[40] *Ibid.*, 87.

Fillefjel in southern Norway.[41] In 1626 peasants in two districts on Funen were forbidden to ring the church bells when someone died, unless permission had been obtained from the minister or the church-wardens.[42] The plundering during the Thirty Years War saw several silver crucifixes surface, which were hollow and supposedly contained the bones of saints. During the same period it was reported that a picture of the holy Regisse was exhibited in the chapel next to her spring, while an image of St Nicholas with three golden apples in his lap could be seen in the church in Helderup.[43] In 1634 the government requested the local administrator and the bishop of Ribe, Jens Dinesen Jersin, to halt an objectionable practice by the peasants in the district of Nørvang, which took place at two old altars in the church in Sindberg, which had been in use in Catholic times.[44] A couple of years later Bishop Jersin published a book, in which he emphasised that the use of charms containing pieces of paper on which the name of Christ was written, was contemptible and constituted a relic of Catholicism.[45]

These examples illustrate the problems which confronted the Prot-estant ministers in their attempt to reform a Christian tradition which had been internalised by the population over half a millenium. The previous centuries had fused together heathen beliefs and Christian teachings. Fatalism, ideas about fertility and the different creatures belonging to nature, farms and houses were inextricably bound up with the life of the peasantry. However, it has to be emphasised that the evidence for these phenomena is scant in the post-Reformation centuries. The chain of continuity is broken between the Middle Ages[46] and the middle of the eighteenth century when we have the first docu-mentary evidence of such beliefs (a fact which does not necessarily undermine the argument). It would, however, give too much promi-nence to these heathen components in popular belief, if we were to accept Jean Delumeau's view that Christianity had never reached the rural population.[47] It would only make us miss the indissoluble unity which over time had been established between Christianity and popular heathen traditions. Even the Lutheran faith fused so firmly with traditional magical peasant beliefs that they are nearly impossible

[41] Rieber-Mohn, 'Reformasjonen', 323.

[42] *RA*, Letterbooks, Fynske Tegnelser, no. 3, f. 913.

[43] Troels-Lund, *Dagligt Liv*, VI, 72.

[44] *RA*, Letterbooks, Jyske Tegnelser, no. 9, f. 63.

[45] J. Dinesen Jersin, *Troens Kamp oc Seyr. Det er: Om alle de Fristelser, med huilcke Troen udi it Guds Barns Hierte anfectis*, Copenhagen 1636, Sig. Cc.

[46] A. Gustavsson, *Forskning om folkligt fromhetsliv*, Staffanstorp 1976, 65ff.

[47] J. Delumeau, *Le Catholicisme entre Luther et Voltaire*, paris 1979, 247 and 267.

beliefs that they are nearly impossible to separate.[48] Likewise, the concept that the peasants should have been so split in their beliefs that they simultaneously worshipped within two different sets of beliefs – a primitive popular one during weekdays and a Christian one on Sundays, seems unlikely. A far more plausible interpretation has been offered by the Swedish theologian, Hilding Pleijel, who described the situation as a manifold unity (*complexio oppositorum*).

Undoubtedly a considerable proportion of Catholic parish priests and lower clergy shared their parishioners' beliefs, often lacking the necessary theological insight into such matters. They saw the rituals of the church on a par with the means with which they themselves, or cunning people, tried to heal humans and animals or prevent accidents.[49] When it is borne in mind that, on the one hand, most of these Catholic priests continued in their jobs after the Reformation and, on the other, that they and their new Lutheran colleagues were recruited from the peasants who formed the bulk of their congregations, it is hardly surprising that some of them caused the government some anxiety.

In 1559 the monks in Dueholm monastery were under suspicion of heterodoxy and the royal administrator of Mors was instructed to prevent them from serving the local community and to recruit a good, learned man who would provide the pastoral care.[50] In 1568 the ministers on Funen received an injunction to stop offering the sick consecrated wine 'against watering eyes'; clearly, ministers still felt obliged to assist their parishioners with the potent means they administered.[51] The minister in Jørlunde lost his post in the mid-1570s and was put in custody in the monastery in Sorø, where he was kept under observation, and restrictions were imposed on the visitors he was allowed and the books he was permitted to read. This had come about because of the unchristian conduct, including among other things blessings and witchcraft, which the minister had long used, causing a great scandal in the church.[52] He had previously been the parish clerk and may well have continued to use practices already begun before he became a minister. He might even have escaped charges had he not chosen to take his case to the king, claiming to be the innocent target of some spiteful locals.[53] Only some

---

[48] Pleijel, *Hustavlans värld*, 25.
[49] A. Wittendorf, *På Guds og Herskabs nåde 1500–1600*, Gyldendal and Politikens History of Denmark, VII, Copenhagen 1989, 62ff.
[50] *RA*, Letterbooks, Tegnelser no. 5, f. 405.
[51] Wittendorf, *På Guds og Herskabs nåde*, 264.
[52] *RA*, Letterbooks, Tegnelser no. 5, 167b and 228.
[53] K. S. Jensen, *Trolddom i Danmark 1500–1588*, Copenhagen 1982, 29.

ten years earlier a group of women who were suspected of having bewitched a nobleman, confessed that the minister in Ringe had been in concert with them.[54]

The fact that most ministers came from the peasantry helps explain why, for such an extended period, they continued to assist in the performance of fertility rituals, such as *korsebør*, the Catholic tradition of carrying the crucifix out to the fields on certain days (*gangdage*) in order to bless them. Clearly, the ban against such rituals was perceived to constitute a considerable threat to the peasants' livelihood. Ministers were continually admonished to bless neither the fields and meadows nor the crops of the peasants on Easter Eve at local and provincial synods during the sixteenth century.[55] Towards the turn of the century the meaning of the word *korsebør* became synonymous with charity,[56] though the actual carrying round of the crucifix continued illegally well into the seventeenth and eighteenth centuries.[57]

The tradition that certain ministers knew more than the Lord's Prayer survived well into the seventeenth century, not least because of the moderate theological training received by the average clergy in the countryside. In the new constitution of the University of Copenhagen (*Novellæ Constitutiones*) from 1621 it was stated that nobody could hold a living without having studied for two or three years in the faculty of theology at the University of Copenhagen, or for at least one year if they had studied at a foreign university.[58] Thus in 1622, the bishop of Lund was ordered to interrogate the minister in Gjerslev, Christen Pedersen Væver, at the forthcoming provincial synod. Væver had apparently, while in Copenhagen, used magic in order to still a fire.[59] In 1626 the local, royal administrator was ordered to prosecute a former minister in southern Jutland, because he had been concerned with witchcraft and ghosts.[60]

It is not until the seventeenth century that cases are mentioned which, according to modern usage, can be classified as belonging to the category of superstition. In 1626 Gertrud Peder Frandtzens in Lidemark was accused of having taken cobweb from the pulpit in the church. She

---

[54] *RA*, Letterbooks, Koncept.
[55] Wittendorf, *På Guds og Herskabs nåde*, 263.
[56] Wittendorf, 'Fire stolper', 225.
[57] E. Jørgensen, *Helgendyrkelse i Danmark. Studier over Kirkekultur og kirkeligt Liv fra det 11. Aarhundredes Midte til reformationen*, Copenhagen 1909, 3.
[58] J. Glebe-Møller, 'Det teologiske Fakultet 1597–1732', in S. Ellehøj *et al.*, (eds.), *Københavns Universitet 1479–1979*, V, Copenhagen 1980, 130–1.
[59] *RA*, Danske Kancelli, Skånske Tegnelser, no. 4, 395.
[60] *Ibid.*, Jyske Tegnelser, no. 8, 7.

claimed there was no superstition involved and that cobweb was an excellent antidote against fever. Nevertheless, Gertrud was ordered to confess her sins in public; it is, however, remarkable that the sentence specifically stated that the minister should inform the congregation that she was not accused of sorcery.[61] There are considerable gaps in the copies of the minutes from the provincial synods. Bearing that in mind, however, the shortage of cases concerned with superstition is still remarkable. In 1645 the authorities in the Danish Chancellery were worried about a case which had been reported to them. A woman had offended by placing her child on a horse in order to heal it. The theological faculty in Copenhagen was requested to produce a report about how to punish this phenomenon, since nothing had been 'expressly determined'. Two weeks later letters were sent to the bishops warning them against this particular form of ungodliness, which was described as 'superstition'.[62] The following year rural deans and ministers at the provincial synod of the diocese of Aarhus were instructed to keep an eye on this particular form of superstition.

Considering the general attack on Catholic remnants by the Lutheran church, it is thought provoking that we hear so little of that part of popular religion which was connected with the popular religious festivals. In his *Visitation Book* Peder Palladius only stated that 'you are not allowed to hold vigils at the may tree ... neither on St Valborg's night if you want to lead summer into town',[63] and in 1570 some clergy demanded that the traditional 'May vigil on the nights of St Valborg and St Hans should be stopped'.[64] Such issues were evidently not considered significant or dangerous enough by the new Lutheran clergy to merit any special attention. Likewise, the Lutheran clergy does not appear to have paid any attention to those aspects of popular religion which were concerned with the concept of spirits/creatures of nature, farms and houses, whose existence we only know of through the folklorists of the nineteenth century.

This is undoubtedly due to the fact that Nordic popular religious festivals were very different from most of those celebrated in the rest of

[61] The Royal Library, Copenhagen, Gl. kgl. Samling 2190, 4vo, *Synodalia Dioccesana Conventum Roskildiæ*. This case is known from a copy taken by the synod from the diocesan minutes. In 1728 the episcopal archive was burnt and all diocesan minutes were destroyed.
[62] *RA*, Danske Kancelli, Sjællandske Tegnelser, no. 28, 445b and 455b.
[63] *Palladius' Danske Skrifter*, V, 87.
[64] A. Wittendorff, ' "Evangelii lyse dag" eller "hekseprocessernes mørketid"? Om Peder Palladius' historieopfattelse', in G. Christensen *et al.* (eds.), *Tradition og kritik. Festskrift til Svend Ellehøj den 8. september 1984*, Copenhagen 1984, 109.

Europe, especially the carnivals. The weather was unsuitable in Scandinavia for large outdoor celebrations at this time of the year; and what
took place did not incorporate the same dangerous combination of food,
sex and violence, nor the excitement of 'the world turned upside
down'.[65] Christmas is probably the festival we are best informed about,
but it appears to have been a relatively quiet affair. Thus, in the busy
harbour town of Elsinore, at the entrance of the Sound, only one brawl
directly associated with the Christmas celebrations was reported in the
first quarter of the seventeenth century.[66]

One aspect of popular belief is conspicuous by its absence in the
reformers' and the Lutheran church's fight against superstition. There is
no mention of holy springs in the sources. Only one slightly peculiar and
incomprehensible ban is known; in 1565 the citizens of Elsinore were
ordered to warn their servants who washed their laundry at the spring
outside the town that they would be prosecuted if they washed 'in or over
the spring'.[67]

However, holy springs are only mentioned infrequently in late medieval Danish sources. For example, the shrine and chapel in Karup in
Jutland is mentioned in the 1480s while nothing is said about the holy
spring.[68] After the Reformation information suddenly becomes abun-
dant about holy springs: such as the Regisse chapel and spring in Frørup
on Funen and the Helene spring in Tisvilde on Zealand. The spring of
the Holy Trinity on the island of Lolland is not mentioned until the 1570s,
but whether the chapel was built at the spring which was already a place
of pilgrimage or whether the spring first became important after the
chapel had been built, is impossible to say.[69]

It was not until after 1620 that considerable information about
holy springs became available. It was included in the reports which

---

[65] P. Burke, *Popular Culture in Early Modern Europe*, London 1978, chapter 7.

[66] J. Chr. V. Johansen and H. Stevnsborg, 'Hasard ou myopie. Réflexions autour de deux théories
de l'histoire du droit', *Annales E.S.C.*, 46 (1986), *passim*.
   In Elsinore during 1555 a ban was issued on the wearing of masks and on public plays in the
streets during carnival, see The Provincial Archive of Zealand. Town Clerk of Elsinore's Archive.
Stadsbog 1554–5, 18 February 1555. There is no further mention of the ban. It is, however,
revealing that these festivals did not cause enough disturbance in the eighteenth century to make
much impact in the surviving legal sources, but continued to be known solely through the clergy's
animosity towards them, see B. Løgstrup, *Bundet til jorden. Stavnsbåndet i praksis 1733–1788*, Odense
1987, 134–41.

[67] The Provincial Archive of Zealand. Town Clerk of Elsinore's Archive. Stadsbog 1561–5, 20 July
1565.

[68] S. Andersen, 'Helligkilder og valfart', in E. Waaben *et al.* (eds.), *Fromhed og verdslighed i middelalder og
renaissance*, Odense 1985, 39.

[69] *Ibid.*, 38.

Danish-Norwegian ministers had been ordered to produce for the professor of medicine and famous antiquarian, Ole Worm, in Copenhagen,
informing him of historical and antiquarian details in their parishes. It
should be noted, however, that the holy spring at the pilgrimage church
in Kippinge was first mentioned as late as 1707, and by then it had only
been worshipped for a few years,[70] even if Kippinge, as a place of
pilgrimage, had already been famous in the days of Peder Palladius, as
can be seen from his *Visitation Book.*

Evidently, people's faith in miracles did not suddenly disappear with
the Reformation. Instead, they focussed on those holy springs which in
Catholic times had only played a rather unobtrusive part in the wealth of
possible expressions of belief in saints and miracles. Undoubtedly the
growing belief in holy springs must be considered a way of compensating
for the loss of other avenues,[71] but at the same time it also demonstrates
the relative success of the reformers and the Lutheran ministers in
combating superstition.[72] This, of course, does not mean that all Catholic rituals disappeared, but only that they were rendered harmless and
no longer constituted a threat. That is why worship of springs proved
acceptable. Likewise, worship of saints and the Maria cult continued
quietly long after the introduction of the Reformation, not as an underground alternative to the official Lutheran faith, but rather as a supplement to the authorised faith.[73]

Another way of compensating for this loss can be seen in the 'lay cult',
especially attached to individual kings and queens, which was, if not
encouraged, then certainly tolerated. Thus, the Norwegian minister,
Absalon Pederssøn Beyer, who died in 1575, and who actively promoted

[70] *Ibid.*, 40.   [71] *Ibid.*, 42.
[72] Recently, J. M. Kittelson has concluded that towards the end of the sixteenth century 'the
Reformation received little resistance and much approbation from the vast majority in the
villages under the authority of Strasbourg'. See 'Successes and Failures in the German Reformation: The Report from Strasbourg', *Archiv für Reformationsgeschichte*, 73 (1982), 163ff. T. Dahlerup has reached similar results for Denmark: 'It could be claimed, that this gradual and
piecemeal Reformation did have some sort of success. Around 1600 we have a rather ugly infight
between the orthodox clergy and those suspected of crypto-Calvinism. In this situation Jesuit
missionaries began to work in Denmark – but they had to start from scratch. There were no
underground communities, no priests' holes, no living tradition of the past. Even if ideas often
had to come to terms with realities in the two generations from 1563 to the end of the century, the
new system was totally accepted and considered a matter of fact'; see 'Sin, Crime, Punishment
and Absolution. The Disciplinary System of the Danish Church in the Reformation Century', in
L. Grane and K. Hørby (eds.) *Die dänische Reformation vor ihrem internationalen Hintergrund*, Göttingen
1991, 287.
[73] It is a central conclusion, in V. Helk's thesis about the Catholic church's attempt to reclaim
Denmark and Norway, that Lutheranism was by then so firmly established that it was a futile
exercise, see V. Helk, *Laurentius Nicolai Norvegus S. J. En Biografi med bidrag til belysning af romerkirkens
forsøg på at genvinde Danmark-Norge i tiden fra reformationen til 1622*, Copenhagen 1966.

the Reformation in Norway, was strongly attracted to the cult of holy Olav.[74] Similarly, a dress which allegedly had belonged to Queen Margrethe, was kept in the cathedral of Roskilde, until it was carried off by the Swedish king, Charles X in 1658. While there, the dress proved highly popular with visitors to the cathedral.[75]

During the second quarter of the seventeenth century, Bishop Jesper Brochmand expressed the opinion that visits to springs ought to be discouraged, but he never tried to intervene to stop them.[76] The growing attraction of springs had found an additional rationale. Thus, more and more people were directed to the spring of Helene, not only because of the miraculous healings which its water was supposed to bring about, but also because of the water's medical, curative potential. Visits to springs were acceptable, but the superstition which continued to be associated with such visits was not. This aspect is illustrated by the punishment of the man who, in 1627, had erected a cross at the spring of Helene,[77] and the argument raised by several ministers that the spring should not be allowed to be used during midsummer night. One of the explanations for the mild judgement of the use of the springs, should undoubtedly be sought in the prominent place allocated to the creation in Reformation theology as a consequence of the renaissance's positive view of nature. This led to the idea that water contained a healing power created by God.[78] During the seventeenth century the idea that God had created simple remedies or medicine which he had then revealed in nature gained prominence. Theologically it represented a gift from God which Man should neither doubt nor despise. There were in other words neither theological nor medical reasons for forbidding visits to springs which had acquired the reputation of being curative. Instead, visits appear to have been encouraged, as was the search for new springs. This attitude helps to explain the popularity of the Helene spring in the post-Reformation era.[79]

A royal letter of 1645 to Dr Fabritius, Dr Fincke, Dr Ole Worm, Dr Pauli, Dr Christian Fabricius, Dr Niels Foss and Dr Sperling demonstrates the considerable interest generated by the Helene spring. The

---

[74] Rieber-Mohn, 'Reformasjonen', 314.
[75] K. Erslev, 'Studier til Droning Magrethes Historie', *(Dansk) Historisk Tidsskrift*, V, part 3, (1881–2), 398.
[76] Wittendorf, 'Fire stolper', 223.
[77] Troels-Lund, *Dagligt liv*, VII, 236.
[78] B. Arvidsson, 'En helig källas teologi före och efter reformationen. Helene kilde i Tisvilde och Erich Hansens "Fontinalia Sacra" 1650', *Kirkehistoriske Samlinger* (1991), 98.
[79] *Ibid.*, 103.

seven physicians were requested to check the water from the spring for metals and minerals and to assess whether or not it was 'fit' to be used against diseases. Many people had already used the water with great profit.[80] Their inquiries must have had a positive result since only a couple of months later, the royal administrator on Kronborg Castle was told to construct a good road between Frederiksborg and the Helene spring.[81] The official approbation of the spring came a little later when the king wanted a building erected near it, for the use of visitors.[82] A by-product of this growing interest was the unhindered continuation of popular beliefs.

The next major attack on popular superstition in Denmark-Norway did not happen until the 1730s. This time it was generated by Pietist ministers who had been inspired by Bishop Erik Pontoppidan's work, *A Broom to sweep out the old Leaven or the revealed Remains of Paganism and Papism in the Danish Territories.*[83] It should be noted that Augustine's interpretation that superstition equalled paganism[84] and the language of the reformers remained in use; the connection between popular superstition and paganism and papism remained in place.

The reformers' stand against superstition and the resulting witch-hunts should be seen in the context of their expectation that the Day of Judgement was imminent.[85] The connection between superstition, popery and witchcraft had been beyond doubt for Peder Palladius; in his *Visitation Book* he wrote about witches that 'she knows endless long strings of words which she has been taught by the devil and the monks'.[86] Basically, many of the blessings which 'cunning folk' knew had a Catholic content, for example from the invocation of saints or directly copied from Catholic rituals. A few years later Palladius underlined the close connection again when he stated that 'the popish sorcerers are only the devil's dupes ... strengthening false worship, the invocation of saints and

---

[80] *RA*, Danske Kancelli, Sjællandske Tegnelser, no. 28, 362b.

[81] *Ibid.*, no. 28, 405.

[82] Wittendorf, 'Fire stolper', 222.

[83] The original Latin edition was published in Copenhagen in 1736.

[84] Delumeau, 'Les réformateurs', 453.

[85] It was emphasised by Bishop Jørgen Erickssøn in 1592 when he wrote: 'likewise we see how in these last days God has dealt with a considerable part of Christianity, how the anti-christian Pope in Rome with his cardinals, bishops, monks and other vain people during some centuries has deceived several thousand people with false teachings and diverted them from the road of truth towards the kingdom of the devil, to the prevalence of idolatry and infidelity'. Erickssøn, *Jonæ Prophetis*, sig. P.

[86] *Palladius' Danske Skrifter*, V, 110.

other impiety'.[87] Bishop Hans Tausen was in total agreement with his colleague when he wrote that the moment a fortune teller arrived, she was immediately sought by the local population, and Tausen continued by warning against such prophecies, describing them as 'notorious idolatry and an obvious, great sin against the first commandment'.[88]

One of the evangelical reformers, Oluf Chrysostomus, took direct action shortly after he had become bishop of the diocese of Vendelbo, when he scented a connection between papism and magic acts. In northeastern Jutland, the monastery of Mariager had installed a certain Oluf as minister in one of the parishes in their possession, though he was possibly not ordained. This Oluf supplemented his income through 'all kinds of superstitious magic'.[89] He claimed that the sick were possessed, and that he could heal them; he knew how you could force the herring into the fishermen's nets, and the 'superstitious' population used him willingly. Since Oluf technically belonged to the diocese of Viborg, but worked mainly within Chrysostomus' diocese, the latter complained to his colleague, Bishop Kjeld Juel, in Viborg, who dismissed Oluf in February 1550.

The concern of the Protestant church with those aspects of witchcraft which belonged to magic and healing is striking. Thus Peder Palladius wrote in his *Visitation Book* that impious people fetched witches for themselves and their animals when they fell ill,[90] and even if their cows recovered they themselves were in danger of having their souls damned. The sick should rather seek the blessing of Jesus Christ through prayer. Naturally, Palladius was also convinced that sorcerers could cause damage. However, that did not cause him the greatest concern. There was a dual problem, caused on the one hand by the widespread activity of 'cunning folk', and on the other by the population's unwillingness to repent when confronted with God's anger and punishment. The population needed 'cunning folk' and refused to assist in their prosecution.[91] Implicit in the popular attitude to the hidden powers is the alternative idea that Man, in spite of everything, could do something to

---

[87] Ibid., I, Copenhagen 1911–12, 382. Palladius' pamphlet was entitled, *En vnderuisning huorledis der kand hanlis met dem som erre besette.*

[88] Tausen, 'Sendebrev', 242 and 245.

[89] H. F. Rørdam, 'Bidrag til Vendelbo Stifts Kirkehistorie siden Reformationen', *Kirkehistoriske Samlinger*, Series 3, 3 (1881–2), 393.

[90] *Palladius' Danske Skrifter*, V, 110.

[91] J. Chr. V. Johansen, *Da Djævelen var ude ... Trolddom i det 17 århundredes Danmark*, Odense 1991, 159; see also Jensen, *Trolddom*, 25, 27, and 30.

alleviate the dangers and problems of life. Something could be done about disease and disaster apart from obediently accepting the Church's explanation that they were God's punishments for sins for which only repentance and penitence could help.[92]

It is within this context that we must consider the legislation against witchcraft in Denmark-Norway. Before 1584, when Bishop Jørgen Erickssøn was able to force through special legislation for the dioceses of Bergen and Stavanger which dealt specifically with 'wise arts', rules of procedure which forbade the use of torture and allowed the right of appeal, had been introduced. The reason for this special statute covering only part of Norway was that

within the dioceses of Bergen and Stavanger in our kingdom of Norway great unchristian impropriety and considerable abuse of the name of God is being perpetrated by some vain people, who, in order to alleviate their disorders, use unchristian remedies forbidden by God's holy word, such as having crosses cut on their bodies together with ungodly blessings, fables, and readings, not to mention other vanity and witchcraft used against the Christian religion.

The perpetrators, 'who either seek, or use, or perform such scandalous, unchristian acts, either with crosses, blessings, readings, and other such impious and unchristian acts', should be executed. This statute was made valid for the whole of Norway in 1593,[93] but was never introduced in Denmark.

It was during that year that the royal historiographer and canon of Ribe, Anders Sørensen Vedel, published his fierce attack on 'cunning folk' and their popular support. He described how people were prepared to be cured by such people, though they knew full well that they were sent by the devil.[94] Thus, some scholars have argued that accused sorcerers were no more than 'cunning folk', who, in a period with no veterinaries

[92] Wittendorf, *På Guds og Herskabs nåde*, 70.
[93] H. E. Næss, *Trolldomsprosessene i Norge på 1500–1600 tallet. En retts- og socialhistorisk undersøkelse*, Stavanger 1981, 78f. See also H. E. Næss, 'Norway: The Criminological Context', in B. Ankerloo and G. Henningsen (eds.), *Early Modern European Witchcraft: Centres and Peripheries*, Oxford 1990, 368.
[94] A. Sørensen Vedel, *Den XC. Psalme, Mose Guds Mands Bøn*. Ribe 1593, sig. D3b–D4a. H. E. Næs expressed surprise that the statute of 1593 was only introduced in Norway, especially since the famous Danish theologian Niels Hemmingsen had also been strongly opposed to the use of conjuring, see *Trolldomsprosessene*, 80. It should, however, be borne in mind that Hemmingsen had already fallen from royal favour by 1593 because of his crypto-Calvinism, and that Anders Sørensen Vedel did not occupy a position of comparative inportance within the Danish church to that of Bishop Erickssøn in Norway.

and few physicians,[95] complemented their talents with magic rituals and made them available to the society in which they lived.[96]

The situation in Denmark was similar to that of England, where 'generally speaking, the cunning folk and the maleficent witches were believed to be two separate species'.[97] This is evident in Jutland where only 36 out of a total of 463 people accused in the years from 1609 to 1687, in other words less than 8 per cent could also be considered to have been 'cunning folk'. There are, however, ambiguities in a number of these cases which makes it difficult to interpret them.

Most of those who are known to have been 'cunning folk', were not accused of these activities. Thus, when one witness in the case of Maren Piersdatter stated that the accused had cured her of a disease of her legs and feet a few years previously, another eight witnesses spoke solely of bewitchment, following the pattern known from Danish trials of 'maleficent witchcraft'. Undoubtedly, it was commonly held that those who had bewitched somebody could undo the bewitchment. From the case of Maren Piersdatter it appears that the accused possessed both abilities, but that one had prevailed.

Similar evidence can be found in the case against 'Lange' Maren Lauridsdatter. Here twenty men gave evidence that she had been notorious for witchcraft and conjuring in the decade she had lived in the village; however, the decisive evidence for her conviction centred around her being accused of having bewitched a child. Nothing in the accusations brought against these two women supports William Monter's conclusion, that 'a *guérisseur* could be arrested for black witchcraft after one of his cures had dramatically failed'.[98]

In the case against Maren Brandtiis, however, there is some evidence to support Monter's conclusion. Witnesses stated that for payment she had promised to heal a sick man who had subsequently died. Two witnesses may well have thought their evidence would have benefited another accused, Mette Lauritzdatter, when they told the court that she had made the sign of the cross over their sick cattle, which had then been cured. Another four men gave evidence that a man was unable to attend a court hearing because he was paralysed and confined to bed. This paralysis had been brought about by Mette Lauritzdatter, who, after the

[95] J. Brix, *En sammenlignende studie af udviklingen indenfor lægestanden i kongeriget og hertugdømmet Slesvig indtil året 1864*, Åbenrå 1992, 24ff.

[96] Johansen, *Da Djævelen var ude*, 88–91.

[97] A. Macfarlane, *Witchcraft in Tudor and Stuart England*, London 1970, 127ff.

[98] E. W. Monter, *Witchcraft in France and Switzerland. The Borderlands during the Reformation*, Ithaca 1976, 184.

man had fallen ill, had made the sign of the cross over him several times, apparently with no effect, because she had given him a drink, which should be drunk on a Sunday morning before sunrise. Having followed the instruction he was paralysed the following Tuesday. Similarly, in the case of Anne Nisdatter, a man claimed that she had tried to cure his wife, who suffered from 'fear and terror', but every time she had tried, his wife's condition had deteriorated further. Both these cases fit Keith Thomas's conclusion about witches, 'that their white counterparts were unlikely to find themselves in the court unless their activities had been fraudulent or otherwise harmful'.[99] Still, this might happen in extraordinary circumstances. In 1624 a number of statements were taken to the effect that Maren Jørgensdatter had approached a man in the autumn of 1623, offering to cure his wife of her eye disease. Maren had told him who was responsible for the disease and she had fetched consecrated soil into which she had laid the man's wife. According to the local minister, the 'sick woman' had then informed him of Maren Jørgensdatter's acts. Undoubtedly, the minister was behind the case, since no one accused Maren. However, since the statements made it impossible for the high court judges to convict Maren of any evil acts, they banished her.

Apart from this case, it was typical for 'cunning folk' only to be accused in cases similar to those of Maren Jørgensdatter and Anne Nisdatter. Accordingly, it is not clear to what extent people like 'Lange' Maren were used; or if the population was gradually realising that their healing potential was limited. Thus, Paasche Rasmussen, who had for years been used as a 'cunning man', continued to be consulted by people until the court case against him started, in spite of the fact that the effects of his undertakings were widely recognised to be ambivalent. One witness explained that when she fell ill she had asked Paasche Rasmussen for help which he had promised for payment. He was going to show her the person who caused her the damage, but she had only been able to see Paasche Rasmussen.

This ambiguity may help explain why bewitchment came to the front when 'cunning people' were charged. All testimonies, with the exception of one in the case of Anne Simmensdatter, are concerned with bewitchment; she confessed, that she only conjured, when asked by others and that she made evil crosses. She was sent to the stake, and the only difference between her and Birte Lauersdatter, who was banished, was that in the latter case the high court judges found that no evil had been

---

[99] K. Thomas, *Religion and the Decline of Magic*, London 1971, 245.

attempted. That the population had no intention of accusing the 'cunning folk' unless the witchcraft element had taken over, can be seen from the court rulings of the high court which gradually became the norm during the 1620s. In 1619 Bergette Mikkelsdatter was accused of bewitchment, but the high court judges found that it had not been proved that she intended any evil to others. Accordingly, she was convicted with an *absolutio ab instancia*. However, she had confessed that she could conjure and the high court judges were of the opinion that if she had used invocations after the issue of the decree of 1617 she should be tried by her venue. However, the case never reached the high court, where the judges appear to have been indecisive about what action to take. In 1620 a number of witnesses stated that Anders Chrestensen had the reputation of being able to blind thieves, to cure impotence, to prevent the milk from becoming sour, and to churn. In spite of the high court judges being able to banish Anders Chrestensen with a clear conscience, it did not happen.

The high court judges did not decide to change their practice until the following year. Johane Jensdatter had been brought before the district court by mixed testimonies, claiming that she could heal magically and exercise the *maleficium*. The judges were not convinced by the latter part of the evidence and accordingly did not send her to the stake. Nor did they grant her a re-trial; instead she was banished immediately. Since the high court judges had received no instructions about how to deal with these cases, it is more than likely that the judges in Viborg had agreed between themselves to follow the above-mentioned procedure. They knew that a 'cunning woman' would never be accused of 'cunningness' solely at her district court. In a society short of physicians, the 'cunning folk' offered the only prospect of cure for most sick people. Any attempt to eradicate them was doomed to fail.

The case against Kirsten Poulsdatter from the island of Læsø provides an insight into how 'cunningness' was perceived by common people. She claimed that she did not consider it to be witchcraft to take away somebody's 'milk-fortune' and to return it. It was undoubtedly in accordance with her own view, when one witness stated that she had told him that a certain person would suffer ill fortune because he had accused her of sorcery. That the borderline between 'cunningness' and witchcraft was a narrow one is illustrated by the evidence given by another witness. He testified that Kirsten Poulsdatter had told him that if he handed her some grain before he sowed, she would make sure that he would harvest a thousandfold. He admitted that his yield had been excellent that year, but because it had been disastrous the subsequent year, he was of the opinion that she was the cause of that too, since she had walked across the field while he was sowing.

In spite of this fine dividing line between 'cunningness' and witchcraft most 'cunning folk' managed to avoid crossing it. According to the wording of the decree of 1617, the number of 'cunning folk' must have been large enough to worry the authorities. From the surviving evidence it is impossible to say what made witchcraft come to dominate. When only 36 out of a total of 463 cases in Jutland operate with concepts which make it possible to classify people as 'cunning folk', it can be concluded that these people were only included in the witch-hunts in exceptional circumstances. Of the thirty-six cases from Jutland, seventeen were sent to the stake (all of them women), while sixteen were banished (including two men). Thus, the thirty-one 'cunning women' and five men who were prosecuted constitute 7.5 per cent of the total accused of witchcraft.[100] Undoubtedly they only represented a fraction of the 'cunning folk' active at the time. Every village or parish must have had 'cunning folk', most of whom never came into contact with the authorities.

In Norway conjuring constitutes part of the accusations in 263 of the known witchcraft cases. Most of the cases were concerned with the healing or curing of humans. The practitioners did not consider themselves to be criminals. In case after case they willingly provided information about their activities. Of special importance to conjuring was the use of rituals or objects; the exponents made ointments from herbs, soil, nails and hair with which they rubbed their patients. Simultaneously, they would read prayers which contained invocations of God, Jesus, the Holy Spirit and Mary.

In 1594 Anne, the wife of Kristen Jyde, confessed that a local official (*lagmanden*) in Stavanger had called her to his wife, in order that she could 'read over' her. In 1634 Lisbet Pedersdatter confessed that she owned an eaglefoot which she used for healing people, and that she used the jaw of a wolf to cure small children who had sore throats.[101]

It was only in a small number of the cases that the accused were said to have used conjuring, as well as *maleficium*. In 1622 Barbro Bjelland confessed that she could heal humans and cattle. But the common people, who were present at the district court, were of the opinion that

---

[100] These figures are in accordance with Alan Macfarlane's results from Essex: 'of forty-one definite Essex cunning folk, only four were later recorded as accused of "black" witchcraft, while less than half a dozen of a total of 400 persons accused of black witchcraft are known to have been "cunning folk" '. Macfarlane, *Witchcraft*, 127f.

[101] Næss, *Trolldomsprosessene*, 122ff.

she could perform *maleficium*. They based this on the assertion of Lauritz Ollestad, who, when asked by the local official to collect tithes from Barbro, had responded that he would rather walk ten miles, because she was in the habit of casting evil spells on people.[102]

It would appear that Bishop Jørgen Erickssøn used the cases concerning 'cunningness', which were brought before the cathedral chapter in Stavanger in 1584, as a lever for the special legislation which he convinced Frederik II to introduce. However, according to the legislation these cases were to be prosecuted by the lay authorities and there is every indication that the desire to deal firmly with 'cunningness' failed in Norway, not least because the cathedral chapters were excluded from prosecuting such cases.[103] This may well explain why the death penalty for 'cunningness' was ruled out when, in October 1617, unified legislation concerning crimes of witchcraft was issued for Denmark and Norway. Possibly in the expectation that more cases could be brought involving this aspect of witchcraft, the penalty was to be banishment. However, as already mentioned above, this approach did not produce the desired results either.

In general, the population was decidedly hesitant in bringing 'cunning folk' to court, whereas it had no similar qualms about the many maleficent witches. In this people were assisted by a decree which not only defined the content of the crimes, but also stipulated the different punishments. Through the witchcraft legislation of 12 October 1617, the demonological aspect of the crime came to dominate; the covenant with the devil, the serious heresy and apostasy from God became the central points in accordance with developments on the rest of the continent. The real sorcerers were seen to be those who associated with, and made covenants with, the devil.[104]

The issue of the decree in 1617 can probably be explained by the interaction of a number of circumstances. The king, Christian IV, had become increasingly worried about the dangers of witchcraft. During 1612–13 around fifteen women in the town of Køge, south of Copenhagen, were accused of witchcraft. Christian IV took an active interest in the case and had one of the women, who had been given the death penalty, transferred to the royal castle in Copenhagen, where she was subsequently tortured. Furthermore, the period after 1615 was

---

[102] *Ibid.*, 130.   [103] *Ibid.*, 292 and 21.

[104] Johansen, *Da Djævelen var ude*, 23. See also J. Chr. V. Johansen, 'Denmark: The Sociology of Accusations', in *Early Modern European Witchcraft*, 341.

characterised by a general hardening of religious attitudes. When the elderly bishop of Roskilde, Peder Winstrup, died, he was succeeded by Hans Poulsen Resen, who became the central figure in the doctrinal re-orientation of the Danish church towards orthodox Lutheranism. This period of doctrinal hardening was also characterised by what amounted to a moral crusade. On the day the decree against witchcraft was issued, two additional decrees were published: one against unnecessary luxury and the other against 'looseness'. Furthermore, it was no coincidence that the centenary celebrations for the publication of Luther's ninety-five theses seemed to give added weight to the decree against witchcraft.[105]

The decree appears to have generated a considerable increase in the number of witchcraft trials in Denmark. Lack of proper sources, however, makes it impossible to give a precise estimate of the number of trials before 1610. For the subsequent years, detailed data are only available for Jutland, where all the minute books of the high court in Viborg are preserved. Thus we know that only seven trials took place in the region of Jutland in 1616, while the number had grown to eighteen in 1617, reaching 41 in 1618. Evidently, the population had realised by then that the authorities took a grave view of witchcraft and wanted determined action to be taken. In Jutland 494 trials involving witchcraft took place in the period 1609–87.[106] It is not the figure, however, which is remarkable, but the actual distribution of the trials; no less than 297 trials took place during the eight years from 1617 to 1625, constituting 60 per cent of the total number of trials for the period. It was not unusual for the number of witchcraft trials to fluctuate, but compared with other countries where the trials fluctuated over a considerable time, the fact that 60 per cent of all trials took place within only eight years must be considered astonishing. Furthermore, a considerable number of the trials was geographically concentrated along the west coast of Jutland.[107]

It is almost impossible to get any impression of the number of trials in Norway before the beginning of the seventeenth century.[108] The surviving evidence appears to confirm that the joint legislation for the two countries also made an impact in Norway. Eighteen per cent of all known Norwegian trials took place between 1561 and 1620, while no less than 36 per cent occurred in the period 1621–50.[109] For Norway, however, it is

---

[105] *Ibid.*, 37f.   [106] *Ibid.*, 40f.   [107] *Ibid.*, 67.

[108] The survival of minute books from the local courts in Norway is closely connected with the employment of clerks (*sorenskrivere*) at the courts (*bygdeting*) from 1591.

[109] Næss, *Trolldomsprosessene*, 20f.

striking that 46 per cent of all witchcraft trials took place in the second half of the seventeenth century.

A similar picture can be drawn from Icelandic data. Here 120 trials took place between 1604 and 1720, with the majority in the second half of the period and geographically concentrated on the northwestern part of the island. However, conditions in Iceland appear to have been exceptional when compared with other European witchcraft trials. The idea of the 'black' Sabbath was unknown, women were only involved in 8 per cent of the trials and only one woman was burned at the stake. This is undoubtedly explained by the fact that magic was closely connected with the concept of *knowledge* in Iceland, and, at least, since the introduction of Christianity *knowledge* had primarily been a male prerogative.[110]

Similarly, among the leaders of the Swedish church there was a strong desire to stamp out 'cunningness'. Archbishop Abraham Angermannus undertook a detailed visitation of the sees of Skara, Växjö and Linköping in the spring of 1596. In theory, Angermannus made a distinction between witchcraft on one hand and superstition and conjuring on the other, but in practice he took strong measures against both. The most serious cases were dealt with by the lay courts, while the lesser offenders were flogged. In the see of Linköping alone, 140 people were accused during the Archbishop's visitation, even if 60 per cent were only accused of conjuring. Angermannus's brutal conduct caused considerable outrage among both nobility and peasantry.[111]

In spite of popular resistance to the actions of the church, bills were introduced in order to generate more forceful legislation against conjuring and superstition. It was suggested in the so-called 'Rosengrenske' bill, which never became law, that conjuring should also be punished by burning at the stake.[112] This was a policy similar to that which Jørgen Erikssøn had managed to have introduced in Norway.

Bishop Angermannus's initiative was based on the Swedish church's claim to be entitled to exercise ecclesiastical jurisdiction over a number of crimes. Swedish church laws, including the Church Order of 1571 and the Articles of Örebro of 1586, implied that the church had been given great scope to determine and punish a considerable, but indefinite, group of crimes. Accordingly, Duke Karl quickly realised that the church had been given too much power. Thus in the mid-1590s, the chapter in Uppsala was severely reprimanded because it had called a meeting of the

---

[110] K. Hastrup, 'Iceland: Sorcerers and Paganism', in *Early Modern European Witchcraft*, 385–8.
[111] B. Ankarloo, *Trolldomsprocesserna i Sverige*, Stockholm 1971, 58.
[112] *Ibid.*, 59.

ministers in the diocese and dealt with criminal cases which correctly should have been dealt with by the lay courts. In 1619 the new king, Gustavus Adolphus, refused to confirm the church's right to exercise ecclesiastical discipline which the bishops claimed to have been given in the Articles of Örebro by Duke Karl. Consequently, the ministers complained in 1617 and 1643 that conjuring and superstition were not punished severely enough, but only fined.[113]

The chronological parameters for the prosecutions in Sweden and Finland correspond with those in Iceland. As in Denmark and Norway, it is impossible to estimate the number of prosecutions in sixteenth-century Sweden precisely. Up to 1615, a little over 170 cases can be verified. In the three provincial towns of Stockholm, Jönköping and Vadstena, which together offer unbroken records from the middle of the fifteenth century, a low frequency of prosecutions appears to have dominated until 1579. The number of prosecutions increased towards the turn of the century in these towns, while the frequency in the countryside does not appear to have increased until after 1600. However, these figures are low compared with the 856 accused in the so-called Blåkulla trials, which took place between 1668 and 1675.[114]

The situation in Finland was identical to that of Sweden; between 1520 and 1639, 144 witchcraft cases are known. They constitute 20 per cent of all known cases in Finland. The majority of cases did not take place until the second half of the seventeenth century, with a chronological concentration in the two decades from 1670 to 1689. The overwhelming majority of cases in the sixteenth century were geographically spread along the west coast of the country, clustered around the harbour towns. During the first half of the seventeenth century these areas continued to be affected by witchcraft cases, while inland settlements in general escaped both accusations and prosecutions. It is fascinating that the same high proportion of the accused were men in both the Finnish cases and the Icelandic cases. Towards the end of the sixteenth century, men made up 60 per cent of the accused, and only from then on did the proportion of women increase. Thus women only made up half the number of accused in all Finnish cases. In Karelia, in the eastern part of Finland, nearly all the accused were men. This is probably explained by the fact

---

[113] *Ibid.*, 57 and 85.

[114] *Ibid.*, 270. See also B. Ankerloo, 'Sweden: The Mass Burnings (1668–1676)', in *Early Modern European Witchcraft*, 294ff. Blåkulla was a name for the island of Jungfrun in the sound of Kalmar. Since the later Middle Ages the island had been connected with magic ideas. From the end of the sixteenth century a combination of notions about witches' Sabbath and Blåkulla can be traced in Swedish court cases.

that the witchcraft cases were concerned with traditional magic. This should also be considered in the context of Finnish folk traditions and ancient Finnish religion, where supernatural powers were associated with men.[115]

A new and different interpretation of the Scandinavian witchcraft trials follows from the above. Until the early seventeenth century, most trials were concerned with 'cunningness', such as sorcery and popular magic. This is demonstrated by the trials in Iceland and Finland where the accused were men who, traditionally, had been concerned with magic in these countries. In Denmark and Norway, ministers attempted to root out such beliefs and vehemently attacked them, while in Sweden, Bishop Angermannus focussed on precisely this aspect of superstition during his visitation. Furthermore, it is a picture which corresponds with the results reached by Stuart Clark in his research into Protestant demonology: 'Above all, the pastor demonologists made up for any caution regarding malevolent witchcraft by their sustained and bitter attacks on its "benevolent" equivalent – popular magic.'[116] By the early seventeenth century, this inter-Scandinavian pattern was collapsing. In Finland and Sweden a gradual shift of emphasis took place, towards focussing on demonology, which finally culminated in the 'Blåkulla trials'. Norway did not remain insulated from this tendency which made an impact in the country in the second half of the seventeenth century, while the trials in Denmark focussed exclusively on *maleficium*.

The concentration of the Swedish and Finnish trials in the second half of the seventeenth century is explained by the fact that they were definite Sabbath trials, which resulted in a high number of accused, generated by the stories told by witnesses to the proceedings on Blåkulla. The growth in the number of Norwegian trials can likewise be explained by the increasing number of people accused of diabology. Simultaneously in Norway and Sweden there is the traditional use of the 'co-oath' in

---

[115] A. Heikkinen and T. Kervinen, 'Finland: The Male Domination', in *Early Modern European Witchcraft*, 321–5. See also M. Nenonen, 'Hexenglaube, Mensch und Gemeinschaft in Finland. Spätmittelalter und frühe Neuzeit', in C. Krötzl and J. Masonen (eds.), *Quotidianum Fennicum. Daily Life in Medieval Finland*, (Medium Aevum Quotidianum XIX) Krems an der Donau 1989, 67–9.

In his book, *Noituus, taikuus ja noitavainot* (English summary: *Witchcraft, Magic and Witch Trials in Rural Lower Satakunta, Northern Ostrobothnia and Viipuri Carelia, 1620–1700*), Helsinki 1992, M. Nennonen explains the increase in the number of cases from the beginning of the 1670s, by pointing to the increase in cases involving 'benevolent magic' which primarily involved women (435). This is explained by the authorities' growing ambition to exercise social control, because 'the practice of magic was an offence to the faith taught by the authority' (442).

[116] S. Clark, 'Protestant Demonology: Sin, Superstition, and Society (*c.* 1520–*c* 1630)', in *Early Modern European Witchcraft*, 77.

witchcraft trials, whereby an accused, together with a certain number of people of the same sex, who were willing to swear with them, could prove his or her innocence. Three forms of the 'co-oath' were used: one, where the accused was supported by the oath of twelve people; another, where six people were required; and finally one where only three people were needed. In serious criminal cases, however, only the first option was available to the defendant. During the last decades of the sixteenth century, a number of accused women in Norway successfully used the 'co-oath' formula to be acquitted. In cases where the oath could not be met, this may well be explained by the fear of friends of being suspected of collusion with the accused, and thus guilty of witchcraft.[117]

That the chronological focus for the witchcraft trials in Finland, Iceland, Norway and Sweden lies in the second half of the seventeenth century, while in the case of Denmark it is centred in the early seventeenth century, radically changes the discussion about centre and periphery which was initiated at the Symposium on Witchcraft, Sorcery and Crime in Early Modern Europe which met in Stockholm in 1984.[118] Here Denmark was placed unequivocally, geographically as well as chronologically, in the periphery. The cases above, however, underline that Denmark belongs to the centre of European witchcraft trials rather than the periphery.

Further problems, however, emerge when the typology of the Danish trials is considered. In central Europe, the centre of the European witchcraft trials, the trials, like those in Sweden, Finland and to some extent in Norway, were Sabbath trials. This was not the case in Denmark, where only very few traces of the Sabbath idea can be found,[119] and where all the trials were concerned with *maleficium*, as they were in Iceland. Consequently, it must be concluded that to consider the European witchcraft trials within a chronologically based centre–periphery model is unproductive.

Instead, it is far more important to try to establish a typological model which may help to explain how the Sabbath concept could leap across Denmark and reach Finland and Sweden from central Europe. It is, in my opinion, necessary to return to the role of the ministers in order to answer this question, which may also give us a better understanding of

[117] H. E. Næss, 'Mededsinstituttet. En undersøkelse av nektelsesedens utbredelse og betydning i norsk rettsliv på 1600-tallet', *(Norsk) Historisk Tidsskrift*, 70 (1991), 192 and Ankerloo, *Trolldoms-processerna*, 47.

[118] See *Early Modern European Witchcraft* where some of the contributions originite from the Symposium in Stockholm.

[119] Johansen, 'Denmark', 361ff.

one of the greatest issues in the history of the European witchcraft trials: why the trials came to an end.[120]

The trials in Sweden and Finland ceased because the authorities suddenly realised that confessions about Blåkulla were pure fabrication. The Swedish trials began in the north and spread southwards where they reached Stockholm in 1675. Here, like everywhere else, a commission was established to investigate the matter and several people were condemned to death. By August 1676 the members of the commission had started to disagree among themselves. Initially, it was the three clerical members who, in their capacity as spiritual advisers, had misgivings about handing out death sentences. The chaplain, Noraeus, stated that the confessions were of dubious value since they had been extracted under torture. Then the accused, who had admitted to having led others to Blåkulla, began to retract their confessions, one of them claiming that 'he had lied about himself and led the children to the same mendacity'. Consequently, the interrogations changed and the accused were enjoined to speak the truth and beware of false confessions. The chaplain, Noraeus, demanded far more extensive enquiries before he would be prepared to hand out the death sentence; this led to the interrogations which made the commission realise that not only some, but all of the evidence was false.[121]

In Norway a gradual scepticism developed among the judges of the court of appeal about the procedures used at the lower courts. This change in attitude coincided with the increased incidence of private citizens undertaking the defence of women accused of witchcraft. They substantiated the use of illegal methods such as forced examinations, torture, swimming and false denunciations. A number of local judges, ministers and bailiffs were heavily fined for their actions. In the course of a few years this was sufficient to discredit the trials for witchcraft altogether.[122]

In Denmark the witchcraft trials ended for different reasons. The origin of their disappearance should be found in the early sixteenth century. It is more than twenty years since H. C. Erik Midelfort proved that until the end of the sixteenth century, Catholics and Protestants in southwest Germany had shared a view of providence developed by the Catholic, Martin Plantsch, which emphasised that suffering came from

---

[120] For the argument that belief in witchcraft is not only something of the past, see J. Favret-Saadas, *Deadly Words. Witchcraft in the Bocage*, London 1981.

[121] Ankerloo, *Trolldomsprocesserna*, 207ff.

[122] Næss, 'Norway', 380.

the hammer of God and not through the evil deeds of witches.[123] Later Plantsch's ideas were taken over and developed by the Protestant, Johannes Brenz, from Schwäbisch Hall. According to this tradition God was the source of all human suffering, because of Man's sins, and that old women should not be accused of witchcraft even if they themselves believed in it. Towards the end of the sixteenth century, the Catholics dropped this doctrine in an attempt to establish an unambiguous confession, and at the start of the Thirty Years War, the Protestants went down the same avenue and began to intensify their persecution of witches.

However, several Danish ministers appear to have stayed with the old providence tradition which saw God as the cause of all suffering. The minister on the island of Fur, Daniel Dirksen, had been of the opinion that he had been bewitched by Kirsten Petersdatter, but according to evidence given by his colleague in Åsted, Dirksen had followed the example of Job and accepted his pain from the hand of God. Some years later during a trial against a man accused of black magic, the minister in Kirketerp, Niels Jacobsen, stated 'that if you have bewitched me I am sure you will be rewarded in time. I, however, will accept it as coming from God.'[124]

These clear statements are supplemented by the extraordinary passivity among other ministers. In 1623 the minister in Elling, Oluf Madsen, testified that 'Hose' Mette Jensdatter had been notorious for witchcraft since 1602. That he had nothing to add is surprising. He had, after all, tolerated the existence of a known witch in his parish for more than twenty years without attempting to bring her to trial. Among the witchcraft trials in Jutland are no less than twenty-six similar cases of local ministers having demonstrated an identical passivity. This is even more surprising, when it is borne in mind that the decree of 1617 described witchcraft as primarily a religious crime. In May 1618 during a provincial synod in Roskilde, Bishop Resen had emphasised ministers' obligations to watch out for sorcerers. Similarly, in the diocesan archive in Aalborg the printed version of the 1617 decree, containing the signatures of a considerable number of the bishopric's ministers, has been preserved.[125] No fewer than twenty-two of the passive ministers became involved in the trials from 1618 to 1625, which was the period when the majority of trials took place in Jutland. Thus 8 per cent of the trials in this period

---

[123] H. C. Erik Midelfort, *Witch Hunting in Southwestern Germany 1562–1684. The Social and Intellectual Foundations*. Stanford 1972.
[124] Johansen, *Da Djævelen var ude*, 148.   [125] *Ibid.*, 145.

show that local ministers took no action against sorcery.[126] Only the minister in Snedsted, Mads Petersen, found it necessary to apologise. He was well aware that a certain woman was notorious for sorcery, but, as he pointed out, he was an old man.

Evidently the behaviour of these ministers indicated that they had little if any appetite for the witchcraft trials. In many cases, however, they were in no position to take action had they wished to do so.[127] Thus during the trial of Apeloni Thamiskone, the minister in Præstkær, Søren Pedersen, pointed out that before the start of the trial he had never heard her accused of sorcery. Similarly, the minister in Viuf, Jens Jensen, testified that Ane Jenskone was not accused of witchcraft as asserted.

It is possible that the two ministers had been directly inspired in their belief in providence by the writings of Johannes Brenz which were widely read in Denmark. However, they are far more likely to have drawn on the published sermons of Jørgen Erikssøn and Anders Sørensen Vedel. In his sermons on the Book of Jonah, Erikssøn pointed out that adversity should never be attributed to the devil or sorcerers, because it was God's punishment for sins.[128] In his third sermon on the ninetieth Psalm Vedel wrote that sorcerers should not be given the honour of being thought able to cause death or disease. Man only suffered such inflictions through the providence of God.[129] Vedel did not deny the existence of sorcerers, but he spiritualised the question of guilt, sin and fate. Accordingly the demand for prosecution of sorcerers was significantly dampened. In fact, it could be questioned if anyone could justifiably be prosecuted for witchcraft.

After Vedel, sorcery did not re-emerge as a topic in subsequent Danish theological writings, as opposed to the spiritualisation of the relationship between sin and adversity which was extensively covered. During the first two decades of the seventeenth century this aspect was given only moderate attention by theologians, but from the start of the 1620s it became more and more dominant, coinciding with the growth of the pre-Pietist movement.

It was hardly a coincidence that Erikssøn had chosen the Book of Jonah and Vedel the ninetieth Psalm as their points of departure. Luther

---

[126] J. Chr. V. Johansen, 'Om helte, skurke og Guds forsyn: De danske trolddomsprocessers ophør – et opgør med en tradition', *Fønix*, 16 (1992), 161.

[127] Many ministers may have opposed witchcraft trials in their parishes in order to secure peace in the community, see A. Soman, 'Decriminalizing Witchcraft: Does the French Experience Furnish a European Model?', *Criminal Justice History*, 10 (1989), 10.

[128] Quoted in Johansem, 'Om helte', 162.

[129] Vedel, *Den XC. Psalme*, sig D3.

had emphasised in his sermon on the ninetieth Psalm that under no circumstances should man link his misfortune and death to a demonic power.[130] Similarly, in his commentary on the Book of Jonah, Luther had underlined that God visited Man with all sorts of plagues and finally even with death.[131]

Perhaps it is time to reconsider Luther's attitude to witchcraft and sorcery in general, and his influence on the attitude of Danish parish clergy to these questions in particular. Luther was convinced that covenants with the devil and *maleficium* existed,[132] and he supported witchcraft trials initiated by the authorities. However, he dismissed the possibility that the common people could start the trials,[133] as was the case in Denmark where the trials were built on accusations. When the population had trials initiated out of fear of sorcerers, Luther pointed out that only the Book of Job was valid and not Exodus 22:18. In his writings from 1520: *Eine kurze Form der zehn Gebote*; *Eine kurze Form des Glaubens*; *Eine kurze Form des Vaterunsers* and in *Betbüchlein* from 1522, Luther underlined the exclusion of the use of witchcraft and sorcery as explanations for personal misfortune.[134] For Luther the matter was simple: the evil experienced *maleficium* as punishment, while the righteous considered it a cross on a par with Job.

A late Danish example of this idea can be seen in the trials which took place in eastern Jutland in 1686, which had been initiated by the local noble administrator, Jørgen Arenfeldt. From the start several ministers had been actively involved in the interrogation of the accused, but when Arenfeldt's own minister, Niels Rasmussen, realised that the nobleman was not conducting the trials because of his duty to do so as lay authority, but out of personal fear of witchcraft, he immediately backed out and refused to be involved.[135]

The popularity and wide distribution of pre-Pietist devotional literature from the 1620s, with its repeated references to the Book of Job and the Psalms, was decisive in bringing to a halt the witchcraft trials in Denmark. It has to be emphasised, however, that a conscious choice lay behind this interpretation of the Book of Job. Different interpretations argued for more determined action against witches. Thus in 1632 in Zurich, Ludwig Lavater argued in his commentary on Job that God

---

[130] P. Althaus, *Die Theologie Martin Luthers*, Gütersloh, 1962, 148f.
[131] *Ibid.*, 154f.
[132] R. van Dülmen (ed.), *Hexenwelten. Magie und Imagination vom 16.–20. Jahrhundert*, Frankfurt 1987, 32.
[133] J. Haustein, *Martin Luthers Stellung zum Zauber- und Hexenwesen*, Stuttgart 1990, 181.
[134] *Ibid.*, 105.   [135] Johansen, 'Om helte', 165.

demanded forceful action against everyone who served the devil.[136] In 1629 it was emphasised in Saint Jean de Luz, that if anyone refused to assist God in burning a witch, God would let those who had refused to help him feel his anger.[137]

Before the extensive trials which followed the 1617 decree against witchcraft, the parish clergy in Denmark had had twenty-five years to study the writings of Erickssøn and Vedel. The popular demand for witchcraft trials was, however, so relentless, that even if the ministers preached the providence concept, they were forced to keep a low profile. Faced with this popular witchcraft frenzy, the ministers chose to be silent and passive. The majority of sorcerers and witches were prosecuted before the end of 1626. That the number of trials fell dramatically thereafter is related to the fact that it took a number of years for a rumour about witchcraft to take hold without which it was impossible to have anyone accused.[138] This lapse, however, gave the ministers a chance to promote their concept of providence to the population during the next few decades. In this they proved successful: in Jutland only 4 per cent of the trials took place from the mid-1650s until the end of the 1680s when the last witchcraft trials occurred.

Thus the Danish witchcraft trials were suppressed by the parish clergy through their preaching and promotion of a tradition which had its roots in the early sixteenth century.

CONCLUSION

During most of the sixteenth century a constant battle against superstition was undertaken by the Lutheran clergy in Scandinavia, which eventually proved successful. In Sweden the ecclesiastical situation remained unsteady until the end of the sixteenth century, but from then on the church and its leaders intervened, using house visitations. In Denmark and Norway success in this confrontation came somewhat earlier. Catholic traditions were suppressed to such an extent that any attempts to recatholicise the country were futile. However, it quickly became evident that the population needed some form of replacement for the rituals and traditions which they had lost with the introduction of the Reformation. This explains how and why a cult developed around the holy springs which was grudgingly accepted by the Lutheran church,

---

[136] D. Meili, *Hexen in Wasterkingen. Magie und Lebensform in einem Dorf des frühen 18. Jahrhunderts.* Basel 1980, 42.

[137] D. Desplat, *Sorcières et Diables en Béarn (fin XIVe–debut XIXe siècle)*, Pau 1988, 141f.

[138] Johansen, 'Denmark', 353ff.

not least because of changes in theological thinking. In one area, however, the Lutheran clergy in Denmark and Norway encountered solid resistance from the population: the attempt to suppress 'cunning-ness' failed abysmally. Under no circumstances was the population prepared to stop using 'cunning people'. They refused to help prosecute such people since they represented their only access to healing for themselves and their livestock.

The witchcraft trials, however, took distinctly different routes in the Nordic countries. The trials in Denmark were unique in their total emphasis on *maleficium*. This meant that the heresy aspect of the crime became less prominent, which made it possible to bring the trials to an end through the teaching of providence. This was not the case in Finland and Sweden, where the demonological aspects were given increased emphasis throughout the century. In these countries the prerequisite for an end to the witchcraft trials was the realisation that the phenomenon rested on delusion and fraud.

Index

Uppsala, 5, 46, 49, 50, 55, 71, 74, 98, 101, 102, 103, 106, 107, 111, 113, 161, 166, 168, 176, 185, 202; Uppsala Assembly (1593), 5, 148, 153, 156, 166, 169, 177, 185; Uppsala Resolution (1593), 157, 158–60, 162–4, 178; University of Uppsala, 6, 168, 175

Urne, Lage, 77, 79, 80, 81, 85, 86, 88

Vadstena, 48, 53, 105, 107, 185, 203; parliament in, 156

Væver, Christen Pedersen, 188

Valkendorf, Erik, 95, 97

Västerås, 46, 50, 71 n., 72, 101, 102, 106, 108, 110; parliaments in, 51, 55, 63, 84, 103, 108, 109, 144, 184; Succession Parliament (1544), 61, 144, 145

Västgötaherrarnas' rebellion (1529), 54, 110

Växjö, 46, 71 n., 101, 111, 202

Vedel, Anders Sørensen, 115, 195, 208, 210

Vejle, Hans Knudsen, 132

Verden, 141

Viborg (Denmark), 20, 22, 23, 71 n., 80, 82, 85, 88, 194, 201

Viborg/Viipuri (Finland), 57, 65, 68, 172, 174, 175, 178

Vilna, 133

Vladislav, son of King Sigismund, 162

Vormordsen, Frants, 23, 26, 86, 180, 181

Weidensee, Eberhard, 15

Wenth, Johann, 15

Weze, Johan, 74

Winstrup, Peder, 131

witchcraft, 11, 140, 179–211; trials, 11, 195–210

Wittenberg, 5, 15, 16, 40, 45, 57, 63, 65, 68, 120, 121; University of Wittenberg, 8, 38, 47, 128, 180; Wittenberg Church Order, 173

Worm, Ole, 191, 192

Worms, Diet of, 14

Württemberg, 58; Church Order, 147

Zealand, 33, 38, 40, 41, 91, 139, 141, 182, 190

Zurich, 209

Zwingli, Huldrich, 164, 181